the tea drinker's handbook

François-Xavier Delmas

Mathias Minet

Christine Barbaste

the tea drinker's handbook

Abbeville Press Publishers

New York   London

CONTENTS

THE WORLD'S 50 BEST TEAS

China

INTRODUCTION

We have been visiting the mountains where the world's premier teas
are grown ever since we first began selecting the rarest blends of tea
for Le Palais des Thés. We spend several months every year walking the
plantations from Darjeeling to Shizuoka and from Taiwan to the Golden
Triangle. We always experience the same sense of wonder and joy on seeing
their mist-wreathed summits, and the vast expanses of green that are so
patiently worked by the men and women who carry out the same task
every day, plucking buds and leaves between forefinger and thumb,
in a ritual that hasn't changed for centuries.

In our twenty years of visiting the plantations, we have built up some very
precious relationships with the plantation owners and workers and as a
result have had many professional secrets confided in us. But we felt that
it would be pointless acquiring all this knowledge simply to store it and
not pass it on. In fact, it was our desire to pass on some of what we had
learned and our passion for tea, that led us to set up L'École du Thé
(School of Tea) in 1999. The courses the school offers have enjoyed
continuing success, reinforcing our conviction that the world of tea, with
its many different facets, is capturing the imagination of an ever-growing
public. It is against this background that this book has been written.

We believe that tea, with its wonderful range of flavors, has been ignored
in gastronomic circles for too long. Rather than simply giving an account
of all its many aspects—a number of books have already done this,
suitably bathed in nostalgia for the old days—we prefer to take you on
a visit to the tea gardens. There cannot be a better way to discover how tea
is grown than to meet the people who, with patience and love, every day
devote their knowledge to pleasing tea aficionados the world over.

To ensure the consumer is satisfied, an intermediary is needed: the
professional taster, whose role is similar to his counterpart in the wine
trade, using his expertise to evaluate thousands of teas every year.
As with wine, this skill can only be acquired after a long and absorbing
apprenticeship. Nonetheless, the art of tasting is open to everyone, and
anyone who is interested in tea will discover the basic information in this
book, together with a variety of indispensable tips about preparing it.

And since every taster loves to pass on their enthusiasm, we could not resist
the pleasure of sharing with you our choice of the world's fifty best teas.
Happy tasting!

François-Xavier Delmas and Mathias Minet

What is tea?

- **THE TEA** BUSH
- **THE ECOLOGY** OF TEA
- **THE CULTIVATION** OF TEA
- **THE PLUCK**
- **THE COLORS** OF TEA

WHAT IS TEA?

Tea is a plant that is cultivated extensively across the world. The use of its leaves in an infusion was widespread long before it made its way to the West and long before it became the focus of scientific study, taking on significant political and economic importance for the countries involved in its trade. Prescribed by apothecaries and used in temples during sessions of meditation, it helped to inspire artists, poets, and potters, and travelled with the caravans to the remotest regions of Asia.

A Chinese legend places the "discovery" of tea in the year 2737 BC. Shen Nong, the legendary emperor and equally legendary father of Chinese medicine, commanded his subjects to boil all drinking water for health reasons. One day, while he was boiling his water beneath the shade of a tree, a few leaves fell into the pot and he was captivated by the resulting flavor of the water. This poetic little story, while not offering a reliable date for the discovery, does give a valuable indication that tea may been known in China for perhaps almost five thousand years. Certainly, the most ancient Chinese writings show that the leaves were in use at least eight hundred years before our era.

A species native to South East Asia, the tea tree originated in a region situated on the frontier between Laos, China, and Myanmar (Burma), but it was not until more than a thousand years later, in the fourth century, that the Chinese began to cultivate it on the first plantations in Szechuan. Until that time, the leaves to be used were simply collected in the wild. It was the start of a great adventure.

THE TEA BUSH

The tea bush is a member of an extensive family which groups together thirty genera of plants and no less than five hundred species—the *Theaceae*. It belongs to the genus *Camellia,* of which there are some eighty-two known species. The tea bush (*Camellia sinensis*) is a cousin of the horticultural camellia (*Camellia japonica*) and is divided into three principal varieties: *Camellia sinensis* var. *assamica*; *C. sinensis* var. *sinensis*; *C. sinensis* var. *cambodiensis.* Due to hybridization, either spontaneous or initiated by man, these varieties have given rise to a great number of hybrids. Sources reveal that there are now between three hundred and six hundred different types of tea bush, each with its own characteristics, descended from the three principal varieties.

LEAVES AND BUDS, FLOWERS AND FRUIT

The tea tree is an evergreen that can reach a height of between 15 and 50 feet (5–15 m) in the wild, depending upon the variety. Its leaves are alternating and eliptical in shape, with finely dentellated edges. According to variety, they can be anything from ¼ to 10 inches (5 mm–25 cm) long. The upper surface, which is exposed to the sunlight, is shiny, while the underside is matte and lighter in color.

Like many cultivated tropical plants, tea bushes alternate phases of intense growth with long dormant periods. These phases are essentially regulated by the plant itself and as many as five growth phases and five rest, or dormancy, periods may be seen in the course of a year, in a tea plant that has been left to grow unhindered.

Unusually, where the cultivation of perennials is concerned, tea is grown for its foliage (the bud and the two leaves below it on the stem), rather than its fruit or seeds. The tea planter's objective, therefore, is to keep his tea bushes producing new growth for as much of the year as possible.

When the tea bush starts producing new growth, the buds begin to form and develop in length, and leaves unfold all along its stem. The fine

Taiwan. These very young tea bushes have not yet been harvested, but receive the meticulous care that ensures ideal development.

19

silvery down that covers the young buds takes the name of pekoe from the Chinese *pak-ho*, meaning "fine hair" or "down." These unopened buds and young leaves are plucked regularly and make up the harvest.

A frequent misconception

The term *Orange Pekoe* does not refer to an orange-flavored tea, but to a type of pluck, so-called by the first Dutch importers in the seventeenth century to honor the Dutch royal family, the house of Orange-Nassau.

The fruit of the tea bush contains up to six seeds.

The trunk of a tea bush can reveal its age. It is often older than its height would suggest.

The foliage of cultivated tea bushes is dense and uniform. The young shoots are easily distinguished from the other leaves.

The bud and the first two leaves are the parts that are harvested.

During these phases of vegetative growth, as soon as a bud is plucked another begins to form. But once a branch has produced five leaves, the bud becomes exhausted, stops growing, and fails to open. In the tea world, this dormant bud is referred to as *banjhi*. By extension, the word is also used to describe the periods when these dormant buds are plucked. When these *banjhi* form, that branch stops growing and the next new growth will begin with shoots from which new branches will grow. Repeated plucking of the tea bush increases the number of times these growth phases occur.

It is important not to confuse these phases, when the buds arrest their growth, with the periods of winter dormancy that occur in some of the world's tea-growing regions. As the hours of daylight grow shorter and the atmospheric temperature steadily drops, the growth of the tea bush slows down to the point where it seems to have ceased completely. In the colder regions, this "hibernation" stage can last up to four months. When growth begins again after this rest period, the first buds and leaves to be harvested are, as will be seen, particularly prized for the powerful aromatic properties they contain. The low temperatures and sparse rainfall, together with the hours of sunshine in the winter, will have combined to concentrate the aromatic molecules and essential oils in the buds and leaves. The opposite occurs at the time of the monsoon, when the buds and leaves that form are of a good size but are essentially swollen with water.

The white flowers that grow on the tea bush each have five petals, pale yellow stamens between ¼ and ½ inches (5–9 mm) long and a pale green pistil. They grow either singly or in clusters of two to four. It is rare to see bushes in flower on the plantations because the repeated harvesting of buds and young leaves inhibits the flower growth. The fruit that develop from the flower have a hard shell and contain spherical, brown seeds of a diameter of anything between ¼ and ⅝ inches (4–15 mm).

They are grown either for planting or for their kernels, which are crushed to produce an excellent quality oil that has been used as a food product in China for more than a thousand years. In Kerala, in southern India, it is also used to make soap and cosmetics. The residue left after the tea tree oil has been extracted is used as a pesticide or goes into the making of fertilizer. Tea tree oil is also used in the production of certain green teas, such as Long Jing.

THE VARIETIES

The *Shijing* (Book of Songs) tells us that tea leaves have been used to produce beverages in China since the eighth century BC. The word *tu* refers to tea leaves, as it does to the other bitter herbs used in medicinal decoctions. The Chinese claim—and they are supported in this by historical and literary sources—that the tea tree undoubtedly originated in their lands, more specifically in Xishuangbanna, a region of Yunnan Province, where there is still a high concentration of wild or semi-wild tea trees.

On the other hand, among Europeans, who discovered it more than two millennia later, the botanical classification "tea tree"—as it was called then—was the subject of a great deal of speculation. Tea was immensely popular in the capitals of Europe from the middle of the seventeenth century onwards and, as the subject of a significant and lucrative trade with China, also became an important economic factor for a considerable part of the eighteenth century. More than one European power of that era sought desperately to uncover the secrets of the cultivation and manufacture of this exotic commodity, in which the Chinese held a total commercial monopoly.

The flower of the tea bush is hermaphroditic, with both stamens and pistil. Usually it is self-sterile, able to produce seeds only through cross-pollination.

The first written account of the tea by a "Westerner" was in 1712 by the German scholar Dr. Kaempfer who travelled around Asia and lived in Japan for a time. He gave it the name *Thea japonense*. Some forty years later, the Swedish botanist, Carl von Linné, renamed it *Thea sinensis*. Such differences of opinion among experts nevertheless did nothing to further the discovery of its cultivation or the use of its leaves in an infusion. The Western world had to wait until the middle of the nineteenth century for the detailed observations of botanist Robert Fortune (see below) and Major Robert Bruce's discovery of an indigenous tea tree growing in the Assam jungle in India.

 Robert Fortune: the British spy

By the nineteenth century, tea had become a serious source of revenue for the British economy, and like several other great European powers at the time, the British did everything they could to free themselves from the restrictions the Chinese monopoly imposed on their trade. Dubious strategies were employed, beginning with the introduction of opium into China with the aim of creating a dependency among the population, then using the currency this trade generated to buy tea at a lower price. Britain also sent a botanist into China as a spy. In 1848,

Sir Robert Fortune's mission was to uncover the secrets of the cultivation and manufacture of tea. Disguised as a Chinese tea merchant, Fortune meticulously recorded everything he saw in a diary and did eventually succeed in lifting a corner of the veil cloaking certain aspects of the "mystery." He discovered, for example, that contrary to current belief, both green tea and black tea were produced from the same plant. But more importantly, at the end of his daring journey, the "tea thief" brought back thousands of seeds that were to be sown on plantations in India.

In accordance with the International Code of Nomenclature for Botanical Species, since 1959 *Camellia* has been used in preference to *Thea* to designate the species, and the three species that exist in the wild have been recognized officially. Each has its own distinctive physical characteristics:

→ The Chinese tea plant
(*Camellia sinensis* var. *sinensis*)

A specimen of *Camellia assamica* planted in the late nineteenth century, now 45 feet (14 m) tall. (Darjeeling, Botanical Gardens).

Originally from Yunnan, in the wild this variety can reach a height of up to 20 feet (6 m). The crown of a mature tree is dome-shaped. The growth of its numerous straight, flexible branches begins almost from the base of the trunk, unlike the *assamica* variety. It has an abundance of flowers and small, thick, dark-green leaves.

Though the *sinensis* variety, which gives a somewhat perfumed tea with relatively little body, produces a smaller yield than the *assamica*, it is robust and fairly resistant to drought and frost. This tolerance of low temperatures means it can be grown in Japan, China, the former USSR states, Iran, Turkey, and on plantations at high altitude. It also has a longer lifespan. At Darjeeling, in the Nilgiri Hills and in Sri Lanka, certain examples of this variety have been in production for more than one hundred years.

→ The Assam tea plant
(*Camellia sinensis* var. *assamica*)

In the wild, this variety can grow to a height of 32 to 50 feet (10–15 m). Compared with the *sinensis*, the *assamica*'s structure is more open and widely spaced, and it has a distinct trunk. Its flowers are more widely distributed and its leaves, which can grow to 8 inches (20 cm) in length, are supple, shiny, and pale in color, with a fleshy texture. The *assamica* produces a quite robust liquor, strong and of a good color.

Less hardy than the *sinensis* variety, the *assamica* can fall victim to drought or frost and has a lower tolerance of pests and disease. This variety, together with its hybrids, is resistant to heavy rains and can therefore be grown in monsoon regions. Its lifespan of around thirty to fifty years is shorter than that of the *sinensis* variety.

We should point out that Assam tea plants are not found solely in Assam, nor are Chinese tea plants restricted to China: the names *sinensis* and *assamica* simply reflect the fact that one variety was discovered in China and the other in Assam.

→ The Cambodian tea plant
(*Camellia sinensis* var. *cambodiensis*)

Halfway in size between the *sinensis* and *assamica*, the Cambodian tea plant grows to between 20 and 32 feet (6–10 m) in the wild and is conical in shape. Its leaves are yellowish-green. This variety resulted from the natural hybridization of the other two varieties and is not cultivated for tea production but serves to provide new cultivars.

🌱 Family quarrels

The classifications proposed by the International Code of Nomenclature have failed to convince the Chinese who prefer to stick to their own classification—only one variety of tea is recognized, the *sinensis*, which is divided into two sub-varieties (Yunnan and Bohea), each generating several sub-sub-varieties. In this genealogical chart, the *assamica* features as a distant descendant of the sub-variety Yunnan ... and anyone who casts doubt on the legitimacy of this lineage, in a country wedded to the conviction that it is the sole cradle of tea, runs the grave risk, even today, of seriously upsetting Chinese sensibilities.

Nowadays, apart from these three main varieties, there are also vast numbers of hybrids or cultivars. Given this great ability to hybridize, and the ease with which it is able to adapt to its environment, *Camellia sinensis* now covers a wide variety of naturally occurring examples. The *sinensis* variety has mutated spontaneously since it was first cultivated in China. In the nineteenth century, when the British first introduced tea plantations to India, the *sinensis* and the native *assamica* variety were often grown in close proximity to each other resulting in natural crossbreeding. It is therefore not unusual today to find tea plants that combine the characteristics of both varieties. To these can be added those varieties created by the planters as well as those created later at research centres. Tea is a thriving species, very far from the threat of extinction. In China, for example, the official plant list cites

The dark, tough foliage of *Camellia sinensis*.

Camellia assamica: the leaves are broader, lighter, and more supple.

A seedling, a hybrid of both varieties.

ninety-five cultivars, but in the forests of Yunnan there are more than 250 sub-varieties of wild or semi-wild plants.

Faced with such a wide range of possibilities, it is not always easy to establish the genealogy of a given tea plant, so it is difficult to enumerate with any degree of accuracy the total number of hybrids or cultivars under cultivation in the different tea-producing regions of the world.

A cultivar

This word is a contraction of "cultivated variety." A cultivar results from the selection, hybridization (crossbreeding of two species or two genera), or spontaneous mutation between plants. The basic difference between a cultivar and a variety lies in the fact that the unique characteristics of a cultivar are not generally transmittable from one generation to the next by the seed. These plants can only be reproduced from cuttings.

→ Wild tea trees...

In 1823, Scotsman Robert Bruce discovered that in Assam, in Northern India, the native tribes chewed the leaves of trees that grew two or three times higher than the tea trees seen in China, but which nevertheless bore a disconcerting resemblance to them. Once it was established that these really were tea trees, though of a different variety from those already known, disputes and speculation about *Camellia sinensis* flared up again. Naturally, from the Chinese point of view the inopportune arrival of this cousin from India provoked a great deal of both indignant and skeptical protest. The British, thrilled by the discovery of this native tree in one of their colonies, saw it as a major trump card to use against the Chinese. Many other Western botanists set off in search of further wild tea trees that had not been planted by man. Their travels took them to China, Vietnam, Cambodia, and even Japan, and it was during this era that first tea herbaria and the earliest collections of seed were formed.

A Chinese farmer harvesting a semi-wild variety. (Menghai, Yunnan Province).

Is it theoretically possible that truly wild tea trees could still be found in Assam, China, or Cambodia, as against those planted by man, and could they be regarded as the original ancestors of all tea plants? We still don't know the answer, but what is certain is that given that the cultivation of tea began close to three thousand years ago, these celebrated original wild tea plants would be a rare find indeed.

It is not unusual, however, in Yunnan, on the frontier with Myanmar (Burma) and Laos, to find forests of tea growing wild, sometimes reaching a height of 20 feet (6 m). These are ancient tea gardens, cultivated in the nineteenth century by minority groups such as the Dai, the Hani, and the Bu Nang, and then abandoned. In their case it is more correct to call them semi-wild tea trees. As for Assam, where the jungle has been totally tamed and cleared, nothing is left of the tea forests discovered by Robert Bruce.

→ . . . and ancient tea trees

In China, which claims to be the original cradle of tea and boasts that it possesses the oldest tea plants in the world, another subject gives rise to passionate debate—the age of the old trees that are still to be found in certain regions of the country. As with many things in China, their estimated ages, the result of spicing up history with a pinch of legend, provoke a mixture of both awe and doubt. The oldest tea trees in the world are undoubtedly those found in the forests of Xishuangbanna, in southern Yunnan Province—trees of a truly impressive size, the oldest survivors of abandoned ancient plantations which are still thriving in the wild—but the ages claimed for them, often by local minority groups, should be viewed with caution.

Scientific carbon dating has been carried out on some of these imposing trees: in the forest of Menghai, in Xishuangbanna, the "Bada," a giant tea tree 105 feet (32 m) high with a trunk diameter of 4½ feet (1.38 m), was found to be 1,700 years old. In the mountains of Nannuo, also near Menghai, a tea plant estimated to be about eight hundred years old is the oldest surviving example planted by man.

Even though this dating has a sound scientific basis, when dealing with trees plants claimed to be the "oldest tea plants in the world," it is not always easy to make allowances for national and regional honor (the autonomous Chinese prefecture of Xishuangbanna, is very touchy about the question of its minority groups and regional identity) and commercial opportunism. The district of Fengqing, the other important area for the production of Pu Er tea in competition with Xishuang-banna, recently declared itself home to the biggest tea tree in the world with foliage covering an area of 732 square feet (68 m²), and claims that this tree is 3,750 years old.

Nevertheless, it is true that this region in south China does contain 37,000 acres (15,000 hectares) of semi-wild tea trees, many of them more than a century old, whose leaves are being harvested once again. Given the publicity that surrounds these crops and the price that the leaves command, the question of whether or not ancient tea plants, like ancient vines, have a special aromatic potential, is a matter of some interest.

THE ECOLOGY
OF TEA

At the end of the seventeenth century, a few European countries began to toy with the idea of acclimatizing young tea plants for cultivation in their own lands. Not surprisingly, the few experiments that were tried ended in fiasco. Tea may be able to adapt well to its environment, but the climates of countries such as England and Sweden could never provide it with the right conditions. Two ecological factors are vital for the success of its cultivation: the climate and the quality of the soil.

THE CLIMATE

Cultivated tea bushes grow between the latitudes of 42° North and 31° South, and can adapt to climatic conditions ranging from equatorial to damp temperate. The ideal conditions for their cultivation include a hot climate and constant, high levels of humidity, a minimum of several hours of sunshine daily, and regular rainfall, preferably throughout the year.

The typical climate prevailing in high-altitude equatorial regions, where two rainy seasons alternate with two dry seasons, is ideal for tea cultivation, especially if the days are sunny and the rain falls during the night. Outside the tropics, a lack of sunshine and temperatures below 53 to 54°F (12°C) are inhibiting factors both to the growth of the bushes and their productivity.

→ Temperature and rainfall

Tea bushes grow well in a constant temperature. In Yunnan, for example, the average temperature is between 55 and 77°F (13–25°C) throughout the year, which allows the tea to be harvested for all twelve months of the year. Zones where tea is grown now extend from tropical regions to temperate ones, so the air temperature can be anything from 46 to 95°F (8–35°C). While tea can survive at low temperatures, it is not frost-resistant and if exposed to temperatures below 23°F (–5°C) for more than seventy-two

A vast green and undulating expanse punctuated by tall shade trees is typical of Sri Lankan plantations.

hours, the bushes will die—unless it happens to be one of certain hybrids specially selected to grow in those conditions. The *sinensis* can withstand low temperatures better than the *assamica*. Tea does not like the temperature to be too high either—its rate of photosynthesis is at its highest between 86 and 95°F (30–35°C). Above that it drops rapidly and it ceases altogether once the temperature goes above 107°F (42°C). The leaves can no longer absorb carbon dioxide and are damaged irreparably.

In many respects, the temperature of the soil is as important as the air temperature, as it also influences the growth of the tea bushes and their yield—if it is too high it lowers the soil's reserves of the oxygen that is necessary to enable the roots perform their function of absorbing water and nutrients.

Tea also needs abundant and evenly distributed rainfall. It requires at least 59 inches (1,500 mm) of rain per year, and in tropical conditions the dry season should not last longer than three months. Young tea bushes especially are sensitive to frost, which damages their leaves and shoots, slows down their growth, and severely reduces the harvest. Abundant rainfall acts simultaneously on the volume and the quality of the crop. In the monsoon period, for example, tea grows at an astonishing rate and can be plucked every four or five days, but the quality and aromatic content of the leaves produced is inferior. On the other hand, a period of drought can often produce a quality crop.

Another factor that is essential to the growth of the tea is a humid atmosphere, the ideal hygrometric level being between 70 and 90 percent. Often situated at a high altitude so that they can benefit from more clement temperatures than are found in the valleys, tea plantations can be enigmatic places, wreathed in cloud and mists.

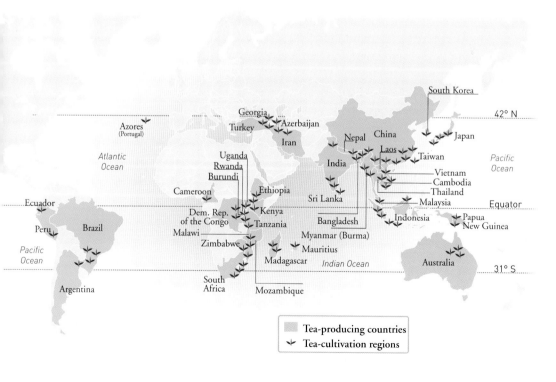

→ Shadow and light

Tea bushes need at least a few hours of sunlight daily for their development. Light plays an important role in developing the essential oils that give the infusion its flavor, but diffused light is preferable to direct. On almost all plantations, groves of large trees are planted at regular intervals to filter the sun's rays, help the soil retain its moisture during the dry season, and protect the bushes from winds or excessively heavy rain.

The apparent effectiveness of the planting of these large trees always takes the first-time visitor by surprise. Planted relatively far apart, they do not appear to be shading the tea bushes and on a hot day there is little shelter from the sun to be found beneath their foliage. They play a decisive role in many plantations, however; the small amount of shade they do offer helps to regulate the temperature of the bushes' leaves which, on sunny days, is often much higher than the temperature of the air around them.

The choice of these trees is not a random one. Their root systems must penetrate deep into the soil so that they do not compete for nutrients and moisture with the those of the tea bushes. In addition, they should not deplete a soil that is often already exhausted from being used to grow a single plant species, but rather should contribute to its balance. This is why deciduous trees, whose fallen leaves will enrich and regenerate the soil as they rot, are generally chosen for this role.

THE QUALITY OF THE SOIL

In the same way as it flourishes in a wide range of different climatic conditions, tea grows equally well in a variety of different soils—proof, if any were needed, of its great ability to adapt to its physical environment.

The geological composition of the soil is not so important. Tea plants can adapt equally well to recently deposited alluvial soils, such as those found in Assam or Dooars, as to soil derived from granite or gneiss, such as in China, Georgia, Indonesia, Sri Lanka, and the Darjeeling region, or to that found in the Rift valley in Kenya, Uganda, and Burundi, which is formed from solidified lava or volcanic ash. They do best, however, in young volcanic soil, neither chalk nor clay.

Shade trees, often of a leguminous variety, are introduced to new plantations at the same time as the tea plants.

What is tea? → The ecology of tea

In Japan, in winter, fans are used to keep the air in motion, preventing the build-up of a layer of freezing air at the level of the crop.

Typical high-altitude plantation, where patches of mist drift in and out throughout the day.

In drier regions, spray irrigation is used to provide necessary moisture.

Tea only grows well in acid soil with a pH between 4.4 and 5.5. Acidity plays an important role; it governs the use and absorption of the nutrients the plant needs, two factors which in turn influence its growth.

Because its root structure needs to be able to extend to a depth of up to 20 feet (6 m) to maximize its intake of nutrients, tea needs a loose, permeable soil that is deep and rich in humus, without any hard barrier layers.

The composition of the soil must also allow water to drain away rapidly from around the roots in periods of heavy rainfall. A very clay soil, for example, would slow down the drainage and the resulting accumulation of water would limit the growth of the roots and even damage them. The soil must, nevertheless, have good retentive qualities that allow it to hold on to sufficient water to maintain an optimum evapo-transpiration rate right through the growing season—particularly in the dry season.

The fertility of the soil is measured by the amount of nutrient elements it holds available for the roots. Potassium, for example, which the plant draws from particles of clay and humus, reinforces its resistance to drought and disease and encourages photosynthesis. Magnesium, which is one of the basic components of chlorophyll, plays an important role in most of the tea plant's vital functions. The lack of magnesium affects photosynthesis and therefore the crop yield. As to trace elements, though only absorbed by the plant in very small quantities, they still play an important role. Zinc, for example, is a factor in growth, and copper helps with the assimilation of potassium and nitrogen.

Thanks to its highly developed root system, tea is little affected by relief, at home on even the most rugged of slopes.

Tea and the "terroir"

Thanks to tea's great ability to adapt to very different soils and geographic conditions, a parallel with the vine and its cultivation can be drawn, raising questions about the influence which the "terroir"—the total natural environment of an area—can exert over the organoleptic qualities of a particular tea.

While there is little doubt that the physico-chemical composition of the soil does influence the performance of the plant, it is still difficult to determine to what degree it is able to lend a particular characteristic to the tea produced. This stems, in part, from the extreme compartmentalism that reigns in the world of tea. Between countries and even sometimes between regions, planters rarely interest themselves in what is happening on their neighbors' plantations. The result is a strong regionalization of cultivars. Since tea bushes from one plantation are rarely acclimatized on another, it is difficult to make comparisons based on examples of a particular cultivar produced according to exactly the same rules but grown on different soils.

Unlike wine, where the terroir (soil and geographic conditions) is seen as playing an important role in its quality, the bulk of world tea production is still not approached in this way. We do discuss it a bit with the planters with whom we work, but the influence of the natural environment on the teas they produce is not yet a primary issue for them.

ALTITUDE AND GRADIENT

Tea should ideally be grown on sloping ground that drains naturally. Unlike rice, tea bushes cannot tolerate stagnant water, so networks of irrigation ditches are dug in those plantations situated on the plain to prevent the ground from becoming waterlogged.

On the other hand, with its spreading root system, tea is perfectly adapted to growing in the steepest mountain regions. Along with the vine it is one of the rare plants that can be cultivated in the extreme conditions found on steep gradients. It is not by chance, therefore, that many tea gardens are planted on mountainsides. As well as providing good natural drainage, the mountain slopes offer near perfect climatic conditions for the cultivation of tea because of the lower temperatures that occur at high altitudes. The temperature drops between 43 and 45°F (6–7°C) for every 3,300 feet (1,000 m) of altitude: if the temperature is 95°F (35°C) in the valley it will be 77°F (25°C) in a plantation situated 5,000 feet (1,500 m) higher up.

Tea's remarkable resistance means it is possible to plant it in places that are so steep a person could lose their balance. Anyone making a tour of the tea plantations of the world will see some spectacular mountain landscapes that have been completely "domesticated" by the cultivation of the tea bush. Plantations can be found at altitudes as high as 6,650 feet (2,000 m). The highest of all are in Taiwan, in the Li Shan range, where they grow at 8,000 feet (2,450 m). At such altitudes, the temperature affects the rhythm of bud growth and minimizes the yield, but it also influences the quality of the manufactured leaves and the infusion. In fact, in a given region, among teas produced from the same cultivars, those grown at altitude are more fragrant than the ones grown on the plain. This is particularly evident in the *Camellia sinensis* var. *sinensis* and its hybrids.

In Darjeeling, plantations even cover the crests of mountains and 45° slopes.

On the plains (here, the Terai region), the flatness of the land is offset by using ultra-sophisticated irrigation systems.

Terracing provides natural drainage, and a level surface to assist harvesting.

THE CULTIVATION OF TEA

Climb up a mountain slope in one of the tea-growing regions of the world and you will probably encounter several different kinds of crops as you ascend. Setting off from the palm trees, exotic orchards, and fields of pineapples sweltering in the heat of the plain below, as you reach the first slopes you could be greeted by rubber plants and banana palms. Beyond these lie plants that give us spices such as pepper and cardamom, and perhaps some coffee plants too. If the land levels out for a few miles, it might be covered with paddy fields. As you climb, the higher you go, the thicker the mist enveloping you becomes. But once you have climbed up through the mist, a spectacular scene unfolds before you—endless acres of bushes of an intense green, clinging precariously to the mountainside, the neat, geometric patterns in which they were planted, still just visible.

Plantations vary in size considerably throughout the world, from one tea-growing region to another, the average is about 2½ acres (1 hectare); in China they vary from small (150 acres/60 hectares) and medium (150–500 acres/60–200 hectares), to large (more than 500 acres). The large plantations are not owned by a single person but by the individual workers, who each have between 3 and 5 Mu (15 Mu = 2.5 acres) to work and are obliged to sell the fresh leaves exclusively to the plantation's factory.

In the Darjeeling province of India, while the size of the plantations averages 500 acres, there is a big difference between large and small; some consist of barely 197 acres (80 hectares), while others are spread over 1,730 acres (700 hectares). In Assam, plantations take up at least 740 acres (300 hectares) of cultivated area and employ, on average, 600 workers. In the south of the country, while some plantations cover an area of 1,235 acres (500 hectares), there are also some as large as 12,355 acres (5,000 hectares). In the two latter regions, however, the term "plantation" does not refer to a single cultivated area like those of Darjeeling, but to geographical zones organized around a factory. So, in Assam, as in the Nilgiri Hills, several tens of thousands of small farmers each own a few hundred square yards of tea plantation and sell their crops to the local factory. In Sri Lanka, the plantations cover between

Shizuoka, Japan. A worker sucks up droplets of rain from the foliage of the tea bushes.

3,700 and 6,177 acres (1,500–2,500 hectares) and employ just 10,000 workers.

TEA THROUGHOUT THE WORLD

As we have already stated, there is a great diversity of tea plant cultivars throughout the world. When replanting existing plots or developing new ones, it is essential to choose those cultivars that are suited to the particular environment and climate, that are resistant to disease and pests, have good productivity and will produce the quality of tea required.

Cultivars and varieties

As with the different varieties of vine that are grown, certain types of tea bush are more suitable for the production of green tea, others for the production of black tea, etc. But unlike the wine-producing sector, where the varieties are given acclimatization tests when planted outside their area of origin and have become relatively globalized, the different varieties of bush have, characteristically, been largely confined to a given tea-growing zone. This regionalization is due, above all, to the lack of communication between the different tea-growing regions of the world. The lack of curiosity, even the disinterest, of planters with regard to what is going on elsewhere, hardly encourages experimentation in acclimatization, and there is little chance of finding the same cultivar being planted both on the hillsides of Darjeeling and the island of Taiwan.

→ What is available?

AV2 (Ambari vegetative 2), popular for its vigorous growth and resistance, was developed in the 1960s.

P312 (Phoobsering 312) is particularly adapted to exposed north-facing slopes and high altitudes.

Nowadays there are research centres in all the large tea-growing regions—as there are for all agricultural or industrial activities involving important socio-economic issues—these include TOCKLAI in Northern India, UPASI in Southern India, TTES in Taiwan. These research facilities study tea plants, develop new cultivars and generally work towards the improvement of the varieties. As a result, focusing either on yield or aromatic quality in the cup, cultivars have been developed to suit every tea-producing region in the world. These cultivars are

specifically developed to suit the soil that exists in each region and to produce the color of tea required.

In the Darjeeling region, planters use thirty-three different cultivars, the most popular in terms of quality being the AV2, the P312 (see photograph below opposite) or the T78 (Tukdah 78).

In Japan, there are forty-three official cultivars for the production of green tea. While the main one, Yabukita, is grown on nine-tenths of Japanese plantations, planters are beginning to introduce others, such as the Sayamamidori or the Kanayamidori, in order to re-establish a balance (see page 194).

In the Nantou region of Taiwan, the cultivar TTES12 (Taiwanese Tea Experiment Station no. 12 or Jin Xuan) is used in the production of certain Dong Dings; with their buttery and very intense vanilla aromas, sometimes bordering on pronounced floral notes of ylang-ylang, this particular variety has striking organoleptic characteristics (see page 189).

These cultivars are named after the plantation where the clones, obtained by selection originated (Tukdah, Phoobsering, Ambari, etc.), or after the research station which perfected them (TTES); the numbers correspond to an in-house classification allocated by the site.

→ Creating new strains of tea bush

Throughout the hundreds of years during which the history of tea has been charted, growing from seed has been the dominant method of cultivation. But from the point of view of modern agriculture, this offers a serious disadvantage. Bearing in mind the tea plant's propensity for crossbreeding with its neighbors and mutating to adapt to its environment, it has a very mixed heritage. This means that growing from seed produces plants that differ greatly one from the other. In the days when plantations were sown with seed, the result was haphazard plots, with tea bushes that varied in productivity, grew foliage of varying degrees of density, and produced tea of an uneven quality.

In the nineteenth century, when the British introduced tea growing to India (first in the province of Assam then, around 1840, in the Nilgiri Hills and finally in the province of Darjeeling, in 1859), they fully expected to compete with China in terms of quality. They concentrated their efforts, therefore, on improving the inherited features of their plants and achieving more uniform quality in the teas they produced, without losing sight of yield.

The very first method they tried, based on the principle of crossbreeding, involved the creation of hybrids by controlled pollination between hand-picked parent plants and the subsequent harvesting of the seed. The initial stage involved the selection of two parent tea bushes, which were raised in isolation, well away from the other tea plants on the plantation to avoid the danger of unwanted pollination. The transfer of pollen could have been left to the goodwill of the wind or insects, but it was generally done manually. The seeds obtained from this cross-pollination were used to create mini-plantations and the resulting harvests were tested and judged on characteristics and quality. When carried out on a larger scale by selecting several pairs of parent tea plants from different varieties, it enabled comparisons to be made and the finest plants to be picked out. The main problem with this method of selection was the length of time it took. Two years were taken up with the cross-pollination, a further ten years were required to build up an adequate stock of seed and then it took ten to fifteen years to set up the mini-plantations and study the result. Despite being a simple and practical method, in all it took at least twenty-five years, along with a great deal of effort and experimentation to perfect it.

In the 1930s, in India, methods of selection underwent a decisive change when the technique of propagation by cuttings began to be used. From then on, cuttings that were taken from tea bushes chosen for their morphological and organoleptic characteristics were planted, and grew into new tea bushes identical to the mother plant. By saving the years of work previously spent on pollination and amassing a stock of seed, this cloning technique reduced the process of selection to a dozen or so years.

Propagation by cuttings remains the method most commonly used today. Cuttings are taken from adult tea plants that have been screened to establish certain criteria (physical aspect, behavior in the environment, the quality of the tea they produce, and so on). The plants selected are grown on a mini-plantation, their crops harvested, made into tea, and then tested. Only a few of the very best are kept as "propagators," destined to provide either seed or cuttings.

Recent advances in genetic research now make it possible to study the DNA sequence of each candidate tea plant. Establishing their genome characteristics has made it possible to quickly select those new plants that are the most resistant to pests and disease.

Nevertheless, improvement by crossbreeding is still an issue. There are several techniques that enable the characteristics of two selected tea plants to be combined. One of the conventional ones is to graft a leaf from one tea plant onto the rootstock of another, but more recent developments in microbiology enable the genetic heritage of two tea plants to be merged at cell level. All these techniques are aimed at creating new cultivars which combine the characteristics of both parent plants—such as good structure, disease-resistant foliage, a longer lifespan, high yield. Once created, these hybrids need to be tested rigorously on mini-plantations, and taken through micro-cropping and manufacture. If

The cutting is taken using a sharp knife from a stem that is neither too pliant nor too ripe.

The cuttings can be planted out in individual pouches filled with a medium rich in nutrients...

...or inserted directly into the nursery plot. Here they have already put out young shoots.

this testing and observation phase proves conclusive, the newcomers will then rise to the rank of "propagators" and provide either seed or cuttings, as appropriate. Note that some hybridization techniques result in sterile tea plants which can only be propagated by cuttings.

TEA BUSHES GROWN FROM SEED OR CUTTINGS?

The advantages and disadvantages of tea plants grown from seed are different from those of tea plants grown from cuttings. In order to produce a well-stocked plantation and avoid exposure to certain dangers, the planter must take a number of factors into account and follow certain recommendations regarding choice of stock.

Since they have a distinct genetic heritage with all the accompanying strengths and weaknesses, plants grown from seed offer the advantage of a longer lifespan and a greater resistance to the vagaries of climate, particularly because their root system is more developed and penetrates more deeply into the soil. However, they also present some drawbacks. The difference in their inherited characteristics leads to differences in quality and yield, and of two seeds sourced from the same parent plants, one may give satisfactory results according to these criteria, while the other may not.

A tea bush grown from a cutting on the other hand, is an exact copy of the mother plant—a clone. It has exactly the same qualities and the same failings as regards resistance to climate and disease as it does with regard to yield and organoleptic qualities. The advantage of tea bushes that are grown from cuttings lies in the fact that they produce a tea that is always identical in quality and yield, but this method does have one major disadvantage: a weakness in one tea bush will be repeated in all those propagated from it and, if one bush contracts a disease, all the others will develop it. A further disadvantage of bushes grown from cuttings is their shorter lifespan and the tendency of their root system to develop laterally rather than go deep. In addition, a plot of land planted with trees grown from cuttings is more exposed to the danger of landslides.

Due to these differences, it is recommended policy to plant an equal number of bushes grown from seed and bushes grown from cuttings in the same plot. The first, with their root system penetrating deep into the soil, will help to limit erosion, and if one of them develops a disease, it is not inevitable that other bushes from the same mother plant will also contract it. For the same reason, it is also better at the planting stage to choose cuttings from five or six different mother plants, so that no more than 10 percent of the cultivated area is exposed to a particular risk (disease or the toll taken by insect infestation). Mother plants come in three categories (quality strain, yield strain, and standard, or balanced, strain) and planters are recommended to include

A grafting experiment at a research center in Yunnan Province (China).

some of each. On the Darjeeling plantations, for example the established proportions are 40 percent quality strain, 20 percent yield strain, 40 percent standard strain.

PROPAGATING BY SEED AND CUTTINGS

Given that 2½ acres (1 hectare) of plantation is made up, according to region, of between five thousand and fifteen hundred tea bushes, each planter needs to produce a large number of young plants to maintain his plantation's stock. To do this he cultivates nurseries for growing seeds and cuttings, but must take particular care to keep them isolated from the rest of the plantation and to respect certain criteria.

Cuttings are taken from various tea bushes that have been carefully selected for their properties as top quality parent material. These are then planted in a nursery garden well away from all other sources of tea pollen. Pollination is left to the wind and insects and the young plants are left to grow freely, though the nurseries are tended carefully since the future of the plantation rests, at least in part, with them.

In the case of seeds, these are allowed to fall to the ground during the fruiting period (October to January) and are collected daily. The best seed-bearing tea bushes will produce 5 to 8 pounds (2.5–3.5 kilos) of seed per year (three thousand seeds). The seeds are then sorted according to size (requiring a diameter of at least ½ inch/12 mm) and density. Size and weight are indications of the seeds' physical condition. To test their density, they are immersed in water for twenty-four hours; at the end of this time, any that have risen to the surface—the lightest ones—are discarded and only the heaviest kept for use.

The seeds are first placed in a seed tray until the hard shell has split and the radicle has begun to shoot. Each seed is then placed in a little bag filled with a fertile growing mixture and transferred to a nursery, where the young plant, along with tens of thousands of others, will be tended with great care. Initially the young plants are well-shaded from the wind, bad weather, and direct sunlight, but the shade is then progressively reduced to harden them off before their final transplantation at the end of eighteen months.

Right-hand page: grown from cuttings; the bushes in this plot are seven years of age.

The tea bushes in this nursery have reached the end of the eighteen-month hardening off period and will soon be planted out.

Each section of the nursery is clearly marked: type of bush, number of plants, date of propagation, etc.

An experimental tea garden in Darjeeling, with different varieties in miniature plots.

Just as he keeps a special nursery plot in his plantation for the growing of seeds, the planter also creates a similar area for cuttings. The cuttings planted are from selected cultivars and are tended with the utmost care and attention.

One mother tea bush can supply between fifty and thre hundred cuttings a year. The cuttings are removed with a sharp knife, then the flexible part between the tip and the more woody section, is cut further into 1¼ to 1½ inch (3–4 cm) lengths, each bearing one leaf.

The cuttings are placed in the same kind of soil as is used for seed propagation. The root system forms first and then the young plants begin to develop. They are grown on in exactly the same way as those grown from seed. However, cuttings need more fertilizer and water to develop healthily. In order to promote the growth of the roots, the atmosphere needs to be very humid so they are sprayed with clear water, sometimes several times a day, to maintain the degree of hygroscopicity in the air. The moisture content of the soil is also monitored constantly. As with the young plants grown from seed, the cuttings are sheltered from direct sunlight, their roots developing at ten to twelve weeks after planting. In the following four to six weeks, the amount of shade is reduced and the spraying with water is lessened progressively in order to harden off the plants. A cutting is only ready to be planted out when its root system has developed sufficiently. Like the plants grown from seed, plants grown from cuttings need at least eighteen months before finally they can be transplanted.

This plot (foreground) has just been planted. The bushes are spaced so as to cover the entire surface after five years.

FROM NURSERY TO PLANTATION

Preparing a new plot demands patience, perseverance, and effort. Good management of the soil is essential in order to maintain it and improve its fertility, as well as to maximize the tea bushes' productivity, assure satisfactory root growth and to limit, as far as possible, the toll that this takes on the soil structure. Before it is ready to take the young plants, the plot has to be prepared: it must be cleared of weeds; both the surface and the sub-soil must be drained; the soil surface must be plowed to prevent it being baked to a hard crust in the sun, and leveled to remove any hollows where rainwater could collect and stagnate, rather than draining through the soil to the roots; measures to combat erosion need to be put in place and in some cases it is also necessary to install an irrigation network.

The optimum period for transplanting young tea bushes varies from one tea-growing region to another. Everything depends on the climatic conditions, which must give the young plants time to acclimatize and form a good root system and abundant foliage, before the start of the season that is most favorable to their future development. In Darjeeling, for example, the best time to start transplantation is between March and June, before the monsoon brings heavy rains.

As to the number of tea bushes planted per acre, this varies according to the region. In India, when tea planting first began, tea bushes were planted 7,500 to the acre, as can be seen on some plantations in

Darjeeling where plots planted in the nineteenth century by the British are still producing crops today. Nowadays planting less than 18,750 trees per acre is regarded as unprofitable. The average is between 25,000 and 37,500 bushes per acre, with occasionally as many as 45,000.

The young plant is ready to be transferred to the plantation as soon as it has developed a well-branched root system and some leaves. A healthy plant will have a central stem approximately ⅜ inches (8 mm) in diameter and be 16 to 18 inches (40–45 cm) tall. Any stunted plants are discarded, a loss that can amount to as much as a 25 percent annually.

The young tea bushes are planted in holes approximately 12 inches (30 cm) in diameter and 18 inches (45 cm) deep. The space between them is calculated so that, when they are fully mature, their plucking areas will almost merge to cover the entire surface of the ground below. The young tea bushes are at their most vulnerable just after transplantation, when they need to be protected against the sun, wind, and hailstorms. During the period when the large trees planted to provide shade have not yet grown sufficiently tall, temporary shelters made of leguminous plants and ferns filter the sun and protect the young tea bushes from bad weather. At high altitudes, hedges are planted on the crests of the slopes to act as wind-breaks.

THE FORMATIVE PRE-PRODUCTION YEARS

It takes five years before a tea bush can be brought into production. During this formative period they produce no crop but are tended carefully—straw is placed around the base of their trunks to protect the soil from erosion, limit the evaporation of water by the sun and suppress the growth of weeds.

The young bushes are pruned regularly to help them to develop a robust and low-standing structure and the maintenance foliage that is the basis of the growth of vigorous shoots. Pruning also helps the top of the bush grow into a wide plucking surface that will produce the maximum number of harvestable shoots within easy reach of the pluckers.

At the end of these five formative years, each tea bush will have reached maturity, with a permanent structure of productive branches supporting a leafy mattress of maintenance foliage upon which the young shoots will develop. The trees are now ready to be harvested.

According to the region, the plucking table is maintained at a height of roughly 3–4 feet (1–1.2 m).

Without this table, plucking becomes tiring and awkward.

A tea plant allowed to grow freely for five years would reach a height of some 13–16 feet (4–5 m).

THE LIFESPAN OF A TEA TREE

The lifespan of a tea bush under cultivation is normally around forty to fifty years, but some varieties can live to a hundred. Even old bushes, if well maintained, will continue to produce quality crops.

→ Pruning: a necessity

Along with a number of other maintenance procedures that are vital to their health, tea bushes are pruned throughout their lives in order to boost their strength and stimulate their productivity. There are three types of pruning:

Pruning for production, a light pruning is performed every year or every two years at the end of a harvesting cycle, in order to maintain the plucking table at a convenient height and renew the maintenance foliage that is essential to the formation of young shoots.

Pruning for regeneration, which is generally done every five years, rejuvenates the bush after a few years of harvesting have slowly reduced the thickness of the maintenance foliage and the yield. Carried out at 14 inches (35 cm) from ground level, this practice of hard pruning forces the plant to regrow all its productive wood.

Pruning "in the green" is an exceptional measure used for bushes that have been damaged by hailstorms or frost. It re-establishes the plucking surface and encourages a partial renewal of the maintenance foliage.

On plantations that practice organic agriculture, the plucking surface is regularly lowered to within about 12 inches (30 cm) of the soil to limit its exposure to harmful insect attack and diseases.

→ Supplementary nutrients...

Left and center: a detail and overall view of the effects of hard (regenerative) pruning on *Camellia assamica* in Fujian.

Right: viewed from the opposite slope, recently pruned areas on this mountain are clearly distinguishable.

Continuous plucking throughout the year involves the constant renewal of the young leaves that use up the nutrients in the soil so voraciously. Tea therefore makes considerable demands on the soil in which it grows, often resulting in the soil becoming exhausted. It frequently becomes necessary to supplement the nutrients in the soil with the application of fertilizers.

As with all large-scale crop cultivation, chemical fertilizers are also used in the cultivation of tea. In certain parts of the world these have

been and still are the principal fertilizers used. Apart from rice, more labor is used in the cultivation of tea worldwide than in any other crop. It is therefore not surprising to learn that tea represents an important economic issue for a number of tea-producing countries and the yield is of crucial importance.

However, it is not a good idea to generalize. Following the example of many other agricultural sectors, tea cultivation is no longer solely reliant on chemical fertilizers to improve the soil. In many tea-producing regions of the world, cultivation is carried on in small enterprises which do not have the means to invest in fertilizers. Elsewhere, as we shall see, some planters are being pricked by their conscience and are turning more and more to organic methods of cultivation.

→ ... and preventative treatments

The fight against pests, another threat to the quantity and quality of the harvest, is also affected by the same drive for profitability. The plantations provide a stable environment for all manner of predatory creatures—caterpillars, mosquitoes, aphids, cochineal beetles, crickets, and also termites, larvae, ants, dust mites, etc. To combat the invasion of these unwelcome guests, many planters have gone back to spraying with chemicals. Others, however, have abandoned them, once again under the impetus of organic agriculture.

WHEN TEA GROWING GOES ORGANIC

The concept of organic farming has not yet become widespread in tea-producing countries and does not provoke the same response among local consumers as in Western countries. In the last fifteen years or so, however, a growing number of crops have been appearing on the market that have been produced according to organic methods and certified by organizations generally operating in Europe. Made aware of this issue by their Western clients, some planters have realized that it is in their interests to change their methods of cultivation. Some of them, faced with the problem of soil exhaustion after decades of monoculture, see organic farming as a reasonable solution that would allow them to restore the fertility of their land and avoid condemning their plantations to a slow but inexorable decline in terms of yield and quality. Others see organic certification as an official guarantee that has come along providentially to sanction the methods of agriculture that they have been using all along.

Organic certification represents a big financial investment for plantations. Since it is more labor intensive, organic farming means production costs increase in return for yields that are generally smaller. There are many small plantations which cultivate the land using no

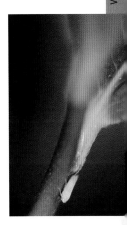

In Taiwan, the damage caused by the paoli is welcomed as assistance from nature (see page 190).

chemical products whatsoever—generally for economic reasons—but whose owners do not have the means to finance this way forward.

Today it is in India, Sri Lanka, China, Vietnam, Japan, and Kenya that the greatest number of plantations certified "organic" are found. The fertilizers used there are principally a form of compost, made from the vegetable matter and animal manure available in the immediate vicinity. In Southern India, for example, the residue from the dross of castor seed after the oil has been extracted is collected. Very rich in nutrients, when spread around the base of the tea trees, this residue helps to improve the soil and increase its capacity for retaining water, also helping to combat soil erosion. Vermiculture, the introduction of earthworms into the soil, is another method of fertilization that is becoming more and more widespread. The earthworms produce a natural fertilizing agent, enriching the soil by releasing large quantities of nutritious mineral elements into it through their casts. In addition to having a significant positive impact on the productivity of the tea bushes, this bio-organic method also helps to improve the drainage and aeration of the soil, and more generally to restore its balance.

As to the fight against parasites, since pesticides, insecticides, and chemical fungicides are strictly prohibited, one solution lies in the introduction of natural insect or bird predators into the plantations, with the help and advice of scientific teams. These are carefully selected so that no one species proliferates and upsets the balance of the ecosystem.

The problems of converting a plantation to organic farming are not just financial. Switching a plot to organic cultivation does not protect it from being polluted by its immediate environment. Airborne pesticides sprayed on a neighboring plantation, for example, may be blown by the wind and contaminate tea trees that are being farmed organically. One of the solutions adopted by many growers in order to limit this problem is to surround their plantations with certain rare tree species, which are selected for their properties of absorption, so forming a screen against airborne pesticides.

When the conversion period is over, and when it has complied with the conditions laid out (see opposite), the plantation is granted a certificate which will allow it to export to Europe as "organically grown tea." The certifying documentation will accompany the tea throughout its journey and could be required for inspection at any time by the certifying organization, the authorities, or even the consumer.

A high population of insects, birds, flowers, weeds, etc., is often the sign of good organic practice.

Right-hand page: on organic plantations, the plucking table is lowered considerably to limit the surfaces exposed to pests.

ORGANIC CERTIFICATION: ESSENTIAL FOR TRADE

Providing official recognition that organic methods are practiced on an estate and a guarantee to the consumer that the product was grown according to European organic standards, certification is essential in organic farming. The work of control and certification is carried out by qualified independent organizations with a mandate to issue the organic farming certificate. The certification of a plantation is a long process. The planter undertakes to comply with and put into practice a contract containing very precise conditions. Here are some of the principal conditions:

- to combat parasites only with natural predators and suitable cultivation
- to employ neither chemical nor transgenic products
- to use only organic-certified plants or seeds
- to separate organic production units from traditional production units
- to observe a transitional period of three years, during which time the plantation will be "in the course of organic conversion" and consequently will be cultivated exclusively according to organic methods, but despite this will still not be considered completely "clean," since it can take several years for the soil to eliminate certain chemical products
- to submit to an annual inspection by the certifying organization which will check all the preceding points

THE PLUCK

As the sun rises over the tea-producing regions of Southern India and Sri Lanka, patches of bright color begin to appear among the intense green of some of the plantations. Often shrouded in a mist blown here and there by a wind that never manages to dissipate it entirely, the tea pluckers are beginning their day. In the time-honored way, they will continue their skilled work of hand plucking for eight hours.

THE HARVESTING CALENDAR

The pluck is the periodic harvesting, either manually or by machine, of the young buds that develop on the plucking surface. Unlike the seasonal crops that we are familiar with (grapes, fruit, and vegetables), the tea is an evergreen plant. As a rule it can supply fresh yields throughout the year in cycles of between four and fifteen days, but since the tea bush grows rapidly in hot and humid weather and more slowly in low temperatures, the harvesting periods vary from region to region and according to season. In Darjeeling, for example, tea is harvested on average forty-two times in the year, but the period between plucks is longer in the spring than during the monsoon, when growth speeds up in a spectacular fashion.

The harvesting calendar also varies according to region and the quality of tea required. In Southern India, Sri Lanka, and also Indonesia (regions that grow mostly black tea), harvesting goes on uninterrupted from January to December. In Northern India, certain Chinese provinces, and on the high-altitude plantations of Taiwan, where the foliage of the tea bushes stops growing during the coldest months of the year, crops are plucked only from April to November. The specific characteristics of teas differ according to the time of year when the leaves were plucked. In certain regions, each period of the year sees the corresponding manufacture of a certain kind of tea. The white teas of Fujian are made only on a few days of the year, at the very start of spring, and

Twice a day pluckers meet at their assembly point where each weighs the contents of his or her basket and notes the result in a register like the one carried by the woman in the foreground. Individual harvests are then collected together.

47

solely from the first buds. When this crop has been harvested, the leaves that continue to grow are destined for other teas, often green teas made from large buds. In India, where many traces of the British Empire still linger, the crop is commonly called a *flush*, a term that means "growth thrust." *First Flush, Second Flush,* and *Third Flush* refer respectively to the harvests of spring, summer, and autumn.

The spring harvests

During the winter, growth slows down, and the young tea bush shoots take advantage of the dormant period to stock up on essential oils. This means that the first harvest of the year, in the spring, is very rich in aromas and highly prized. This is particularly so in China, where the best green teas are produced exclusively from the buds and first leaves of the spring crop, which lasts throughout April in the different provinces (Zhejiang, Anhui, Fujian). They are often referred to as "new season green teas."

In India, the most emblematic of the spring crops is from Darjeeling. The quality of the first pluck of the year depends on the climatic conditions experienced during winter, which is particularly unpredictable in this part of the world. Therefore, work begins somewhere between the last days of February and the third week in March, depending upon the kind of winter experienced, and continues until mid-May. In Assam, too, though more rarely, there is a spring harvest.

In Japan, Ichibancha ("the first crop") is also the most prized for green teas. Its value is enhanced by its symbolic significance, as is everything concerned with the renewal of the seasons in Japan.

THE BUD

During a period of vegetative growth, a bud covered with a silvery down forms at the end of each stem and after a few days develops into a young shoot. The terminal leaf, still curled up upon itself, is the pekoe. It is this leaf bud, the richest in several substances (tannin, caffeine, aromatic compounds), that is the benchmark for quality of the pluck.

After the pekoe, other leaves open out along the stem and it is the number of subjacent leaves that are plucked together with the pekoe that decides the category of the pluck: the more leaves there are growing on the stem that has been cut, the less fine will be the crop, and the younger the leaves, the richer they are in aromatic compounds.

The young shoots must not be plucked too soon during their growth; if only one leaf has developed below the pekoe, the stem should be left until the next pluck, when it has produced at least one more leaf. Providing this rule is adhered to, the next crop will be good.

The type of pluck is decided by the manufacturer and planter, and determines the quality of tea to be produced.

Branch showing well-developed "pekoe" (terminal bud); the lighter, grayish tint is the result of a downy covering.

There are three main types of pluck:

The Imperial Pluck (P+1): the pekoe and the leaf immediately below it are taken. This pluck owes its name to the fact that in the past it was reserved for important dignitaries.

The Fine Pluck (P+2): the pekoe and the two leaves below it are taken. This is an excellent quality pluck.

The Medium Pluck (P+3): the pekoe and the three leaves below are taken. This is the most common type of pluck and produces teas of lower quality than the other two, but it also stimulates the growth of the bush.

Some exceptional plucks take only the bud. This type of pluck is more common in China than anywhere else, mainly for the production of the white tea Yin Zen (Silver Needles) and some very rare green and black teas. This type of harvesting is also practiced in Assam, where it is known as Golden Tips (see page 216).

The fourth and fifth leaves can also be taken, known as "Souchong," resulting in a coarser pluck with less concentration of the chemical and aromatic compounds found in the young shoots. These are not suitable for the manufacture of quality black teas and are generally reserved for Chinese smoked teas.

A tea bush of the *sinensis* type produces around 10½ ounces (300 g) of fresh leaves per year which, when manufactured, will give 2½ ounces (65 g) of tea. A hybrid type tea bush can produce up to 2.2 pounds (1 kg) of green leaves per year.

THE PLUCKING PROCESS

In most cases, the harvesting is done without tools, entirely by hand, and only manual harvesting can guarantee a fine pluck for high quality teas. Another reason why hand plucking is predominant is because many plantations are situated on sloping ground that is only accessible to people, the use of machines being out of the question, although tools such as scissors, sickles, and hedge clippers are sometimes used. Everything depends on the quality of tea that the crop is intended to provide and the time of year that it is harvested. Some seasons, such as the monsoon, for example, produce teas with little aroma that no amount of expertise could turn into teas of quality. These leaves will inevitably end up in teabags or in fragments, so there is no need for very careful plucking.

In Sri Lanka, plucking is a job performed by women. It is the same in India—in Darjeeling, Assam, and the Nilgiri Hills—while the men employed on the plantations devote their time mostly to the maintenance of the soil and the tea bushes (pruning). However, at Kangra, most tasks are performed by both men and women, as they are in China and Taiwan. In Japan, the person driving the tractor or using the mowing machine could equally be a woman or a man, but manual plucking is still done exclusively by women.

Only the bud and the first two leaves are plucked for the finest-quality tea.

The bud and first three leaves are used for tea of medium quality.

A rare type of harvest: these long, silvery buds are destined to make white tea.

→ Manual plucking...

Plucking is done by hand in China and Taiwan, where all the plantations are small, and often family-run affairs, and in India, and—but
exceptionally—Japan (for the finest Gyokuro).

Plucking requires both manual dexterity and a keen eye. The work
is always done facing the slope, with both hands resting on the plucking
surface. The young shoot to be taken is held between the index and middle fingers of each hand, broken by the thumb, and thrown over the
shoulder into the basket or sack hanging on the back of the plucker. In
an eight-hour day a plucker can harvest up to 132 pounds (60 kg) of
leaves which, once dried, will give around 26 pounds (12 kg) of tea.

→ ...or mechanized plucking

Right-hand page:
in Yunnan Province,
a plucker perched high
up in a wild tea tree;
the best leaves are
reckoned to be on the
top branches.

The mechanized pluck is used in regions where the cost of labor is high.
It has no advantage over manual plucking other than to cut down on the
number of people employed. Some machines do provide a good-quality
pluck, collecting only the first leaves, but this is always at the cost of a certain amount of waste. More often than not the plucking machines are
working blind, cutting all the young shoots regardless of the maturity of
the bud. Apart from the damage this can do to the maintenance foliage
and consequently the plucking surface, it can also reduce the value of the
crop. The machine that is the most commonly used, which can only
operate on level ground, is the automatic hedge clipper which straddles
the tea tree and cuts over a width of 5 feet (1.5 m).

After a harvesting cycle of several successive plucks, the bush
enters a rest period and forms a *banjhi* or dormant bud. Plucking the
banjhi when it appears prompts a new spurt of vegetative growth and
consequently a new crop.

Two ways of harvest-
ing: by hand, at
Darjeeling, sometimes
with the aid of a rod so
as to pluck only leaves
above the plucking
table, and using
shears (image on the
right) for a quicker,
less precise pluck
(here in the Nilgiri).

Weight of plucks	Number of shoots/kg of fresh leaves	Number of shoots/kg of dried tea (loss of 70 to 80% of water)
Single bud: 0.05 g	20,000	100,000
Bud + 1 leaf: 0.2 g	5,000	20,000
Bud + 2 leaves: 0.8 g	1,250	7,250
Bud + 3 leaves: 2 g	500	2,500

1 kg = 2.2 lbs.
1 gram = 0.035 ounce

HARVESTS FROM
OLD AND "WILD" TEA TREES

Tea gardens containing tea trees that were planted several centuries ago by Chinese minority groups can still be found in Yunnan Province. They were never greatly exploited but in recent years, these semi-wild trees, which grow freely among trees of other species, have been subjected to regular organized harvesting. Since these trees are never pruned, the pluckers are obliged to clamber about in their branches as if in a second childhood. The leaves from these trees are highly valued—but is this due to the rarity factor (the harvests weigh barely more than a few pounds), or the cost of the labor involved, or perhaps—the answer favored by the Chinese—their exceptional aromatic potential? Whatever the reason, speculation on crops plucked from wild tea trees goes on apace and these leaves sell for the same price as the finest plucks of Fujian or Zhejiang—that is, five times the price of normal leaves. Crops from wild tea trees are always compressed into flat round cakes of green tea (see page 74).

ECONOMIC AND SOCIAL ASPECTS
OF THE TEA INDUSTRY

→ Contrasting economic scenarios

The size of tea plantations around the world varies greatly. From the few hundred square yards cultivated by the Nepalese farmer and his family, to the immense gardens of Sri Lanka which can cover thousands of acres and employ close to ten thousand workers, or the medium-sized plantations that are emerging with the opening up of China, the world of tea offers widely contrasting socio-economic scenarios.

While the low-quality teas (essentially produced by the CTC method, see page 61) reserved for the teabag industry are produced by multinational companies on huge plantations at low altitude or on the plain, where the work can be partially or even entirely mechanized, the production of quality teas covers a very wide range of economic models.

→ A glance at the different systems

In Taiwan, the pluck is conducted mechanically using harvesters; the cutting head runs over the tops of the bushes.

Farmers: In a number of Asian countries, small farms cultivated by a family or with the help of seasonal labor, play a significant role in the tea economy. On these farms the farmer cultivates his land and harvests the crops. Sometimes—and this is often the case in China, Sri Lanka, and Nepal—his work ends there; he then sells his crop of fresh tea on the local market, more often than not to another farmer who has larger premises and is better equipped to process the leaves.

Farmers organized into a cooperative: If, however, the farmer belongs to a cooperative and has joined together with neighboring farmers to invest in the necessary equipment, he can process his own harvest and sell it to a wholesaler. This happens frequently in Japan, India, and Nepal.

Farmer harvesting and manufacturing his own tea: If the farmer has personally invested in the necessary equipment—as happens especially in China and Taiwan—he sells his manufactured tea to a wholesaler, an exporter or sometimes directly to the shops.

Companies that cultivate and manufacture tea: In India, Sri Lanka, and also China, small family concerns co-exist with big organizations that have plantations covering several hundreds or even several thousands of acres, employing thousands of workers. On the Indian subcontinent, more often than not, these very large plantations belong to family groups or to multinational corporations, which have one or several plantations and may have business interests in markets other than tea. In India, these businesses never own the land but rent it long-term

THE ECONOMICS
OF THE **TEA TRADE**

Unlike coffee, tea is not quoted on the commodities futures market. There are two good reasons for this: first, tea, because of its diversity, is, like wine, not a strictly homogeneous product, and second, it can only be stocked for a limited period before it begins to deteriorate. With no one hoarding batches of tea in the expectation of a price rise, the market is free from speculation; essentially it is what is known as an over-the-counter market (OTC) operating in the two possible ways described below, depending on whether "grands crus" or inferior quality teas are involved.

- **Direct OTC transactions between producer and buyer** are always based on a human relationship established over the course of years—one that is often cordial and inevitably based on trust. Producer and distributor know each other well, they meet every year, usually on the plantation. This relationship is absolutely vital: in the case of prestigious vintages or very rare teas, the buyer will always receive samples. The producer, for his part, is encouraged to grow teas of the highest quality as the price offered by the buyer is considerably better than would be offered by an exporter, a wholesaler or even at auction.

There are several steps in OTC transactions. The producer sends a sample of each batch to different potential buyers, but the price is not always mentioned. Each of these potential buyers has one to three days to taste the samples and come up with what he thinks is a fair bid, without knowing what his rivals are offering. The batch goes to the highest bidder, who receives confirmation from the seller; the batch is now his. However, before dispatching the consignment, the seller sends him a second sample so he can make a final check on the quality of his purchase. The consignment is then loaded on to a ship or aircraft according to the buyer's preference. By air, the tea will reach its point of sale in two or three days; by boat, it will take around a month.

- **In the case of an OTC transaction between a broker and a buyer**, the broker keeps the buyer informed of the teas available in his warehouses or to be offered at auction. In the latter case, the broker sends the buyer weekly samples of the lots on offer with an estimated price for each. The buyer indicates his maximum price and the broker informs him within a few days if he has succeeded in obtaining the desired lots on his behalf. Most of the time the brokers also double as blenders: they buy up lots that have failed to find buyers at the auctions, form them into a blend and then offer them to regular customers. The blends in question are usually the cheaper ones.

Limited understanding of these procedures in the West means that many distributors in a particular country claim they are "importers" when, in reality, they do not import tea from the country of production but merely purchase it from a wholesaler on their own continent. In the case of Europe, for instance, the commercial hub of the tea trade is Hamburg, in Germany, home to large-scale tea brokers who supply almost all the so-called European "importers" of any standing. These German importers have gained a reputation for blending original varieties, but above all for the manufacture of aromatic teas.

from the state. There are a certain number of obligations that they must observe—mainly involving providing for the housing, health, and education of the workers in their employ. Each plantation must provide a day nursery, a school, and a hospital, in addition to making a house (often attached to a kitchen garden) available for each employee to live with his family.

In China, in the twentieth century, the state set about organizing the production of a number of teas destined for export rather than local consumption (gunpowder, black teas, smoked teas). Very large manufacturing facilities were built for this purpose. They cultivate large areas and buy fresh leaves from the farms around them. Over a period of years these activities have gradually passed into the private sector and into the hands of companies who rent the land and buildings, both of which remain the property of the state.

→ Fair Trade tea

The Fair Trade movement was set up several years ago to help provide the workers on coffee and cocoa plantations with improved working conditions and decent lives. While the working conditions on tea plantations do differ greatly from country to country, forced labor is no longer involved and the situation of the workers in no way resembles that seen in the coffee and cocoa industries. The quality of the product is what affects the working conditions on a plantation, much more than size or locality. And this has its own impact.

On plantations that focus on the production of lower quality teas, price is the most important factor and the management will seek to minimize their costs without worrying unduly about the effect this has on the quality of the finished product. When dealing with buyers who seek cheap rather than quality tea, the planter has little interest in investing in the skill and ability of his labor force. Seasonal labor is used on this type of plantation, where the harvesting and processing are mechanized and qualified workers are not required, and the management often has no qualms about changing the workforce in the case of a dispute. This is where the Fair Trade movement could make a difference. Most of the plantations that produce inferior quality tea are found in areas where geographical conditions rule out the production of "grand cru" teas. This happens, especially, on plantations situated on the plain

Right-hand page: in Southern India and Sri Lanka, plantations can cover thousands of acres with little access for motor vehicles.

In Kerala, harvesting is primarily the job of the plantations' permanent female staff.

A garden-nursery in Darjeeling. In India, plantations have to make provision for child-care from their earliest years.

A market for fresh leaves at Fuding in Fujian Province. Farmers sell the produce from their own gardens.

where, even with a well-trained labor force, the production of quality teas would be impossible.

Those plantations which produce the great teas, on the other hand, have little interest in obtaining the Fair Trade label. The production of "grands crus" is a particularly lucrative market and the quality batches sell for fifty to one hundred times the price of mediocre tea, so the profit made by the planter enables him to make proper provision for his employees. Since the production of quality teas demands constant vigilance, beginning with the careful tending of the tea bushes through to the harvest and in all stages of manufacture, the planter has every reason to ensure that his workers are well-trained and to help develop a mutual feeling of trust. For him, training is an investment and unless he wants to see his workforce leaving him to work for the highest bidder on the neighboring plantations, he is obliged to guarantee that the working and living conditions he offers are as good as, and perhaps better than, those offered by his competitors. It is no coincidence, therefore, that the plantations that produce teas of excellent quality are also those with the best nurseries, schools, and hospitals, and where work-related accidents are extremely rare. These plantations have long practiced a form of Fair Trade without being certified by any organization.

Unfortunately, even in prime growing areas such as Darjeeling, there are planters who fail to produce superior quality teas and who have trouble finding buyers prepared to pay a proper price for their tea. There are also those who, in search of a commercial market for mediocre teas but unwilling to make the effort to improve their product and better train their workforce, go down the Fair Trade road, because this label makes their teas more acceptable in the eyes of the Western consumer. Since the Fair Trade initiative does not oblige the producer to look into ways of improving his product, it has some unfortunate consequences. Fair Trade labels, after all, reflect only the conditions under which production takes place and not the flavor of the products. Due to this, two of the Darjeeling plantations presently covered by the Fair Trade label turn out some of the least interesting teas to come from this mountainous region.

"Two leaves and one bud:" in many tea-growing regions, this encapsulates the expertise of manual plucking, a source of great pride to the workers.

TEA BUYING IN CHINA

In China, until the period 1995–2000, all teas were produced on state plantations and exported via regional bureaux by the government. In each bureau there would be one negotiator for each variety of tea. For example, the bureau of Fujian Province had one official in charge of black teas and others for Wu Long, etc. If a Westerner wanted to buy Wu Long from Fujian, there was only one person in the whole of China authorized to deal with him. In 1995 the trade began to be liberalized with the encouragement of private enterprise.

Today the situation has altered drastically and many former officials from the state export department have set up their own private companies, working for themselves instead of the government. Additionally, they have often invested in the plantations to gain a stake in production.

Nonetheless, certain rules remain unchanged: today, as ever, Chinese teas must undergo checks before export to validate their trade description.

Before the era of liberalization, every tea destined for sale abroad was checked by government experts specializing in a single category. These professionals went round every plantation, sampled the teas, and attributed a grade to each. The plantation owner was a mere spectator at the tastings and could only await the verdict. He was obliged to accept the expert's decision and on every tea chest and all documentation— bills, certificates of origin, etc.—he had to state the exact grade awarded to each variety.

Nowadays these checks still take place, but at the moment of export. The government tasters no longer visit the plantations but receive samples of teas due for shipment. Each sample is checked for the correctness of its description and grade. It is still true that no tea can leave China without the authority of the official tasters; their opinion carries so much weight that many plantation owners and producers have tried to acquire their expertise by "poaching" them from the government service and offering them posts on their estates.

THE KOLKATA TEA MARKET

In India, with the exception of the best teas which are often purchased on the OTC system, common varieties are sold at auction, the principal markets being in Kolkata (Calcutta). These take place every Tuesday. Only brokers are admitted; accredited guests are allowed to observe the proceedings from behind a glass screen located on one side of the room.

Each broker receives details of the forthcoming sale, including the description and evaluation of each particular lot. On the day before the sale he has the opportunity to taste the tea. Tea auctions are sometimes carried out in reverse: each round starting with a high price that is gradually lowered until a bidder raises his hand to claim that particular lot.

THE COLORS
OF TEA

At the end of a day's harvest, the entire crop is assembled at the farm or the factory and a race against the clock begins to prevent uncontrolled transformation of the leaves. Like all vegetable matter, tea leaves contain oxidizing enzymes (the molecules responsible for the yellowing of leaves in autumn) and as soon as they are plucked, the oxidation of the pigments and tannins they contain begins.

It is this phenomenon of oxidation that will determine the final color of the tea—green, black, or white. It was long thought, among the first Westerners to take an interest in tea, that black tea and green tea came from different plants. And of course, the Chinese, who had the monopoly of supplying tea to the West and jealously guarded the secrets both of its cultivation and manufacture, did little or nothing to correct this misconception.

All these diverse colors, however, come from just one species of plant, the *Camellia sinensis*. It is the planter who determines the chosen color of the tea, either by preventing the oxidation process or allowing it to start then subsequently controlling it.

The freshly plucked leaves can be made into every color of tea: green, black, Wu Long, white, dark, yellow, and so on. In the tea world this phenomenon of color change is known as "fermentation," though it is not, strictly speaking, fermentation at all but oxidation. The cells in the tea leaf contain the enzyme oxidase. When the cells are broken (either naturally, by the deterioration of the cellular structure of the leaf, or deliberately, by rolling), this enzyme is released to begin its oxidizing action. By reacting with the oxygen in the air, it oxidizes and transforms the polyphenols present in the leaf and, especially, metabolizes the catechins in two other groups of molecules: the thearubigins and theaflavins, which are, with others, ultimately responsible for the color of the liquor.

In the case of black tea, the oxidation is allowed to go full term and the leaf is oxidized 100 percent. In the case of Wu Long teas, it is arrested in the course of the process so that the leaf will be 10, 20, 30, and even up to 70 percent oxidized. For green teas care is taken to prevent any oxidation from taking place.

Inside a tea-processing plant. Sieving is a simple way to separate whole leaves from damaged ones.

59

On the following pages we refer to oxidation or semi-oxidation and not fermentation or semi-fermentation. However, there is, a family of Chinese teas—dark teas—which does undergo a process of fermentation proper (see page 74).

The color palette of Chinese teas

While in the majority of countries the choice is between green tea, black tea, or semi-oxidized tea, Chinese teas are subject to a system of classification which is entirely their own and which to some extent avoids these international criteria. It is based on the color of the infused leaves.

This classification is constructed around the six great tea families: green teas, blue-green teas, red teas, black teas, yellow teas, and white teas. It reflects the diversity of tea in China and the Chinese knowledge of oxidation. Each color results from a specific manufacturing process, in the course of which the leaf undergoes a varying degree of oxidation that, in turn, gives the tea its characteristic flavor.

While the green and the white teas correspond to those described in the following pages, the others differ. The blue-green teas are those which are semi-oxidized (Wu Long); the red teas are those which we call "black"—not to be confused with the Chinese black teas, which are the equivalent of those teas known in the West as dark teas; the yellow teas are very rare and are prepared in a similar way to green teas.

Right-hand page: these teabags of Indian tea contain a fine powder that was produced by the CTC method. The tea has little taste, but the color in the cup is instantaneous.

On large plantations, the harvest is rapidly taken to the processing plant by tractor.

BLACK TEAS

Black teas (which the Chinese call red teas on account of the rather bronze color of the infusion) are fully-oxidized teas. Legend recounts that in the seventeenth century, a cargo of tea that arrived in London from China, at the end of a particularly long voyage, had gone moldy in its boxes. Originally green, it had turned black but in spite of this the English found it very much to their taste and immediately re-ordered it.

Though improbable, this anecdote does point the way to China, where this method of manufacturing black tea originated. In the nineteenth century, when they began the cultivation and manufacture of tea in India, the British first made use of Chinese labor, but then quickly perfected the tools needed to mechanize the different stages of this so-called "orthodox" process—as against the CTC process (see opposite).

The leaves are processed in six different operations: withering, rolling, riddling, oxidation, firing, and sorting.

Each batch of leaves is first listed in a register indicating the number of the plot from which it was harvested. Batches deemed to be of exceptional quality and destined for the production of "grand crus" are always kept separate during manufacture.

THE CTC PROCESS

At the end of the nineteenth century in India, the British began to mechanize different stages in the production of tea. The rollers, graders, and other machines that were based on manual processing were used in what came to be known as the "orthodox" production method. Later in Assam in the 1930s, they developed and perfected the mechanized CTC method, or "crush, tear, curl" which describes how the leaves are treated. After withering, they are chopped into tiny pieces then rolled into very regular, tightly packed little balls, varying in size from grains of sand to fine lead shot.

Originally intended for use with low-grade leaves that could not be processed by the orthodox method, CTC gradually revolutionized the production of black tea, beginning with those regions and countries to which tea growing had been introduced by the British. This type of tea is particularly suitable for use in teabags. One of the qualities of a CTC tea is the fact that it almost immediately produces a dark color in the cup... though the flavor is unlikely to be very interesting.

Nowadays the major producing countries of black teas (with the exception of Sri Lanka) almost all use the CTC method. The technology is becoming standard and is also extending to new tea families. Factories in China have recently begun using CTC in the manufacture of some of their Pu Er teas.

Withering: Depending on the variety, a tea leaf contains about 70–80 percent water. When the leaves are withered in the first part of the processing, they lose 50–60 percent of their moisture and are soft enough to be handled without tearing.

Traditionally, withering took place in the open air, with the leaves exposed to sunlight, but nowadays it is almost always done in the factory, in halls that have been specially adapted so that the temperature, humidity, and ventilation can be controlled. The crop is spread in thin, even layers on racks made from cloth, bamboo, or wire, or in tanks with a perforated or grille base, ventilated by a light current of air that prevents the level of humidity from rising too high. The withering hall is always well ventilated and kept at a temperature between 68 and 75°F (20–24°C).

Withering lasts for an average of eighteen to twenty hours but, depending on the region and the climatic conditions, it can go on for up to thirty hours. During this stage a number of biochemical reactions take place within the leaf. The level of caffeine and the amount of amino acids increases, while the carotene content is lowered.

Some of these reactions are responsible for producing the aroma compounds and the halls where the withering takes place are filled with very typically floral scents, reminiscent of jasmine and roses, which are generated by the emergence of molecules belonging to the aldehyde and alcohol family. These molecules, which in turn change during oxidation and give rise to new scented compounds are, to a certain extent, the forerunners of the flavors.

The expertise of the factory manager, like that of the cellar master in the vineyard, is an essential factor. He is the one who, using a combination of eye and nose, will decide when the moment has come to end the withering process.

Rolling and riddling: After withering, the leaves will have softened and become flexible. The next stage, rolling, is intended to break down the cells to release the enzymes they contain, and encourage the reactions produced in them by oxidation. The more the leaves are rolled, the more rapidly oxidation takes place. It is the length and force of the rolling that decides the final result in the cup—lightly rolled leaves give a light liquor with only slight astringency; more energetic rolling produces a more full-bodied result.

Rolling may be done by hand—as for the finest black teas in China—or mechanically. The process lasts about thirty minutes but

A processing plant for black tea in the Anamalai Hills, in Southern India.

In the withering hall, the leaves are spread out on racks, beneath which currents of air are blown.

Rolling is carried out by well-calibrated machines that are able to exert sufficient pressure on the leaves without destroying them.

may go on longer or be repeated after the buds, which are tender and risk being broken by it, have been taken out. The first rolling is always light, the second more vigorous. The total time the leaves are rolled depends on the time of year when the crop is harvested, the temperature of the leaves upon leaving the withering hall, and the prevailing climatic conditions.

After rolling, the leaves will have become sticky and be curled up lengthwise and may have clogged together. If they have become clogged they are passed through a special machine equipped with a form of comb, which separates the clumps formed in the roller. This is the riddling process.

Oxidation: This is the crucial operation that is primarily responsible for governing the quality of the tea. The three most important factors are humidity, temperature, and duration of the oxidation.

Unlike withering, which removes water from the leaf, in oxidation the humidity level needs to be maintained in order to facilitate the process. The leaves are spread on tables in layers 1½ to 2½ inches (4–6 cm) thick, in a well-ventilated but draft-free hall, where the atmosphere is very damp (90–95 percent) and the ambient temperature is kept constant at between 68 and 71°F (20–22°C). If it drops below 68°F, the process of oxidation is slowed or even stopped, but if the temperature rises above 71°F the leaf risks being "burned."

During oxidation, after several hours, the leaves gradually take on tawny and bronze tints, turning to red-brown by the end of the procedure.

The length of time required for oxidation varies from one to three hours according to the quality of the leaves, the time of year, the geographical region, and the color required.

The polymerization of the catechins into thearubigins and theaflavins is accompanied by the appearance of new aromatic compounds, especially those molecules responsible for the woody, fruity (both ripe and cooked fruit), spicy, and vanilla notes.

The oxidation process is closely monitored by experts. The first "odor peak" (or "first nose") occurs after about fifteen minutes, then this surge of intense aroma subsides and the process continues until the arrival of the second "odor peak." This is an appropriate time to halt the process. During oxidation, the color of the leaves changes to red or brown and it is this change of color that indicates to the tea expert exactly when the process should be halted.

Firing: To stop the oxidation process once the desired level has been reached, the leaves must be heated immediately to a temperature which will destroy the heat-sensitive enzymes that cause it. This will have the further effect of reducing the humidity contained in the leaves. This firing or drying-out process, is carried out in machines that expose the leaves to an average temperature of 194°F (90°C) for fifteen to twenty minutes. However, the temperature and the length of time the leaves are exposed may be varied to take a number of factors into account. Firing is another stage which demands great expertise: too little drying-out and the water content of the leaves remains too high so that they risk being attacked by mold; too much (because the temperature is too high

Following pages: ground floor of a tea factory in Sri Lanka. In the foreground black tea—fresh from the drying oven— is transported by conveyor belt to a large "sieve shaker" to be graded. In the background are three rolling-machines.

Right-hand page: today, most Pu Er is compressed into cakes, just as it was in the fifth century.

Grading by hand—reserved for quality teas—involves removing small pieces of twig, badly rolled leaves, dirt, and small insects, one by one.

or the exposure time too long) and the tea will lack flavor—a tea that is dried 100 percent cannot be infused because many of the substances in the leaves are no longer soluble. After firing the leaves must still contain 5–6 percent water.

Firing also plays a part in determining the character of tea. When the leaves are exposed to a high temperature, the interaction between the sugars and amino acids in the leaf is amplified and this leads to the formation of certain aromatic compounds and causes the polyphenols to combine with the proteins, reducing the astringency of the liquor. As soon as it comes out of the dryer, the tea is cooled rapidly since as it must be completely cold before beginning the next phase; if not the leaf will be brittle.

Grading: The next stage involves sorting the tea into different grades. It can be sorted into *broken* and *whole* leaves immediately. The *broken* leaves may have been damaged during the production process, or they can be produced artificially by being chopped by machine.

The *whole* leaves are then graded according to how fine they are. This is done by machine or, for the best qualities, with a hand sieve. The leaves should be graded quickly because tea leaves have a tendency to soak up any humidity in the surrounding air, and in subtropical regions the humidity level may be high. After grading, the tea is put into silos and stored to await packaging.

🌱 Tea grades deciphered

In India, and in all the countries that were involved in the manufacture of black tea under the impetus of the British, there are a whole series of abbreviations that, if you know how to decipher them, give a useful guide to the grade and therefore the quality of the leaves. The following are some of the grades used most often by tea merchants. OP (Orange Pekoe) certifies that the tea comes from a fine pluck (the bud and two adjacent leaves). If the pluck has been carried out early in the year and the bud has not yet opened, that tea will be FOP (Flowery Orange Pekoe) and if the tips of the buds are golden it becomes GFOP (Golden Flowery Orange Pekoe). The more letters that are added on the left of the acronym (T for Tippy, F for Finest, S for Special), the more exceptional was the harvest. When a B slips in before the final OP, this means the leaves are *broken*. As to those leaves reduced to tiny fragments, they are called Fannings (F).

Packaging: When it is packaged, tea should not contain more than 5–6 percent water and is subject to a compulsory check. Under pressure from Western markets, especially in Germany, and in accordance with international regulations aimed at protecting the world's forests, fewer aluminium-lined wooden tea chests are now used. They are being replaced by paper sacks lined with aluminum foil, which provides the best barrier against humidity.

THE HISTORY OF
TEA AND ITS MANUFACTURE

"Like Art, Tea has its periods and its schools," as Okakura Kakuzo stresses in his *Book of Tea*. Preparing tea has not always been a simple matter of infusing a pinch of leaves: for a long time tea was boiled and then whisked—two methods of preparation which were directly linked to the tea-manufacturing techniques that were prevalent until the end of the fourteenth century.

Already highly prized in the court circles of China, from the fifth century onwards, tea gained rapidly in popularity among the population as a whole. At that time the leaves were steamed slowly in bamboo baskets immediately after they were plucked, then pounded in a mortar to obtain a smooth pulp which was pressed in a form. Once hardened, the resulting brick of tea was turned out and dried in the sun to prevent mold from forming. Sometimes the leaves were first mixed with other ingredients, such as ginger, mandarin peel, spices, onions, etc. This technique of compacting tea into bricks served two purposes, it was a useful way to store it and also made it easy to transport. Tea soon began to be traded on a regular basis, especially with Tibet. When it was to be used, it was powdered and dropped into boiling, often salted, water. This method of preparation is still in use in certain parts of Asia and tea bricks continue to be made today.

In order to keep the quality of tea batches consistent, since it is impossible to produce the same tea two days running, two to three weeks production is mixed together. Only certain crops of a very high quality are not mixed with others; these are packaged every day for direct sale in small batches. The best of the Darjeeling teas are dealt with in this way.

In the case of the very high quality Chinese teas (such as the best grades from Yunnan and Qimen), the preparation process remains traditional. As soon as they have been plucked, the leaves are exposed to the sun in large bamboo baskets for about two hours. During this withering period, they are regularly tossed and stirred to prevent those not in contact with the air from starting to go moldy. They are then taken to the handling hall where they are spread out in thin layers and left to cool. Next they are put back in the baskets and rolled by hand for about ten minutes before being spread out again. These two operations are repeated three or four times until the leaves have become supple and have turned brown.

They then undergo a firing process that involves dropping a small quantity at a time (not more than about 2 pounds) into bowls heated to 140 to 158°F (60–70°C) over stoves fired by bamboo. This firing lasts for barely thirty seconds. Next the leaves are rolled into the required shape. Roasting and rolling are done three or four times until the leaves are dry.

The following day they are graded by hand to remove any that are imperfect and are then packaged.

GREEN TEAS

As the Chinese say, firing fresh leaves in a wok "kills the green."

The rolling and drying stages continue in the pan.

Firing green tea takes place in a rotating drum.

The manufacture of green tea has long been the prerogative of China (Fujian, Zhejiang, and Anhui provinces are the birthplace of some of the most famous of Chinese green teas). The tradition of ancestral techniques—which varied from region to region, or even from village to village—still persists to this day. These traditional methods produce a quality of tea which is remarkable for the delicacy of its aroma, the fine presentation of the leaf and the flavor of the liquor.

Tea, along with Buddhism, was introduced to Japan in the eighth century by monks who appreciated its stimulative properties during their sessions of meditation. Japan produces only green tea, with some of the finest rivaling the green teas of China.

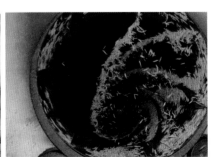

More recently, other tea-producing countries (notably Northern India) have begun experimenting with the manufacture of green tea, but without so far obtaining such exceptional results.

Green teas do not undergo oxidation. While the methods of manufacture may vary greatly in detail according to the region or country where the teas are made, the three manufacturing stages aimed at preventing the leaves from oxidizing remain the same: firing, rolling, drying.

Firing: In order to kill the enzyme which causes oxidation, the leaves are fired immediately after the pluck. The firing can be done in several ways and involves exposing the leaves rapidly to a temperature of not less than 212°F for thirty seconds to five minutes.

In China, depending on the region and the type of tea required, firing is done mechanically in a heated revolving drum, or manually in a pan or wok placed directly over a flame. Prolonged contact with the hot metal sets up a reaction in the leaves known as the "Maillard reaction," after Louis Camille Maillard, who discovered it in 1912—the proteins and the sugars present in the leaves undergo a change and give rise to substances bearing aromas with notes of toast, hazelnuts, and almonds. The tea maker's art lies in not allowing the leaves to burn. Sometimes blisters appear on tea that has been fired in a wok, indicating that the process has not been carried out correctly.

Another method of neutralizing the oxidizing enzymes is steaming. This procedure—first used in Japan in 1738—preserves all the flavors, aromas, and color of the fresh leaf intact. It is the reason why Japanese teas have such fresh aromas, rich in plant notes that evoke cooked vegetables, and why the color of their liquor is so intense, in some cases a quite emerald green. It has also been discovered more recently that the steaming process is the most effective way of preserving the vitamin content. Sometimes, though more rarely, the tea is simply dried in the sun. The green tea cakes that are destined to become Pu Er are also dried in this way, as described later. By the end of this stage the leaves will have become sufficiently supple to be rolled up or folded.

Rolling: This is done manually or mechanically (in a machine of the same type as those used in the manufacture of black tea). In Japan, where most of the tea is manufactured on a large scale, rolling is mechanized. In China, too, certain types of tea (leaves in the form of flakes or shaped into pearls) are rolled mechanically but, more often than not, those that are to be shaped into rods, balls, twists, or even the long, slender bud and leaf combinations found in the Long Jing teas, are rolled by hand. The leaves can be rolled while they are cold or still warm, according to the delicacy of the pluck. Fine young leaves are easily manipulated when cold as they contain more water than more mature ones. Manual rolling requires precise, well-practiced and dextrous movements. Every village has its own methods for producing the same shape of leaf. The shape given to the leaf will influence the notes predominat-

Partially deprived of light, the theanine becomes concentrated in the leaves resulting in teas of great sweetness, the Gyokuro. In Japan, the bushes that are destined to produce certain green teas are covered with large pieces of dark cloth for the three weeks preceding the harvest, which allows the leaves to develop their characteristic notes (see Gyokuro, page 199).

69

ing in the liquor: a lightly rolled leaf will produce softer notes, a more tightly rolled one will be more full-bodied.

Drying and packaging: Once formed into their final shape, the leaves then undergo a more radical form of dehydration which is absolutely essential to their conservation. Chinese teas are generally dried in wicker dryers, around which hot air is circulated for two or three minutes. They are then left to rest for half an hour and are then placed back in the dryer, repeating the process until the leaves contain no more than 5–6 percent water.

Some green teas are processed further after they have been dried. Green Needles, in particular, is treated in this way. It is a tea made solely from long green buds from which the down has been completely re-moved. After being tossed around vigorously in a rotary drum to remove the down, the leaves are shaken in a machine called "one thousand shakes"—the movement straightens the leaves to prevent them from curling up. It also gets rid of the last residue of down. The leaves are then graded and packaged.

A typical plantation in the province of Nantou (Taiwan), known for its Wu Long teas with large pearls.

WU LONG,
OR SEMI-OXIDIZED TEAS

Inaccurately referred to as "semi-fermented" teas, Wu Long teas, which the Chinese also call "blue-green" because of the color of the infused leaves, are semi-oxidized—the oxidation process is interrupted part way through—unlike green teas which are not oxidized at all, and black teas, which are fully oxidized. Still little known outside Asia, Wu Long teas—a specialty of the Fujian and Guangdong provinces of mainland China and Taiwan—constitute one of the great Chinese tea families. There are many different types of Wu Long, the tea being affected by the location of the plantation, the variety of bush and type of leaves used, the time of year of the pluck, variations in the rate of oxidation, the length of firing, the way the leaves are folded, etc.

The origin of the term Wu Long

In Chinese, *Wu Long* means literally "black dragon" and refers to the very dark color frequently taken on by the leaves during drying. However, according to legend, there is a different explanation for the origin of the color: Wu Liang, a Chinese planter, was harvesting his tea one day when he saw a stag. He interrupted the harvest to give chase and, arriving home with the carcass he got busy skinning and cutting it up and quite forgot to put the tea leaves out to dry. A few days later he remembered his precious crop and noticed that the leaves had changed color. He fired them nevertheless, then infused some and was very surprised by the unusually soft and aromatic fragrance they gave off. The secret of his discovery spread around the entire province and the name Wu Liang was transformed into *Wu Long Cha* or "tea of the black dragon."

Traditionally, there are two main categories of Wu Long—lightly oxi-dized teas (10 to 30 percent oxidation), made according to the so-called "Chinese" method, and those that are more oxidized (from 60 to 70 per-cent), made by a method developed in Taiwan. In practice, the param-eters for the manufacture of Wu Long teas are fairly flexible. Each region has its own expertise and produces teas oxidized to a degree that does not necessarily fall within these percentage specifications. Nevertheless, regardless of the local practice, all semi-oxidized teas have to undergo the following processes.

Withering: The leaves are plucked at a precise stage in their develop-ment, when they are not too tender nor mature but instead are fleshy and contain fewer tannins and less caffeine than younger growth. The leaves are withered in the sun or in a withering hall, for a period of one to four hours, after which they are left in a cool, damp room. Repeated twice more, this process tenderizes the leaves.

Oxidation: This occurs during the next and most important stage—"sweating." It is a delicate process during which different aromatic tea compounds begin to appear. Lightly-oxidized leaves develop intense floral and vegetal notes, while heavily oxidized leaves have a fruity, woody, almost spicy character. The difficulty lies in choosing the right moment to halt the process in order to achieve the taste and aroma char-acteristics that are required.

It is called "sweating" because the leaves are literally "sweated" while being stirred constantly in an atmosphere maintained at a temper-ature of 71 to 77°F (22–25°C), with 85 percent humidity. Unlike the oxi-dation of black teas, which occurs when the leaves are subjected to intensive rolling, the oxidation of Wu Long teas is more gentle, begin-ning naturally as soon as the leaves are plucked. It continues while the leaves are stirred and tossed manually, lightly at first but then more vig-orously. The cellular structure of the leaf is gradually degraded and, in the case of black tea, an enzyme is released which reacts with the oxy-gen in the surrounding air. Oxidation then begins in the leaf, starting around the edges, which turn a reddish color.

The planter regularly inhales the scent of the leaves, using his senses of both smell and touch to monitor the operation. When he judges that the optimum degree of oxidation has been reached—that is, when the texture of the leaf is sufficiently supple and the bouquet ideal—it is time to halt the process.

The withering of Wu Long teas begins in the open air. The leaves are raked and shaken constantly.

The leaves are then spread out on large bamboo racks in the "sweating" hall where the withering process continues and oxidation begins.

After a brief period of withering, this bell-shaped roller, rolls the leaves up on themselves.

When using the so-called Chinese method, oxidation is stopped when it reaches a threshold of 10 or 30 percent. This produces light teas with vegetal and flowery notes. The "Taiwanese" method, which involves a longer period of "sweating," allows the oxidation level to rise to 70 percent and produces a darker, more fruity, woody infusion.

Firing: Once the required level of oxidation has been reached, the leaves are then fired in pans or ovens with revolving drums heated to a temperature of around 400°F (200°C), or sometimes increasing to 475 or 500°F (240–260°C) in certain cases. The firing lasts between thirty seconds and five minutes and destroys the enzyme responsible for oxidation. At the end of this "ordeal by fire," by which time the leaves have become malleable and flexible, they are ready for the next stage—rolling.

Rolling, drying, and packaging: Rolling the leaves brings to the surface the essential oils that have been revealed during oxidation. It is carried out immediately after firing when the leaves, which are more fleshy than those used for other types of tea, are still warm. In the case of some teas (Bao Zhong or Shui Xian), the leaf is simply crumpled; in other cases it is shaped into a twist or a ball. Dong Ding is a perfect example of this.

After rolling, the leaves are dried at a temperature of 212°F (100°C) for around twenty minutes in a dryer similar to those used in the manufacture of black tea, or in bamboo baskets (like those used for steaming dim sum, only larger), which are heated over coal fires or electric elements.

Sometimes, as in the case of the famous Chinese Yan Cha tea, the drying period can last for several hours. This produces the chemical reaction known as the Maillard reaction (see page 69) which blackens the leaves and brings out notes of toasting and burning in the infusion. This is the reason why the distinction is sometimes made between those Wu Long teas that have not undergone this final firing and are predominantly vegetal in character, and those that have the characteristic "fire taste," to use the descriptive Chinese term. The teas are then ready for packaging.

Wu Long in pearl form undergoes a special type of rolling; the leaves are packed tightly into a cloth bag, which is then pressed between two plates for several minutes (right); the bag is then shaken and undone. This operation is repeated more than forty times with the same leaves.

YELLOW TEAS

In China, some teas are marketed under the name of "yellow tea." Does that mean that there is another color of tea? However, in this case, yellow does not indicate a color produced by a specific method of manufacture, but is a term generally applied to a green or white tea of such exceptional quality that it is fit for the emperor—yellow being the color symbolic of imperial power. In the days when each Chinese province was bound to pay a tribute to the emperor, the very best of its products, edible and otherwise, was reserved for that purpose. The tea-producing provinces were no exception to this rule and sent their finest crops to the court, which is how, by association, "imperial tea" became "yellow tea." Nowadays, if a visitor is offered a cup of yellow tea he can take it as an indication that he has the status of an important guest. This is a very small family of teas, with characteristics that are somewhere between those of white and green tea. The best known example of Chinese yellow tea is Jun Shan Yin Zen (see page 174), which is only produced in tiny quantities.

WHITE TEAS

Two ways of withering white tea: the traditional withering, on bamboo trays in full sun in the open air, or on racks in a heated and well-ventilated room.

Traditionally, white teas are a specialty of the Chinese province of Fujian. Of all the tea families, it is the white teas that undergo the least elaborate manufacturing process, and yet it is also the white teas that are some of the most delicate of all.

There are two main types of white tea: Silver Needles, made solely from long silvery buds, and Bai Mu Dan, which is made from stems bearing a bud and two—or sometimes three or four—leaves.

The harvest (one bud and two adjacent leaves) takes place just when the bud is beginning to open. In the case of the Silver Needles, the bud is separated from the leaves and stem immediately after the pluck and the leaves undergo a separate treatment.

White teas are made with leaves left in their natural state. They undergo just two processes: withering and drying.

Withering: In order to bring about a moisture loss in line with other teas, the leaves undergo a much longer period of withering varying from forty-eight to sixty hours. Traditionally, the withering is done in the open air and the planter's art lies in predicting the climatic conditions and time the harvest accordingly. In order to control the temperature and ambient humidity more easily, withering is increasingly being carried out in halls that are temperature controlled (86–90°F/30–32°C) and equipped with a sophisticated ventilation system. Oxidation begins during this stage but, because the leaf is not manipulated in any way, it progresses only very slowly.

Drying and packaging: After withering in a heated hall, the humidity remaining in the leaves is no more than 5 to 7 percent but because of

Fujian's humid atmosphere at this time of year, it rises to 15 percent in minutes, so the leaves need to be put through a more radical drying process, either on the shelves of a hot-air dryer or in bowls or pans over a fire. The tea is then graded by hand before being packaged and sent out to the tea merchants.

DARK TEAS

The special feature of dark teas (a Chinese specialty named after the dark brown color of the infusion) is linked to the manufacturing method and the aging properties this produces. They are the only teas that reputedly improve with age. This unique property derives from the way they are manufactured involving true fermentation. Most of the dark teas produced come from Yunnan, but other provinces (Guangdong, Hubei, Hunan, Jiangxi, and Szechuan) also make them. The best-known of the dark teas are the Pu Er, produced exclusively in Yunnan from a variety of tea bush, called Da Ye ("large leaves"), which is peculiar to that region. The official definition of Pu Er—which is rather like the French wine classification *appellation d'origine contrôlée*—is: "Tea produced from leaves harvested from the large-leafed Da Ye tea bushes growing in the Yunnan province, sun-dried and having undergone a process of fermentation, either natural or induced."

❦ A well-guarded secret

The Chinese are not averse to being a little vague and mysterious about the secrets of their manufacturing processes and aging methods, so the information available on Pu Er teas can be contradictory. This probably stems from a desire to protect themselves against industrial espionage, a problem to which they are exposed because of the craze for Pu Er, both in China and—for some years now—the West. The success of Pu Er, which is due to a large extent to the health benefits claimed for it, has had a profound impact on the selling price.

Unlike the teas we have looked at so far, the harvesting and processing of the leaves is carried out at different times and in different places, and, depending on which of the two very different manufacturing processes are used, two quite distinct kinds of Pu Er can result:

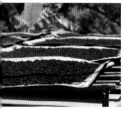

These leaves plucked from the Da Ye tea bush, destined for the production of Pu Er, are drying in the sun.

Compressed green teas, which ferment naturally over a period of years. This traditional method of manufacture, which has been in existence in China for more than three thousand years, compresses the tea into cakes or bricks, which were well suited to the early means of transporting them.

Black, or "cooked" Pu Er, in which fermentation is accelerated artificially. It is marketed either loose or compressed.

In both cases the first processing stages are the same:

The leaves are dried in the sun for about twenty-four hours. The heat needs to be sufficient to destroy the enzymes that cause oxidation, but this is never achieved entirely and the leaves do become slightly oxidized. At this stage, the freshly plucked leaves give off an intense floral note which, as they wither, evolves towards leather and animal notes.

Once dried, the leaves are graded by hand and any defective ones are discarded. They are then packaged and stored before being sold either to big manufacturing concerns or to specialist Pu Er wholesalers who will themselves take care of the processing. Which type of Pu Er will eventually be produced will depend upon the manufacturing method chosen.

→ Compressed green teas

The leaves are compressed into different shapes: flat cakes, birds' nests, bricks, etc.

During the initial stage of the process, the dried leaves are softened by placing the required quantity in a metal receptacle over a jet of steam at 350°F (170°C) for a few minutes. When the leaves have cooled they are put into a cotton bag which is then inserted between the two plates of a hot press, under a continuous flow of steam, to compress the cake into shape.

Once the cake has cooled, it is taken out of the bag and left to dry on openwork bamboo shelves in a heated, well-ventilated hall. It is left for twenty-four hours and then packaged.

The cakes will be stored in order to age them, though not on the premises where they were made. The storage will be handled by specialist wholesalers who buy them in large quantities. Also called "post-fermentation," the aging is caused by the micro-organisms present in the tea (the principal one being *Aspergillus niger*, a yeast that is involved in the fermentation of many foodstuffs). They proliferate freely in a warm, damp, and ventilated atmosphere. Storing in optimum conditions encourages the slow, natural fermentation of the tea leaves, which gradually develop their taste and aroma characteristics. Fermenting naturally during storage, the cakes gradually turn into Pu Er. It takes five years for the astringency and slight metallic mineral note finally to soften, improve, and turn into a harmonious post-fermentation bouquet (nicely balanced damp, woody notes with no remaining trace of the metallic taste in the tea), and for the polyphenols to dissolve into smaller, and consequently less astringent, molecules.

→ The "cooked" or black Pu Er teas

The fermentation process is speeded up in the production of these teas. In this case the method used owes nothing to ancestral traditions but was perfected in the early 1970s by the tea-producing factory of Kunming, the capital of Yunnan Province.

The leaves are spread in layers about 24 inches (60 cm) thick, generally directly on the ground, in a room kept at a constant temperature. They are then sprayed liberally with water and covered with a sheet or

Following pages: Traditionally, tea is formed into blocks by placing it in heavy stone molds which are then compressed— in this instance by two planks.

A factory producing Pu Er, Lincang: a pile of tea leaves, moistened and covered with cloth; the thermometer plunged into the center of the leaves indicates a temperature of 127°F (53°C).

a tarpaulin. The temperature inside the piles of leaves rises rapidly to 140°F (60°C). At the start of the process, the combined effect of the heat and the humidity will cause micro-organisms to multiply and degrade the leaves, forming a film of white downy mold. This stage can last between forty-five and ninety days, according to the degree of fermentation desired. By the end of the operation, the leaves will have acquired their color, which varies from brown to black, and the wide range of flavors that are to be found in the Pu Er family.

When the time allotted for fermentation is finished, the mound of leaves is raked into a thin layer and left to dry for around fifteen days. The white down disappears and the leaves take on a fine brown color of varying intensity. Once dry, the leaves destined to be marketed loose are graded using the same machine used to grade black tea. There are around a dozen grades of Pu Er sold loose. The finest are sorted by hand, the others are mixed mechanically in order to standardize them.

Most of the leaves, however, will be compressed in cakes, bricks, nest shapes, and so on, using the same technique as already described for making compressed green tea. Easy to store, these compressed teas can be consumed immediately or kept for later use. The effects of aging will be less marked than in compressed green tea, but nevertheless aging will bring about the refinement of the tannins and develop more of the sweet taste that is one of the criteria of quality in Pu Er.

This method of manufacturing black Pu Er, which originally aimed at speeding up the aging process used for cakes of green tea, in fact produces teas with quite different characteristics of taste and aroma from those of naturally aged Pu Er: the damp aromas, evoking undergrowth and the cellar, are more in evidence, and the gamy notes more pronounced. As explained in the third chapter, black and green Pu Er are two quite separate tea families.

Freshly made cakes of tea are left to dry for a day in a heated room, then are wrapped in a sheet of rice paper bearing the producer's or factory's logo.

SCENTED, SMOKED AND FLAVORED TEAS

→ Teas scented with flowers

Tea absorbs odors easily, both good and bad—which is why great care needs to be taken with its storage.

In China, the practice of scenting teas with freshly gathered flower petals, natural essences, or fruit peel, harks back to an ancestral tradition: rose, magnolia, chrysanthemum, and, of course jasmine—the most popular of all—are all used to make tea scented with flowers. Various qualities are available, depending both on the quality of the tea used and the amount of care taken during its manufacture.

The leaves for the green tea that will be used for making jasmine tea are plucked in April and manufactured according to the procedures already explained. The tea is then stored until August, when the jasmine is harvested. The best jasmine is gathered in the middle of the afternoon, when the flowers are slowly beginning to open at the approach of twilight. The crop is then left to rest for three to four hours, by which time the flowers will have opened completely and their temperature will have reduced.

The next step is the mixing of dry tea leaves and flowers, which is done by placing four or five alternating layers of leaves and flowers on top of each other, each 4 to 6 inches (10–15 cm) deep. The layers are left in contact with each other for around ten hours and are stirred regularly to reduce the temperature at the center of the pile, which should remain at about 98°F (37°C). The flowers are then picked out by hand, one at a time. The quality of the tea will depend upon how meticulously the workers remove the flowers. The leaves are then left to dry on racks.

This process can be repeated up to seven times to produce the finest quality of jasmine tea, each with a new batch of fresh flowers. The manufacture of 220 pounds (100 kilos) of one of the finest grades of jasmine tea (Yin Hao, also known as Grand Jasmine Mao Feng) requires a total of 620 pounds (280 kilos) of fresh flowers in order to provide sufficient for repeating the process seven times.

→ Smoked teas

Smoked teas are black teas which are said to have been created in Fujian Province around 1820. The story goes that when a planter's farm was requisitioned for service as a military garrison, he found himself obliged to clear out the hall where a large quantity of still damp tea leaves were drying. In order to speed up the process without losing his crop, he placed the leaves on racks above burning spruce tree roots. While this undoubtedly dried the leaves, it also impregnated them with a very unusual smoky perfume which did not suit the palate of his local customers. It did, however, appeal to the taste buds of a foreign merchant who was passing through the area; he took the entire batch back with him to Europe, where the "smoked" tea proved an instant success and has remained so ever since.

The manufacturing process used for these teas is exactly the same as for classic black teas except for one detail. After rolling, the leaves are grilled lightly on a hot iron sheet then spread on bamboo racks over burning pine roots. The amount of time that the leaves spend on the racks determines the degree of smoking.

→ Flavored teas

When Charles Grey, second Earl Grey and prime minister of Great Britain, poured a few drops of bergamot into a cup of tea, around 1830, he cannot have imagined for one moment that he was about to create one of the most famous teas in history: Earl Grey.

Many flavored and scented teas have been developed subsequently, especially during the 1960s, a time when the food and drink industry was experiencing a small revolution in the development of food flavorings and the techniques for fixing them. Tea, and its exceptional capacity for absorbing different scents, seemed an ideal medium for these new flavors, many of them fruity, which until then had been difficult to reproduce.

We don't intend to describe how flavored teas are produced, but at this point it might be helpful to offer a little clarification on aromatization.

In addition to the flowers, fruit or spices that are occasionally used to brighten up teas such as the Indian Chai, tea — be it green, black, or semi-oxidized — can be scented with different substances called flavorings. These have been strictly defined by legislation and most aromatized teas are made from the first two categories below:

Natural flavorings: These are compounds made from entirely natural substances. The compounds — the essential oils, extracts, and concentrates — are obtained by extraction from the scented substances present in spices, citrus peel or flowers, and occasionally fruit, though this contains too much water to lend itself well to the extraction process. A natural flavoring often contains a large number of different molecules which are what give it its depth and richness.

"Nature identical" flavorings: These are flavors that exist in the natural state but which, often for economic or technical reasons, are synthesized (sometimes known as synthetic flavorings). From a strictly molecular point of view these flavorings, while being identical to those present in nature, often contain only the dominant substance that is present in the natural flavoring. The impression left on the palate by vanillin, the principal molecule of the vanilla pod, and one that is easy to synthesize, is much less rich than the natural vanilla flavor which, in addition to vanillin, contains hundreds of other flavor molecules.

Artificial flavorings: Contrary to a widespread belief, these are very rare. They are obtained by synthesis and do not exist in nature. They are often flavors that, while resembling a natural flavor molecule, have been modified to develop its power. Ethyl-vanillin, one of the most common artificial flavorings is, for example, a molecular form three times more highly perfumed than vanillin.

It takes a great deal of skill, expertise and creativity to combine flavorings with tea, a product that already has scents of its own, to produce a good scented tea — more so even than needed to select a good tea crop and master the technique of oxidation. The creation of these teas comes close to the art of the perfumer.

Right-hand page:
harvesting Rooibos
in Cedarberg,
South Africa.

ROOIBOS AND MATÉ:
TEAS THAT ARE NOT TEAS

Regarded as the national drink of South Africa, red tea is made from the **Rooibos plant** belonging to the *leguminosae* plant family. Also known by its botanical name *Aspalanthus linearis*, this plant is cultivated in South Africa, north of the Cedarberg region, which is 125 miles (200 km) north of the Cape. It is bush-like in appearance and can grow to a height of 5 feet (1.5 m), and has a multitude of slender branches covered with long, pale green, needle-shaped leaves growing from its main stem.

Drunk as an infusion by the people of South Africa for the last three hundred years, red tea has been cultivated and marketed since the 1930s. There are two types of Rooibos tea: one is produced by simply being dried in the sun, while the other is oxidized. The oxidized type is the one that is most commonly consumed.

The harvest takes place during the first three months of the year, which are the summer months in South Africa. The plants are cut with a sickle about 12 inches (30 cm) from the ground. The leaves and stems are chopped then crushed between mechanical rollers, heaped up in little mounds outside in a courtyard and sprayed with water. The oxidation that takes place during this time gives the plant its characteristic flavor and red color. The leaves are then spread on the ground to dry in the sun. They are finally sieved to remove any pieces of stem and earth, and are then steamed before being packaged.

Often known as the "tea of the Jesuits" or "Brazilian tea," **maté** is an infusion that is drunk in South America, especially Argentina, Chili, Paraguay, Uruguay, and Southern Brazil. The plant used, the "yerba maté" (*Ilex paraguariensis*), does not belong to the *camellia* family but to the hollies. After firing the leaves are powdered, then infused in hot water to produce a stimulating drink rich in caffeine.

The word maté comes from the Quechuan word *mathi*, which means a receptacle—a type of calabash, traditionally used in the making and serving of maté and which is still in use today.

Tasting

- **THE CONDITIONS REQUIRED** FOR PREPARATION AND DRINKING
- **THE EQUIPMENT AND TECHNIQUES** FOR TEA TASTING
- **THE PHYSIOLOGY** OF TASTE
- **HOW WE EXPRESS** OUR SENSATIONS

THE CONDITIONS REQUIRED FOR PREPARATION AND DRINKING

"The matter of tea," wrote the Japanese tea master Sen No Rikyu, "is really very simple: heat the water, prepare the tea, and drink it with decorum. That is all there is to know."

Yet as many often discover, the art of *less is more* is extremely elusive and a little help in reaching this goal of minimalist perfection may not come amiss.

The tea arrives from the manufacturer with a built-in promise: what is in the leaves is potentially what you get in the cup. So, tea lovers, as you reach for your pot, it's up to you to make the most of them. Bear the following in mind, and those promised joys will be yours.

Essentially, brewing tea involves nothing very mysterious; it's just a matter of bringing dried leaves into contact with warm water for a certain amount of time. Sometimes, however, things go wrong, and the brew turns out to be disappointing or excessively strong. But, before blaming the quality of the tea, we need to look at what is happening in the pot.

A QUICK CHEMISTRY LESSON

Extracted by the action of the heat and water, the soluble constituents of the leaves migrate into the liquor—"form an aqueous solution," technically speaking. The degree to which they dissolve and the speed of the process depends upon the length of time that the leaves are in contact with the water, and the temperature of the water.

Of the constituents present in large numbers in the fresh leaf, certain are destroyed in the manufacturing process: vitamin C, for instance, which is susceptible to high temperatures. Others, on the contrary, are transformed into new compounds, some of which will dissolve during infusion: these include polyphenols, alkaloids, amino acids, glucides, minerals, a number of other vitamins, and aromatic substances. A number of these compounds are perceptible to one of the four senses involved in drinking (taste, touch, smell, sight) but the rest are totally undetectable.

A Chinese expert inhales the aromas of a Long Jing as they briefly cling to the hollowed lid of his zhong.

Also known as "tannins," these belong to the same family as the poly-phenols contained in wine, although some of them, such as epigallocat-echin gallate, are specific to tea. These polyphenols are predominantly represented by the catechins. During oxidation, some of the latter are transformed into two other compounds, thearubigin and theaflavin, responsible for the reddish-brown colorations of oxidized teas.

Certain tannins also govern the texture of tea: it is their presence that gives astringency, sharpness, and body or "thickness" to the liquor in the mouth. Again, a number of them develop a bitter taste. As we shall discover, tannins are only released gradually during the course of infusion.

The bud and initial leaves of a branch are richer in polyphenols than the other leaves; this is one reason why only the bud and first leaves are plucked in quality harvests.

A final point of interest is that these tannins play the major role in scientific research into the benefits of tea.

→ Alkaloids

There are three sorts of naturally-occurring nitrogenous compounds in tea: caffeine, theophylline, and theobromine. Caffeine, the principal alkaloid present, was discovered in 1820 in coffee, then isolated a few years later in tea; at first it was called theine until it was realized that both were the very same substance.

The caffeine in tea acts as a powerful stimulant on the nervous sys-tem and though identical in all ways to that found in coffee, it produces noticeably different effects. When absorbed by the body, caffeine circu-lates very swiftly through the bloodstream to reach the brain in less than five minutes. This produces the famous "pick-me-up" effect asso-ciated with a cup of coffee. But two to five hours later, the effect has dis-appeared. Tea, however, behaves differently. Initially trapped by the polyphenols, the caffeine is released progressively, over some ten hours; the result is that there is neither sudden stimulus nor nervous arousal, but a long-term stimulation—the reason why theine is classed as a stimulant and caffeine as an excitant.

In fact, it was this beneficial stimulating effect, nowadays some-times regarded as undesirable, that gave rise to the popularity of tea when it first began to be drunk in the Far East. In Buddhist monaster-ies, the monks consumed it to keep awake during long hours of medi-tation; it was they who assisted its spread to China and introduced it to many countries of Southeast Asia like Korea and Japan.

The young shoots (buds and initial leaves) contain two or three times as much caffeine as the other leaves. This is rapidly released dur-ing infusion, and, like most alkaloids, lends the beverage a bitter flavor.

It is also in part due to the combination of caffeine and polyphenols that the liquor owes its limpid appearance.

→ Amino acids

Around twenty amino acids have been discovered in tea. The principal one, theanine, is specific to tea and represents about 60 percent of the total amino acids present.

Amino acids increase in proportion during the withering process and are responsible for producing a cloudiness in the liquor. Since they degrade during oxidation—in particular into a family of aroma compounds, the aldehydes—they occur in higher quantities in green and white teas than in oxidized varieties.

→ Glucides

While glucides are present in large quantities in the leaves, only one passes into solution, and then only in minute quantities: monosaccharide, which can lend some teas a very subtle sugary flavor.

On the other hand, it is the sugars present in the leaf which, on reacting during drying with the proteins it contains, give rise to numerous aroma compounds associated with grilling and roasting: the "Maillard reaction," as described in the first part of the book.

→ Mineral salts and vitamins

Tea is a plant naturally rich in vitamin C (around 0.0025 percent by weight of fresh leaves), but this is lost to the end product, being entirely destroyed when the leaves are subjected to high temperatures during firing. On the other hand, tea contains other vitamins, notably vitamin B and bioflavonoids, completely soluble, which find their way into the cup too. Tea is also rich in potassium and fluoride; it contains calcium and magnesium, but very little sodium.

→ Odorous or aroma compounds

These form the tea's bouquet and its "soul." We need to be clear about one thing, though: aroma compounds and aromas are two quite distinct notions. The former are a form of alphabet, the latter a vocabulary. In other words, it is the combination of different aroma compounds that produces aromas: for instance, the aroma of mango or exotic fruit sometimes discerned in a Spring Darjeeling results from the interaction of twenty or so compounds.

Aromas can be counted in hundreds of thousands: some special-

A QUICK RECAP ON THE ORIGINS OF CERTAIN MOLECULES

The fresh leaf contains varietal aromas, that is, those deriving from the specific variety of tea and which differ from one cultivar to another, some of them acting as "aroma precursors;" having undergone modification during manufacture, they give rise to new aroma compounds. Certain varieties of tea plant are extremely scented.

This is the case especially of Yunnan Da Ye, which is used in making Pu Er varieties. Its leaves have a very high linalol content, a compound with the scent of fresh roses, but also reminiscent of coriander seed. Sniff a handful of fresh Da Ye leaves and they could be a bunch of freesias. But as the leaves dry, we discover to our surprise that this bouquet, though preserving a strong floral component, has begun to develop powerful animal scents, with tangs of leather and the stable.

The various aroma compounds in tea do not all form at the same moment in manufacture. A large number appear during the **withering** process: these are the compounds primarily responsible for more or less herbaceous (cis-3-hexenol, t-2-hexenal), green aromas or fresh floral scents like jasmine and hyacinth (phenylacetaldehyde, phenylethyl alcohol). During **oxidation** fruity aromas such as stewed apple (damascenone) develop together with other floral varieties as violets (betaionone) or even those of spices like cinnamon (cinnamaldehyde) or vanilla (vanilline); then, during **firing** (through the Maillard reaction) smells of roasting (pyrazines) and caramelization (furanones), toasted bread (pyridine) or nuts like chestnut and hazelnut. Finally, **post-fermentation** will reveal whiffs of the undergrowth, mushrooms (1-3-octanol), or animal aromas like indole which recalls the greasy, dried perspiration in sheep's wool, the suint.

ists would even put the figure at five million. Aroma compounds occurring naturally number about five thousand; tea has been found to contain up to six hundred. They are present in infinitely small quantities in a cup of tea, representing only 0.05 percent of the solid extract.

These compounds do not dissolve readily and enter the liquor only in small proportions. And because they are sensitive to heat, some are lost in the process of infusion.

So, infusing tea leaves produces a liquor rich in different compounds: tannins, amino acids, aromatic substances, alkaloids. The whole art of tea making consists in obtaining a cup that is balanced between these various elements and, as we shall discover, the conditions under which it is prepared can affect this equilibrium.

BREWING TIME

This must be the factor that we are most aware of; who hasn't at some time forgotten he has made the tea and then grimaced in disappointment on tasting the result?

We should clarify from the start that the different constituents of tea do not all dissolve in water at the same rate: 80 percent of theine is released in the first minute of infusion, whereas some seven minutes are required for a similar percentage of tannins present in the dried leaf— see figure below. As for aroma compounds, the speed of the process depends on their molecular composition.

With this in mind, you can, if you are sensitive to the effects of theine, decaffeinate your tea yourself without impoverishing the liquor too much and still preserve most of its tannins and aromas. To do this, start with a fairly brief initial infusion (20–30 seconds); discard this and proceed to a normal infusion, i.e., the one to be drunk. A handy tip, but not to be used when dealing with a "grand cru" or particularly aromatic teas: the preparatory infusion, however brief, will inevitably destroy part of the bouquet that makes the tea what it is.

Left-hand page: the success or failure of the new harvest and its aromatic potential are revealed during the manufacturing process. Much of course depends on the skill of the planter and his workforce.

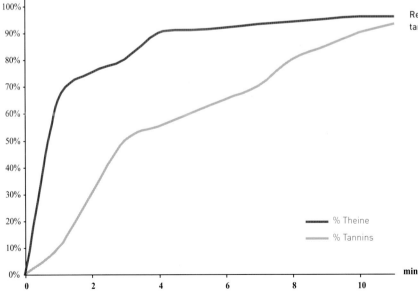

Release of theine and tannins into the water.

% Theine
% Tannins

Contrary to a widespread myth, the color of tea in the cup has nothing to do with the length of infusion. Each family of teas produces liquors of differing colors and intensities, and certain teas lacking strong pigments (white and green varieties) give a very clear liquor. Trusting the color of the liquor to determine progress is a waste of time, and doubling or tripling the recommended brewing time for a green tea because it looks too pale will only end up in a (literally) bitter disappointment; too extended an infusion, in fact, produces an over-concentration of tannins—especially the heavier ones—which will break down the balance between the various constituents and give the liquor a predominantly disagreeable, astringent flavor. Other teas, however, color up very quickly and are even deliberately designed to do so: this is the case, for instance, with teabags and finely ground leaves. The infusion colors rapidly, but usually remains desperately insipid.

Nonetheless, it is not possible to work out a general rule for timing the infusion for a certain color of tea. The chemical composition varies from one blend to another. Why, for example, are Chinese teas less bitter than Japanese? This is to do with the process of oxidase fixation: firing the leaves in the Chinese manner encourages the association of polyphenols and proteins contained in the leaf, and this phenomenon will diminish the astringency and bitterness of the liquor. On the other hand, the steam-heating process used for Japanese teas preserves these polyphenols more efficiently, thus maximizing their taste and tactile properties.

According to type, across the range of colors, brewing time varies between ten seconds and twenty minutes. The secret lies in knowing the tea, not in following some rule of thumb.

THE QUALITY OF THE WATER

For us, with access to safe, pure water from the nearest tap, the business of choosing water may appear persnickety or even ridiculous. In the past, it was far more crucial. The entire history of tea in China is marked by the great importance accorded to springs. Firstly, because pure water was long a scarce commodity, especially in the towns; secondly, according to the Chinese proverb, "Water is the mother of tea." Lu Yu advised preparing tea with water taken from the same source that had watered the tea plant throughout its life: "Water from the same region as the tea is the most suitable." His advice was soon accepted, particularly since water makes up such a large part of a cup of tea, consisting of 99 percent water.

The intrinsic qualities of water therefore have a decisive effect on the brew. Water is not a neutral liquid, and the following characteristics must be taken into account:

- pH
- intrinsic aromas and flavors due to the presence of minerals
- the interaction of the constituents of the water and the tea

Right-hand page: in Japan, as in China, springs are still of vital importance, and the essence of refinement is to prepare a tea with water sourced near the plantation.

The spring known as the Dragon Well (Long Jing) has given its name to China's most famous green tea.

"TEA-FRIENDLY" SPRINGS

John Blofeld, sinologist and today's leading guru where the ancient Chinese art of tea drinking is concerned, relates that, until the early twentieth century, when preparing precious leaves bought at astronomical prices, certain connoisseurs did not hesitate to have water fetched from springs more than 600 miles (1,000 km) away. Chinese folktales and myths surrounding tea abound in such anecdotes: one tradition has it that Dragon Well (or Long Jing) only produces its best when infused in clear water from the famous spring in Leaping Tiger Gorge. We should add that in deference to the example of Lu Yu, one of the first great Chinese tea masters and eighth-century author of *Cha Jing* or *The Classic of Tea*, all connoisseurs agreed that the quality and origin of the water was of prime importance. A table of excellence classified springs in the following order: water from a mountain spring trickling over pebbles or rock devoid of vegetation; mountain springs in general; springs rising on the plains, free from all contamination . . . and so on. Dew collected at daybreak from the leaves of the lotus plant, adds Blofeld, also enjoyed a high reputation, but, for obvious reasons, was rarely resorted to. Anecdote apart, we can conclude that, as far as the specialists are concerned, the quality of the water has considerable influence on that of the infusion.

The pH (potential hydrogen) scale defines the degree of acidity or alkalinity of a solution, the value 7 denoting the point of equilibrium between the two. Pure water has a pH of 7, but tap water, or for that matter spring water rich in minerals, is often mildly alkaline. Experience teaches that pH-neutral or very slightly acid water is the best for making tea; this touch of acidity often lends the water a certain frisson and, on occasion, can enhance the bouquet of the tea, particularly the floral aromas of a Spring Darjeeling.

Whether it comes from the tap or a spring, the varying amount of minerals in the water have a decided effect on the tea. Some contain a flavor, such as the salty flavor of sodium chloride. Others produce an odor, such as the chlorine derivatives frequently used to treat water which produce the smell of bleach, while sulphur compounds, present naturally in some groundwaters, have an unmistakable odor of rotten eggs. These minerals react on contact with the constituents of the tea—especially the tannin—producing a slight clouding of the liquor or a brownish film that dulls the surface. So which water should be used?

Tap water: It is far from being of a standard quality in any one country. Its hardness varies according to the region and the nature of the groundwater—i.e. the amount of calcium and magnesium ions will vary. And to ensure microbiological purity and a pH of 7, it is usually treated with a product that, depending on how much is used, is the sworn enemy of tea and spoils its "aromatic" purity—namely chlorine.

Filtered water: Water can be purified in various ways, both to soften it and to remove impurities. In Japan and Taiwan, purists place bamboo charcoal in the water, while in Europe household filters can be attached directly to the tap or used to filter water in jugs. These filters trap the chlorine and calcium by passing the water through "activated" charcoal.

Spring and mineral water: If you prefer to buy bottled water, for the reasons given above, choose one with a minimal mineral content and with a pH as near neutral as possible.

In tea-producing countries, the variation in water quality from one district to another frequently poses problems for buyers. In the context of professional tastings on the plantations, bottled or filtered water is rarely used; in general people simply take the poor-quality running water and boil it for a long time. (See right for misconceptions about boiling.) So the professional taster has learned to take into account the kind of water that has been used in the tea he is tasting... something that is not always easy to do.

Heat encourages most compounds to dissolve; the hotter the water, the quicker the process takes place. However, it can also destroy some of them.

The essential thing to remember is that a successful tea is not one containing the maximum number of constituents, rather one with a good balance between its tannins, amino acids, and aroma compounds.... Getting the right temperature gives control over this delicate balance, and as each type of tea is different, it varies in each case. Put simply, every tea has its optimum temperature.

But there is one rule that applies to all teas: the water must never be allowed to boil. When heated, the atmospheric gases that have dissolved in the water—including oxygen—evaporate progressively and from a temperature of 104°F (40°C) small bubbles start to form. These gases continue to be released throughout the heating process and at the moment the water boils all the oxygen will have evaporated, so that the boiled water no longer contains any air. However, oxygen plays an important role in tasting as it encourages the passage of aroma compounds to the gaseous state and so affects our perception of a taste when it reaches the olfactory bulb in the brain (see page 130).

In addition, when water boils, the minerals it contains tend to form a skin on the surface of the pan or kettle. This skin reacts badly with tea, mainly because it forms agglomerations with the tannins.

→ The action of water on various compounds

The higher the temperature of the water, the more tannins, including the heaviest, are dissolved. Too high a temperature produces a greater astringency in the liquor, making it sharp and bitter and ruining the bouquet: the liquor is out of balance.

Water that is too hot also destroys certain compounds, particularly amino acids present in large quantities in the green teas. The most volatile aroma compounds, responsible for the "top notes," will "evaporate" or be burned off. For instance, acetaldehyde—an aroma compound with the characteristic odor of freshly cut apples and found in certain Qimen varieties—is destroyed at temperatures exceeding 158°F (70°C).

Because water at too high a temperature can actually burn a tea, in the Chinese method, the leaves of green or white tea are always given a preliminary soaking in cold water. This procedure protects them from the thermal shock that would destroy the amino acids and the fresh, vegetal aromas.

Other teas, however, will only perform well with water at just below boiling point. This is the case with all the Wu Longs and particularly those in pearl or balled form (Dong Ding, Tie Guan Yin, etc.) With these, heat is vital for the gradual expansion of the leaves; harvested lower on the branch, they are often very tough and consequently capable of withstanding higher temperatures. They are sold in the form of extremely dense balls and need heat and repeated infusions to unlock all their aromatic content.

On the other hand, if the water is too cool, the compounds will need more time to dissolve, and not all will pass into the liquor. To obtain an aromatic liquor, it would therefore be necessary to prolong the infusion; even then, it would be impossible to obtain the same results as with warmer water. Nevertheless, the liquor obtained may still have some worth, and you can prepare excellent iced teas from non-scented tea stock (see below).

How to make iced tea

Leave roughly ⅓ ounce (8–10 g) of tea to infuse in 1¾ pints (1 l) of water at room temperature overnight. Next day, remove the leaves and refrigerate the liquor. This recipe works perfectly with non-scented teas. The resulting tea is full-bodied with a very pronounced flavor. Serve with a slice of orange or lime.

For flavored teas and blends, we recommend steeping ½ to ¾ ounce (15–20 g) of tea in 1¾ pints (1 l) of cool water for one hour for blends with a base of black tea. Reduce to thirty minutes for green blends. Remove the leaves and leave to cool.

So what is the correct temperature for the water? Once again: there is no absolute rule! You need to adjust the water temperature according to the variety, and a sound understanding and knowledge of the individual tea is also essential.

A thermometer can obviously be used to help to get the temperature right, or a more sophisticated method is to use an electric kettle with a built-in thermostat allowing you to set the temperature desired. You can also learn to judge the temperature of water by ear and eye. This charming lesson comes to us from the treatise of the Chinese master Lu Yu:

> There are three stages of boiling: the first, when little bubbles like fish eyes rise to the surface of the water; the second, when the bubbles look like pearls tumbling in a fountain; the third, when furious waves begin to dance in the pot.

Even today, the Chinese judge a boiling pot by the size of the bubbles, which they compare to prawn's eyes, crab's eyes, carp eyes.... The Russian samovar was designed to produce a different sound at each stage of the boiling. A word of caution, however: the size of the bubbles depends not only on the temperature but also on the materials from which the vessel is made or with which it is clad and the way these conduct heat. The same is true of using the ear—depending on whether the vessel is made of stainless steel, aluminum, or cast iron, it will emit different sounds at a given temperature. Experience is the answer: you gradually learn to watch your saucepan or listen to your kettle and in a few weeks you will know the right moment to turn the heat off.

In mainland China, this type of glass kettle is widely employed for Gong Fu Cha. In Taiwan, on the other hand, the commonest material is earthenware (see page 98).

GETTING THE PROPORTIONS RIGHT

How do you judge the right quantity of leaves for a particular teapot? Obviously, the more leaves you use, the richer in vital compounds the liquor will be, with the danger of it becoming unbalanced. Here again, there is no hard and fast rule, but instead there are two major schools of thought.

In the Western system, the ratio of leaves to water is one-fifth to one-seventh: producing the well-known routine of 0.07 ounce (2 g) per cup, i.e. per 3½ to 5¼ fluid ounces (10–15 cl) of water. By increasing the amount of water, you can reduce this proportion to one-tenth.

In China, the quantities are worked out to suit the utensils used (the Gong Fu Cha mini-teapots and the zhong, which is discussed later). The amount of leaves is judged in terms of volume rather than mass, with the leaves representing 30 to 50 percent of the teapot or cup.

Tea lovers have a tendency to add extra leaves and reduce the brewing time: this in fact increases the concentration of the aroma compounds, which dissolve very easily—particularly those producing the top notes. But again this is risky: by forcing up the concentration of tannins responsible for astringency or bitterness, you can ruin the balance of the liquor.

In India, tasters often use a 25-paise coin 0.08 ounce (2.2 g) as a weight.

THE RELATIONSHIP BETWEEN LEAVES AND WATER

This is one of the contributing factors that is more frequently overlooked; yet everyone has at some time ended up with a tasteless liquor because the leaves have not been able to expand sufficiently, having been compressed excessively in a metal tea strainer.

Since preparing tea means putting the leaves in contact with water, the greater the area of this contact, the more fully the constituents of the leaves will dissolve. So we need to facilitate as large a contact area as possible to give the tea all the space it needs. When infused and allowed to expand completely, an orthodox black tea (Darjeeling, Yunnan, etc.) increases its volume four times; a Japanese green needle tea seven times, while a Wu Long in pearl form (Dong Ding, Gao Shan Cha, Tie Guan Yin . . .) takes up eighteen times as much space!

Ideally, the leaves should be placed in the pot loose and the tea then decanted into another container to arrest the infusion process. This is the method that is followed when preparing tea in a professional tasting set, a Gong Fu Cha, or Japanese kyusu, the whole of the liquor being poured out at each service.

As for our Western teapots with their larger volumes, the solution lies in making sure there is enough space for the leaves to expand inside the filter, infusion sock, or tea strainer; make sure you take the size of the pot into account when buying your accessories.

Generally speaking, it is best to avoid using a tea strainer with a "grand cru." It is a good idea to use two containers when preparing very special vintages: one for the preliminary infusion with the loose leaves and the other for the decanted liquor.

FACTS ABOUT VOLUME

The volume of tea prepared is closely linked to the "dosage." It is a mistake to begin by assuming that preparing a large quantity of tea simply means proportionally increasing the amount of leaves according to the volume of tea required.

Let us look at a specific tasting example. For a Qimen, infused in two different volumes but maintaining the same proportions:

0.07 ounce (2 g) of a tea in a 3½ fluid ounce (10 cl) set
1½ ounce (40 g) of tea in a large, 3½ pint (2 l) teapot

The comparison is revealing: the first liquor will be light and lively, with a fine leather-and-cocoa aroma, its tannins and aromas well balanced. The second will be flat, insipid, poor in aromas, and unusually astringent for this type of tea. And it gets worse: a half hour later, the liquor remaining in the pot will be undrinkable.

Partly, this is to do with the fragility of the aromas: top notes are extremely volatile, and the larger the surface of tea in contact with the air, the more rapidly they escape. Furthermore, even when the leaves are removed, the tea continues to brew, with interactions between the various compounds continuing in the liquor. Since a large quantity of warm liquid cools less quickly than a smaller volume, the liquor "stabilizes" less rapidly; as time passes, heat encourages the polymerization of the tannins and thus the formation of larger molecules, astringent and sometimes bitter. For this reason a teapot kept warm for thirty minutes will not necessarily bring out the whole quality of the tea.

In addition, it is not incidental that when it comes to appreciating tea on a gastronomic level, small volumes are used:

- Gong Fu Cha: 3½–7 fluid ounces (10–20 cl)
- Zhong: 3½ fluid ounces (10 cl)
- Tasting set: 3½ fluid ounces (10 cl)
- Japanese kyusu: 5¼–7 fluid ounces (15–20 cl)

Using small volumes, in fact, allows the tasting to take place immediately after extraction of the liquor and before it develops too far. With this in mind, the following recommendations can be safely made:

- avoid larger teapots 2½ pints (1.5 l) and over
- for good vintages, avoid pots over ½ pint (30 cl)
- for really great vintages, use a tasting set, or, for Chinese teas, a Gong Fu or zhong teapot

THE EQUIPMENT AND TECHNIQUES FOR TEA TASTING

Assuming we know the conditions required to make good tea, how do we put them into practice and what equipment do we need?

A little earlier we mentioned the two most common methods of preparation: the "Western" and the "Chinese" methods. There are also the more specific techniques involving, for instance, mint tea or the whisked (mashed) tea used in Japanese tea ceremonies. Although these are all interesting we shall just look at the methods applicable to gastronomic tasting, which are designed to get the most out of the leaf.

The fundamental differences between the Western technique and its Chinese counterpart involve:

- the relative proportions of tea and water
- the length of the infusion
- the number of infusions performed with the same leaves

In the Western style, a small quantity of leaves are infused for a relatively long period, and once only. The Chinese take the opposite approach: a large quantity is infused very briefly and the procedure repeated several times. The equipment required for the first method is a tea tasting set or a large-capacity teapot, and for the second a Gong Fu teapot, a zhong or a Japanese kyusu. Neither method is superior to the other: each works better with particular varieties.

Some teas (Wu Long, Pu Er, etc.) are manufactured specifically for preparation by the Gong Fu Cha technique, and their ranking frequently depends on the number of infusions the same handful of leaves can produce.

Other teas, however, need time to release their aromas, and after the initial infusion the leaves have nothing left to offer. These teas are better suited to the "Western" system.

Generally speaking, each tea-producing region manufactures its teas to suit the way they are brewed locally: countries formerly under British influence make teas for Western-style preparation, while in those culturally close to China traditional varieties are produced for the Gong Fu Cha or the zhong methods.

Gong Fu Cha is the Chinese art of infusing tea slowly, methodically, and with attention to detail.

Among the utensils we are going to study, there is one, developed by tea experts, which is used throughout the world at professional level as the most effective way to evaluate a tea: the tasting set.

THE PROFESSIONAL
TEA TASTING SET

In the nineteenth century, the British set up tea plantations throughout the Empire, turning the popular commodity into both a major source of wealth and an important economic factor. Tea markets, organized on highly structured lines, arose in centers such as Kolkata (Calcutta) or Colombo. As the tea trade became more and more professionalized, utensils were designed to allow the tasting and comparison of a large variety of teas under conditions similar to those in the home of the consumer.

The tasting set probably derives from successive adaptations of the Chinese zhong. It is composed of three items:

- a bowl
- a 4¼ fluid ounce (12 cl) cup with a serrated edge
- a lid

Usually made of white porcelain, the tasting set really came into its own at the turn of the twentieth century with the arrival of a profession new to the industry—the tea blender (see right).

In fact, because the tasting set makes it possible to prepare small volumes while maintaining an optimal tea/water balance, tens or even hundreds of varieties can be sampled successively and accurate comparisons made. The pot and its cover are relatively "hermetic;" they are designed to allow the user to sniff and observe the brew by pouring out the contents of the cup into its lid. The bowl is rounded so as not to cast shadows on the liquor. Another practical aspect is that the set is easy to empty and rinse out.

The object of professional tasting is to analyze a tea and compare it to others from the same family. The analysis consists of describing its good and bad qualities and evaluating it in the light of the taster's theoretical knowledge and experience of it: to analyze a tea properly, it is better to have a sound knowledge of its generic characteristics. When

Right-hand page: evaluating teas at the premises of a Colombo broker: an assistant (foreground) is noting the taster's comments. A hundred or so teas are under scrutiny.

Tasting high-quality varieties in Darjeeling: only some ten varieties are submitted to the taster, who samples each with meticulous care.

THE BLENDER:
MASTER CRAFTSMAN OF THE MANUFACTURING PROCESS

With the exception of the "grands crus," which are composed entirely of one variety, most of the teas we come across are blends. The blender puts his nose and palate to work in search of a perfectly standardized mixture of teas. This is a job of primary importance in the tea trade. The first blenders appeared in the 1890s when more and more countries began to produce tea commercially and it became a mass commodity, especially with the birth of the teabag in the USA around 1910. In this context it was vital to standardize products and ensure a reliable supply.

The blender's first aim is to guarantee a year-round provision of tea each batch of which is identical as far as the customer is concerned. The mantra of the big importers and producers is that the true tea lover will not accept the slightest variation in taste,

appearance, or smell and consequently they make every effort to supply a standard and unchanging product.

Given the huge financial investment, they need to guard against markets being adversely affected by unforeseen circumstances related, for instance, to climate or politics. The blenders' second aim, therefore, is to cover themselves by blending several teas—up to seventy in some cases—to make a single product; in the event of a bad harvest or a savage hike in prices, only a small percentage of the final product will be involved and the problem will be resolved without affecting the taste or the price. It is clear, then, that although it requires great expertise, the tasting profession is also in demand at the lower end of the market, including the teabag industry.

closely related varieties are compared, differences and similarities in the liquor will emerge, enabling the taster to pick out the best examples where necessary.

→ A professional tea-tasting session

Just as with wine, professional tea-tasting sessions follow a highly precise ritual whose objective is to highlight the good and bad points of the tea and, in many cases, to compare different batches from the same harvest. Whatever the country, the procedures and utensils are identical. The steps involved are:

- The taster begins by lining up in front of him all the samples to be tasted and compared (photo 1).
- He spreads each sample on a sheet of white paper or a saucer, keeping the envelopes that contained them in the proper order for later reference (photo 2). He then observes the dried leaves and inhales their scent.
- He now lays out in front of him as many tasting sets as there are teas to be sampled. In each cup, which he later covers with its lid, he places 0.07 ounce (2 g) of tea (photo 3), pouring over it 3½ fluid ounces (10 cl) of water at a controlled temperature (photo 4).
- The brewing time varies with the individual tea, but whatever the variety, the professional always allows a longer period than would be applicable to a normal teapot—this helps bring out the tea's characteristics and underline its qualities and defects. The price of this procedure is sometimes a slightly pronounced bitterness, but it is a necessary evil, especially when tasting teas with very similar characteristics, and the professional taster strives to disregard the side effects.
- Once the brewing time has elapsed, the taster pours the liquor into the bowl forming part of the set, keeping the cover on the cup to retain the leaves and avoid them disturbing the liquor (photo 5).
- At this stage the sample exists in three states: dry leaves, infusion (leaves in contact with the water), and liquor (photo 6). The tasting can begin.

In the case of the dry leaves and the infusion, the expert evaluates:

- appearance: the shape and size of the leaves, their color, the skill with which they have been harvested, their preparation
- texture: suppleness or otherwise, their degree of hygrometry
- bouquet: dry and infused

In the case of the liquor, he is chiefly concerned with:

- the color and clarity of the liquid
- the effect on the palate, and tactile sensations
- flavors and aromas
- the aromatic profile

The tasting set is a superb and almost perfect tool for analyzing tea as it enables the different factors affecting the infusion to be controlled very precisely. The "grands crus" designed for preparation according to the Western system can never be evaluated more effectively than when using a tasting set. It is equally effective with Chinese teas, despite their manufacture being geared to produce the best results with the Gong Fu Cha method: a Wu Long prepared in a set often produces a cup with an extremely high aromatic concentration.

However, the professional nature of the tasting set means that it is not used very frequently by the general public. From the point of view of visual appeal, with its air of the laboratory and resemblance to scientific equipment, it can be a little off-putting and the small volumes that it prepares do not really suit the requirements of convivial tea drinking with friends.

Pages 104–5: tasting-room on the Ettampitiya plantation, Sri Lanka.

CHINESE METHODS OF TEA PREPARATION

→ Gong Fu Cha

With the exception of teas mainly destined for export (black and smoked varieties), all Chinese and Taiwanese varieties are prepared in zhong cups or by the Gong Fu Cha method.

"Gong Fu" means something learned with study, practice, and dedication. "Cha" is tea, so the whole phrase could be translated as "the art of tea," signifying both a way of making it and the skills and ceremony of tasting. Traditionally, it is also a convivial and social activity.

Right-hand page: the reserve pot or *chahai*, sometimes equipped with a strainer, is an indispensable piece of equipment; the contents of the teapot are poured into it at the appropriate moment.

The teapots used for the Gong Fu Cha method often surprise Westerners by their small capacity, which rarely exceeds 3½ to 5 fluid ounces (10–15 cl). Since tasting involves making successive infusions, Gong Fu Cha is rather like a journey during the course of which the leaves progressively reveal their secrets.

Varying in its degree of elaborateness according to region, Gong Fu Cha is noteworthy above all for the size of the pots, the quantity of leaves and the duration and number of infusions. With the passage of time, and more especially over the last fifty years in Taiwan, the tasting ritual has developed into a real art form, with every utensil, every gesture designed to celebrate the tea's bouquet and express its virtues and the tasters' appreciation. The aroma or sniffer cup has contributed greatly to the ceremony. It is a tall, narrow vessel that enables the

Three stages in the preparation of tea by the Gong Fu Cha method.

participants to enjoy the bouquet before pouring the tea into a smaller cup. The flared design of the latter helps the liquor cool but more importantly assists the appreciation of its aromas. The aroma or sniffer cup is now an established part of the proceedings and has become the central utensil in a ritual where the ultimate goal is to train the organs of smell and taste.

But the use of the aroma cup should not obscure the essential facts: by using multiple, brief infusions Gong Fu Cha's primary advantage is that it allows the leaves to develop their full potential. Although it is a tasting method that is little used in the West, it is worth learning a little more about it.

[A SMALL LESSON IN GONG FU CHA]

Gong Fu Cha is a method used with Wu Longs and dark teas:

- First prepare the utensils (photo 1). Left to right, top to bottom: kettle and burner; measuring scoop; tasting-cup; aroma cup; tongs and thick cloth; teapot; reserve pot. These items are laid on a tea boat.
- Start by heating the water in a large kettle holding several times the capacity of the teapot. When the water starts to simmer, use it to fill the teapot, which stands on the tea boat—a sort of deep tray, perforated to allow surplus water to be drained into a receptacle underneath (photo 2). It is essential to warm the pot: it is so small that the tiny quantity of water required for the infusion will cool rapidly. The teapot is then emptied into the reserve pot.
- Fill the teapot from a half to a third full with leaves and pour in a little water to rinse them (photo 3). This first water, used only to moisten the leaves, is then decanted immediately into the reserve pot or into the cups to warm them (photo 4).
- Drain the contents of the cups and place the pot in the tea boat.
- Refill the teapot to the top, allowing the water to overflow to expel the froth (photo 5).
- The first infusion should be timed at around thirty seconds. Then completely drain the contents of the teapot into the reserve pot (photo 6).
- Decant the liquor into the aroma cup and immediately transfer it to the tasting cup (photo 7).
- Sniff the aroma cup, which, though empty, retains the tea's bouquet (photo 8).
- Drink the tea in the second cup—slowly, sip by sip.

The best Wu Longs allow the same leaves to be infused sometimes more than ten times by simply repeating the procedure. Because it produces a much more concentrated liquor, tea prepared by this method should be drunk in very small quantities.

Gong Fu Cha is far from being a ceremony with rules that are set in stone: individuals can adapt it according to whatever facilities and utensils are available at the time, while, of course, never losing sight of its essential aim: taking the time to prepare the very best tea.

→ The zhong

The zhong, a handleless steeping cup made of very fine porcelain, with a lid and a saucer (photo 1), is the receptacle most commonly used in China, both at home and in tea houses. Though zhong is the word in everyday use—probably a corruption of the verb *chong*, "to pour water"—the more correct term is gaiwan, or "covered bowl." The zhong was one of many tea-drinking innovations that appeared under the Ming Dynasty. Unlike YiXing earthenware, porcelain is a poor retainer of heat, leaving the zhong more appropriate for fragile teas—greens, yellows, or whites.

The zhong can be used as an individual receptacle or as a "teapot": in fact, the YiXing version is often replaced by a zhong in the method described page 108, particularly when group-tasting very fragile green teas.

[A SMALL LESSON IN USING THE ZHONG]

- As with the Gong Fu Cha method, the zhong is always rinsed with hot water before use, both to clean and warm it (photo 2). This preliminary also has a symbolic value: the receptacle is purified and rendered fit to receive the precious leaves.
- According to their volume, fill the zhong quarter- to half-full of leaves (photo 3): the proportion should be reduced for the densest teas (Long Jing, Jasmine Pearls).
- Pour cold water onto the leaves amounting to about a quarter of the volume of the zhong in order to moisten them and prepare them to receive the hot water (photo 4); then top up with water at just below boiling point (photo 5).
- Immediately pour this water into a bowl or tea boat; it will have served to rinse the leaves and open them slightly, facilitating the release of the aromas during the second infusion.
- You can now sniff the leaves infused directly in the zhong as well as some of the tea's fragrances "clinging" inside the lid (photo 6).
- The second infusion follows the same rules: first the cold water, then the hot. Infusions at this stage can be of widely varying lengths, according to personal taste: after all, the zhong is primarily a personal receptacle. Some people, for instance, prepare their white or green teas in successive infusions of fifteen or so seconds each; others use periods of two or three minutes, in which case they limit themselves to one or two changes of water.
- The lid is used to stir the leaves, check the quality of the infusion (photo 7) and, when tasting, to keep them inside the cup. If you open up the lid slightly, you can even drink straight from the zhong (photo 8). It is always interesting and rewarding to sniff again the inside of the lid, as the fragrances clinging there develop and mature as the infusions proceed.

WESTERN TEAPOTS (LARGE CAPACITY)

Despite the long history of tea in China, teapots did not make their appearance there until the advent of the Ming Dynasty (1368–1644). It is true that the practice of making tea from loose leaves and of artists and intellectuals gathering in teahouses was widespread during the reign of the Song (960–1279), encouraged by an emperor who was something of a connoisseur. But the invading armies of Genghis Khan had put an end to such social niceties—the Mongols drank only brews made from crushed blocks of tea and showed little inclination for more refined preparation; a change of dynasty was needed before tea regained its place in Chinese culture. The Ming, convinced of China's cultural, economic, and spiritual superiority, were anxious to resurrect the Song traditions and restore tea to its rightful place in society. The earliest teapots, delicate artifacts in translucent porcelain, soon encountered competition in the form of YiXing earthenware, named after a region famed for centuries for its clays (see right).

🍃 The "Five Golden Rules of Tea Making"—or The British Method
These were laid down by the British; besides being fairly simplistic,
they are designed to suit certain types of teas and the British way of
consuming them.
1 Warm the pot first; this will help the leaves release their bouquet.
2 Place in the teapot one heaped teaspoonful of tea per cup,
  plus "one for the pot."
3 Pour simmering, not boiling, water over the leaves.
4 Leave to brew for 3–5 minutes.
5 Stir and serve.

The first teapots to arrive in Europe along with consignments of tea had a capacity of around 2¾ pints (1.5 l). To Westerners, these large utensils dedicated to the preparation of a product with such an exorbitant price-tag seemed to verge on the ridiculous. All the same, from the 1670s, when tea drinking became more and more an everyday activity, imports of teapots began to soar, and under the impulse of this new market, Chinese potters and ceramicists started to produce pots of every shape and size, frequently displaying great talent and imagination.

Today Western teapots are found in a large range of capacities. They are used in the same way as the tasting set, but we should remember that even the best teas prepared in a 3½ pint (2 l) teapot will, with due respect to the famous "Five Golden Rules" (see above), always prove disappointing.

But apart from size—in this case big is not beautiful—are there any other criteria to bear in mind when choosing a teapot?

All aesthetic considerations apart, and from the purely gastronomic point of view, the fundamental factor governing the nature and quality of a tea is the material from which the pot is made. As tea is

Right-hand page:
YiXing earthenware
teapots are invariably
handmade. Seasoning
takes several months
as the pores in the clay
of the pot absorb
aromatic residues
progressively.

YIXING:
THE TELLTALE SIGNS

YiXing (pronounced *ee-shing*) earthenware is so famous that people try to fake it. But there are one or two telltale signs to distinguish fakes from the real thing:

- The density of the material, which feels almost like metal. When you tap a YiXing teapot or rub the lid against a sidewall, it emits an unmistakable singing note.
- The signature, always found on the base, sometimes inside the lid and occasionally under the handle.
- The shape: handle, spout, and mouth form a kind of long, horizontal line (with the exception of pots with a removable handle or with the handle on top).
- The very fine-grained clay, uniquely tactile.

To get the best out of a YiXing teapot, stick to the following rules:

- Don't use too many types of tea in the same pot: a variety with powerful aromas will leave a taste that lingers and lingers, smothering that of subsequent, lighter varieties.
- Don't drink the very first brew: a pot that has never been used is highly absorbent as it begins to season, and the initial brew will have its taste significantly affected by the clay. Sacrifice this brew to the pot.
- Never use any kind of cleaning products as the pot will absorb their taste. All you need to do is rinse it with clean water between teas.

brewed repeatedly in the pot, the tannins in the tea form a brown deposit on its inner walls, and the pot becomes "seasoned" rather like a tobacco pipe. To what extent the pot is stained and how permanently depends on the material.

Those teapots that retain tannins well are said to possess a "memory": others, unable to do this because their walls are too smooth, have "no memory." The distinction is far from being simply incidental. A teapot becomes more and more efficient with time. As it becomes more familiar with the tea that is habitually infused in it, it becomes richer in "memories" allowing the leaves to release their best aromas.

One problem, though, is the matter of incompatibility of different types of tea "characters;" a "grand cru," whether black or green, will not reveal anything of its individual character, richness, or aromas in a pot that has been used continually for Earl Grey, smoked teas, dark teas—or any other tea with very definite characteristics. To avoid this kind of personality clash, connoisseurs keep more than one teapot, each reserved for a particular group of teas.

Teapots are available made of earthenware, porcelain, glass, cast iron, and other materials. Here is a brief survey of the respective merits of each type.

→ Earthenware teapots

Since clay is a porous material, these teapots season more readily, and in China, some connoisseurs will pay a small fortune to acquire seasoned pots once owned by tea masters. Today as ever, the best examples come from YiXing, a Chinese town in the south of Jiangsu Province, famous since the time of the Ming Dynasty for the exceptional quality of its clay which assumes a purplish-brown coloring during firing. The superiority of YiXing clay and its fascinating characteristics derive from the unusually high iron and silicon content. Extremely porous, it encourages oxygenation of the tea and allows a more complete release of the aromas than any other receptacle. And because, unlike most clays, it is not granular, it does not lose heat so quickly.

YiXing teapots with a capacity of around ½ pint (300 ml) and designed for export.

Earthenware teapots are ideal for preparing black Chinese teas and dark varieties, their porous structure being well suited to the rounded and full-bodied nature of the liquors. On the other hand, a clay that is too porous will destroy certain very fragile aromas and impose its own odor on the tea. All clays are not identical, and a poor-quality one will contaminate aromas of the floral and vegetal types.

→ Porcelain teapots

Like tea, porcelain has its origins in China: the Middle Empire was making porcelain ware as early as the sixth century. Fascinated by the objects that the Chinese made and their dazzlingly fine, translucent construction, Westerners strove persistently to obtain the secret of porcelain manufacture. They finally achieved it in the eighteenth century and today, porcelain is one of the most highly prized materials used to make teapots. Their smooth interiors do not retain the memory of previous infusions, and because the delicate material retains heat less readily than earthenware, it is kinder to certain fragile aromas and consequently ideal for not only green and white teas but also some black varieties with vegetal aromas—Darjeeling, for instance.

→ Cast-iron pots

These are descended from kettles whose traditional uses were adapted by Westerners. They first appeared in the Iwate region, in the northeast of the Japanese island of Honshu, and were made by local craftsmen on traditional lines dating back to the twelfth century.

Most of the models imported nowadays to the West have glazed interior surfaces that are non-porous and do not allow seasoning. Over the course of time, the build-up of tannins may form a black film that has no effect on the taste of the tea and will gradually crumble away if the pot is left to dry out for several days in the open air. These pots, therefore, have no "memory."

Unglazed examples do have a memory, but this is offset by what to our Western eyes is a severe drawback: cast iron is an alloy of carbon and iron, and the iron content rusts. Traditionally, the Japanese are happy to let their teapots rust: far from presenting a danger to health, it actually adds an iron supplement to their diet.

One detail is important when brewing: because cast iron retains heat well, pots made of this material are liable to influence the development of the liquor.

Cast-iron teapots straight from the mold; before painting they have a bright metallic sheen.

Below:
the molten cast iron is transferred from the crucible (left) into molds made of compacted sand (center). A firing process is sometimes used to impart deliberate protrusions and imperfections to special models (right).

🌱 Looking after a teapot—to keep a cast-iron teapot looking good and working efficiently, follow these tips:
- Don't leave water or tea too long in the pot.
- To avoid spots and stains, remove any water or tea splashes from the outside at once.
- After each use, rinse the pot in detergent-free hot water; wipe the walls while still warm.
- Always allow the pot to dry in the open air, without its lid; don't put it away until perfectly dry inside and out.

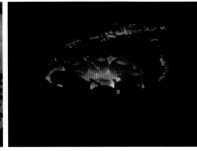

→ Metal and glass teapots

Whether elegant British silverware teapots dedicated to the national afternoon ritual, pewter teapots given pride of place by desert-dwellers, or a simple utensil made of enameled metal, metal teapots all have something in common: they are unbreakable. This is an important factor for nomadic peoples, though for people living a settled life the disadvantages of teapots made out of metal becomes a more sensitive issue: some metals give a disagreeable taste and aroma to the tea, particularly acidity.

The smooth interiors of glass teapots mean that no seasoning can take place, and in any case people normally scour them to keep them clean and maintain their transparency. However, because glass allows the leaves to be observed during infusion in the pot, glass is the ideal material for teas in which the shape of the leaf as it unfurls is important.

Although it is worthwhile considering the advantages and disadvantages of the various materials used to make teapots, to make tea properly, the important thing is to be familiar with your own teapot and its merits.

THE JAPANESE TEAPOT OR KYUSU: A HYBRID PREPARATION SYSTEM

The kyusu is a small teapot made of earthenware or porcelain and sometimes, today, of glass. Equipped with a metal grille to retain the leaves and a hollow side-handle for easy use, it is traditionally used for green teas. The usual capacity is 12¾ fluid ounces (36 cl), but for the finer teas it is best to limit the contents to 3½ to 7 fluid ounces (10–20 cl). The matching cups contain only a fraction of this. The set is often completed by a pot known as the yuzamashi whose purpose is to cool the water before it is poured over the leaves; in this case it replaces steps 4 and 5 described on the following pages.

Because it combines the quantities associated with the Chinese method with a brewing time that is more similar to that used in the West, tea making in Japan is a hybrid of the systems described previously. The Japanese push elegance and refinement to the point of insisting on ideal methods of preparation for each type of tea. This includes following precise rituals that are often symbolic in nature and investing the preparation of a Sencha with the complexity of the national Cha No Yu

Series of kyusu pots fresh from the wheel and ready for firing.

ceremony (see page 195)—but without, however, any of its spiritual dimension.

The method described below applies to the preparation of Gyokuro, Sencha, and Tamaryokucha varieties. For Bancha, Hojicha, and Genmaicha, quantities are similar to those used in the West, but with a single, relatively short infusion of thirty seconds.

There are two basic rules for using the kyusu:

- The better quality the tea, the cooler the water should be.
- Use three successive infusions of decreasing lengths; the Japanese consider that the leaves can only absorb a certain amount of water.

[A SMALL LESSON IN USING THE KYUSU]
- Prepare the utensils (photo 1): the kyusu and three cups, the tea box and its measuring scoop.
- Warm the water in the kettle to just below boiling point.
- Place the loose tea in the kyusu (photo 2).
- Fill two of the three cups with warm water for a Sencha—or just one of the three for a Gyokuro (photo 3).
- Using the third (empty) cup, cool the water by transferring it from cup to cup (photo 4). Each time, the temperature of the contents drops by around 50°F (10°C). Using this formula, it is easy to bring the water to the desired temperature.
- When this temperature has been reached, tip the contents of the cups over the leaves in the kyusu (photo 5).
- With the infusion complete, pour the contents of the kyusu into the three cups, taking care to distribute them equally—the final drops are the most concentrated (photo 6).
- Repeat the identical procedure for every service, but reduce the length of the infusion by a third each time.

Japanese green teas at a glance

Type of tea	GYOKURO	SENCHA
Number of persons	3	3
Quantity of tea	⅓ oz. (10 g)	⅓ oz. (10 g)
Volume of water	3½ fl. oz. (10 cl)	7 fl. oz. (20 cl)
Brewing temperature	140°F (60°C)	176°F (80°C)
Length of first infusion	2½ minutes	2 minutes
Tasting temperature	95°F (35°C)	149 °F (65°C)
Number of services	3	3

2

4

6

Metal tea canisters at a Darjeeling street market.

PRESERVING TEA

In theory tea is a dried product—manufactured leaves contain only 3–4 percent water); however it behaves like a fresh product in that it ages badly. To preserve the full aromatic bouquet of a Spring Darjeeling or the freshness of a Long Jing, the right storage conditions are essential. For reasons that will become clear, tea should always be kept in an airtight, opaque container.

Tea acts rather like a sponge, absorbing moisture and ambient odors readily, hence the need to seal it tightly. It is also affected by the oxygen in the air: when tea comes into contact with oxygen, the constituents of the dried leaves (polyphenols, pigments, and aroma compounds) continue to oxidize and change.

Finally, tea is also susceptible to light and high temperatures. When subjected to ultraviolet rays and heat, the leaves lose their color through oxidation of the pigments; they dry out and their bouquet fades as the aroma compounds degrade and evaporate. Tea must be allowed to retain the small amount of moisture present in the leaves or it will not brew properly; once completely desiccated, the leaf becomes brittle and crumbles to the touch.

→ How long can tea be kept?

Because individual teas react differently to aging, the length of time it is possible to keep a tea will vary from one to another. Those rich in top notes (floral, fresh vegetal, and iodized aromas) deteriorate more rapidly than the more opulent teas where base notes predominate (woody or animal aromas).

With the exception of a single family—the dark teas, which, as we have seen, improve with age—all teas eventually degenerate. The popular conception that tea reaches maturity after a few months' storage is an old wives' tale.

"Grands crus" should always be consumed in the few months following harvesting: a Spring Darjeeling, for instance, will only hold its promise for ten to twelve months, even less with the most floral varieties. New season green teas from China and Japan are best drunk immediately, and at the latest eight to ten months after picking.

Generally speaking, tea should not be stored at home for more than a year.

→ Storage tips

The Japanese keep their finest green teas in the fridge in meticulously sealed vacuum-packs. However, this method is not ideal for teas in daily use: to prevent the tea absorbing too much water through condensation, it is necessary to wait until the packet has reached room temperature before opening it. Would-be purists, however, may resort to the following solution. Divide a batch of tea into several small vacuum-packs, each holding a week's supply; keep these in the refrigerator, apart from the one in current use, which should be stored safely in an airtight container.

In Taiwan, as in mainland China, the professionals (manufacturers and retailers) preserve their best Wu Longs in heat-sealed vacuum-packs stored under refrigeration at between +5°F and –4°F (–15°C and –20°C). In addition, they often slip a dehumidifying agent into the pack.

As regards tea for drinking at home, the best way to store tea destined to be drunk within a month or so is to use packs made with aluminum foil, coated with plastic on both sides, with a zip closure—but remember to expel the air from the packet before resealing it.

If you prefer to use caddies, they must also be air- and water-tight and impervious to light and odors.

→ The aging of dark teas

Dark teas are an exception since their organoleptic qualities develop over time (see pages 68–70). So what are the best conditions for conserving this type of tea and encouraging fermentation? The Chinese have been pondering this question for decades, and the answer is still of interest to every tea drinker.

The aging process is optimized by a warm atmosphere—at 82°F (28°C) and above—and a high level of humidity, i.e., at least 70 percent. Nonetheless, under these conditions constant vigilance is essential to prevent the formation of mold that will ruin the tea's taste. Note that such conditions are difficult to reproduce naturally, including in subtropical climates where dark teas are manufactured and stored.

This no doubt explains why many Chinese claim that "what is good for Man is good for tea." In other words, tea should be aged in conditions approximating the normal living environment.

As for our temperate climates, the following guidelines will help:

- Keep the tea in a clean, well-ventilated place, away from direct light and any environmental odors.
- Remove bricks or cakes of compressed teas from their outside packaging (boxes, tins, etc.) and store them in their rice-paper wrappers on wooden shelving.
- Dark teas, whether compressed or loose, can be stored in ceramic pots covered with a cotton material; this allows the air to circulate and protects the tea from dust. Never use hermetically sealed containers.

THE PHYSIOLOGY
OF TASTE

The act of tasting in the context of eating and drinking is something we do countless times a day, quite spontaneously. But despite the fact that it takes place more or less unconsciously, it is a far more complex mechanism than we might imagine.

To appreciate the full value of a tea, it is worth trying to understand how our mouths, noses, and various senses function when we taste things. The aim of this chapter, then, is to cast a brief glance at the theory behind the various physiological processes involved.

To taste something we need the use of our five senses, to differing degrees. What we commonly (and incorrectly) call taste involves not only tastes (gustatory sensations) but also odors (olfactory sensations). The aromatic richness of a tea derives, as the term suggests, from aromas, which are the olfactory substances contained in the leaves that are perceived retronasally.

When we sample a tea, several small events take place, each associated with a different sense.

To begin with, the cup of tea appeals to our visual sense, offering us the initial image of what we are about to drink. Then, as we sniff the contents, we form the earliest impression of smell. The first contact with the lips primarily tells us the temperature of the liquid. And once the tea has entered our mouths, the tongue relays its taste. A certain number of substances (aromas) enter the gaseous state and are perceived internally (retronasally) through the nasal cavity. The linings of the cheek, the palate, and the tongue also tell us about texture and give us other information relating to touch.

Our sense of smell is infinitely more developed than our tastebuds and a large part of what makes up the richness of a Darjeeling or a Sencha is what we perceive as its bouquet. We all know how food seems tasteless when we have a blocked-up nose due to a cold or flu.

To define the two sensations of smell and taste, professional tasters use the world "flavor." The flavor of a tea is composed of sour, bitter, and sweet tastes, depending on the variety, plus a great number of aroma compounds. Note that the flavor is fleeting and unstable, i.e., its effect is usually of a very short duration. In addition, contact with saliva

As soon as the bowl or cup is raised to the lips, the initial aroma reveals the contents.

123

modifies the flavor of the tea, making tasting an ongoing process: it has to adapt from second to second in response to developments in the targeted flavors. So, before they vanish, we need to catch these sensations and keep up with the emerging sequence.

The inside of the mouth, the teeth, and the lips play a fundamental part in "taste." Heat, a liquid state, astringency, and oiliness are all sensations that are felt in different parts of the mouth and help to shape the image that the brain forms of a particular tea.

So when we introduce tea, or any foodstuffs or drink, into the mouth, three of our senses are called into action—at any rate as far as what goes on in the mouth is concerned—and not just taste alone. As these sensations occur simultaneously, it is not always easy to separate them; nor were we taught in childhood to do so.

So far, this concept is easy enough to understand, even if, particularly where smell is concerned, we have never really thought about it before. Where things get complicated is that, starting from these different series of sensations, which are often extremely powerful, our neurons create a unique image, a kind of synthesis, which they transmit to the brain. It is enhanced by two additional dimensions: one linked to the pleasure (or displeasure) produced by the taste in question, the other to language—the words that we use to describe what we are tasting. Each of these dimensions involves a specific area of the brain.

Neuroscience has begun to study how we experience taste, particularly the manner in which our brains perceive the tasting of food and drink. As a result, for the first time some light is being shed on the qualities needed to be a good tea taster. The best taster is not someone who is especially well endowed with sensory receptors (nose and tastebuds) but rather someone who can keep his bearings amid all this complexity, make allowance for his emotions, and understand the relationship between the three elements that are combined in the taste process—the sensations (experienced by the three senses mentioned), the mechanism of consciousness (verbalizing the sensations), and pleasure (the emotional dimension).

A good taster will be able to strip down the unique image into its various components. To do this, he needs to have an excellent understanding of what sensations are involved and how they work.

TASTE

Our sense of taste can recognize five different qualities: sweet, salty, sour, bitter, and *umami*—the last-named, sometimes translated as "savoriness," being the least familiar to Westerners as it plays little part in our diet (see page 126). Within these major categories, which might seem rather too rigidly defined, there are various degrees and nuances forming a continuous scale; "continuum," in fact, is the technical term.

Indian *chai* consists of tea, spices, and milk and is consumed daily throughout India.

Umami

The taste quality known as *umami*—the original Japanese meaning is "delicious"—was described in certain works on Asian gastronomy as early as the thirteenth century, but not officially classified until 1905. Associated particularly with Chinese and Japanese cuisine, *umami* results from a combination of natural substances including monosodium glutamate (MSG), an amino acid found in certain oily fish like mackerel or sardines and in soy sauce, but also in cheese, milk, and mother's milk. When added to food, MSG acts as a flavor enhancer, and is thus highly prized by restaurateurs and foodstuff manufacturers: experiments with animals have shown that adding MSG to a food gives it a more-ish quality—something that seems to hold equally true for humans.

Essentially it is the tongue, the only organ in the body to possess taste-buds, that recognizes these elements. There are four different types of tastebud, and each of us has around two thousand on our tongue. They have a brief lifespan of around ten days, but they regenerate on a regular basis, as you will have discovered whenever you have accidentally burnt your tongue. On the other hand, as you get older, they diminish in number. These tastebuds are cellular structures situated on the end of tiny protrusions ("papillae"), whose function is to capture taste sensations. When we put something in our mouths, its sapid constituents dissolve in the saliva in our mouths and are recognized by the tastebuds, which in turn send a message to the brain saying "salty," "bitter," etc. A certain number of tastebuds also exist in areas close to the tongue: the soft palate, the upper pharynx, and the epiglottis. Note that the information dispatched by the tastebuds does not travel down a specific nerve-path: unlike the optic nerve, there is no "taste nerve," and taste sensations are transmitted along the same nerves that relay information about the temperature of the food and its tactile qualities.

Our tastebuds are not able to make a distinction between one taste element and another, but instead they react to the intensity of the stimuli in varying degrees. Some are more responsive to salty flavors, others to sweet tastes. It is possible, in fact, to construct a "taste map" of the tongue (see right-hand page): for instance, sweet tastes are perceived on the point of the tongue, salty ones on the point and edges, sour ones on the edges and middle section, and bitter on the back. *Umami*, however, is felt all over the tongue, but more intensely at the back of the mouth.

This taste map holds true for everyone with slight variations in terms of intensity (see Anosmia and Aguesia, page 131). It is of special interest in the context of tea tasting in that it can help us neutralize certain excessive taste sensations, particularly bitterness; a person who finds a bitter flavor unpleasant, for example, can lean forward to concentrate the liquor at the front of the mouth and consequently concentrate on other aspects.

A taste is rarely, if ever, perceived in isolation but rather in association with another: sweet and sour, sweet and bitter, for instance. A case in point is grapefruit, the taste of which is a combination of sweet, sour, and bitter. The actual impact of a taste depends upon this association: lemon juice tastes less bitter if mixed with sugar, which is also used as a palliative by those who do not appreciate the characteristic bitterness of tea.

The degree to which we experience a taste also depends upon temperature. Sourness is felt to an identical extent at 50°F (10°C) and 105°F (40°C), but the effect of sweetness is intensified if the temperature of the food or drink is raised, while saltiness and bitterness increase with a drop in temperature. This explains why tea tastes less bitter when drunk very hot.

Trying to isolate the sensations produced by various tastes is often extremely difficult since we experience them in a complex olfactory and tactile environment. For example, we have to learn to dissociate bitterness (an element of taste) from astringency (a tactile sensation). Again, sweetness is a function of taste, but "vanilla" is perceived by our sense of smell. The fact is that because of cultural associations, connections arise between aromas and tastes: iodized aromas conjure up salty tastes, scents of fruit imply sweetness, while smells arising from smoking or preserving processes often cause us to think of salt by reminding us of pork products.

→ The taste of tea

Tea is classed as a bitter drink. Bitterness is normally viewed unfavorably, but actually is not a fault unless it is so pronounced that it spoils the balance. It is not a taste we enjoy spontaneously but one we gradually come to appreciate and to which all of us are receptive in varying degrees. In the case of very young children, of course, sweet tastes will always elicit a smile, while anything bitter or sour will be greeted with expressions of disgust and probably vehement protestations.

Bitterness is present to some extent or other in virtually all teas owing to the presence of theine—all alkaloids are bitter—and espe-

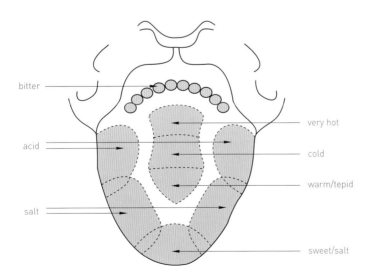

The sensation of tastes on the tongue. Even if not specialized in tea tasting, our tastebuds are receptive to different tastes, which makes it possible to draw up a taste map of the tongue.

cially certain polyphenols. Linked with aromas, the taste is persistent and lingers in the mouth. Actually, a slight element of bitterness is an integral part of the profile of certain aromatic teas.

Sour tastes are frequently associated with a number of black teas, notably Spring Darjeeling, Qimen Mao Feng, and Assam varieties.

A very slight sweet taste is typical of Bancha Hojicha, Bai Hao Wu Long, and Pu Er—in China, when present in Pu Er slight sweetness is an indicator of quality.

To a very small degree, *umami* is also characteristic of certain Japanese teas, such as Gyokuro, or the Spring Darjeelings manufactured from cultivar AV2.

Saltiness is completely absent from tea—although tea drinkers in Tibet actually make a habit of adding salt!

SMELL

As we have already mentioned, aroma compounds comprise the second constituent of flavor.

In scientific terms, when an aroma compound is perceived directly through the nose (direct olfaction), we call it a smell, but when it reaches us through the mouth (retronasal olfaction) it is known as an aroma. In most foodstuffs, these compounds are present in seemingly insignificant quantities. In the case of tea, they represent a mere 0.03 to 0.05 percent of the dry residue and 0.003 to 0.005 percent of the liquor.

Yet their infinitesimally small presence is compensated for by their diversity—scientists have identified up to six hundred different compounds in tea. Our sense of smell is far more developed than we imagine and easily detects these minute quantities: in fact, with its 100 million nerve cells—compared with the one million that produce our sight, the 100,000 our hearing and the 10,0000 our sense of taste—our sense of smell is the best endowed of all our senses.

→ Direct olfaction (through the nose)

When we sniff the leaves of a tea or the bouquet from a cup, the odor-bearing molecules travel via our nostrils to the nasal cavity, at the top of which they strike a sensitive area (the olfactory epithelium) where receptors are located.

Only about 10 percent of odors inhaled along this external path reach the receptors since our noses are equipped with a protection system that partly filters out unpleasant smells and atmospheric pollution in general.

A greater percentage of odors can be inhaled by sniffing in short bursts; this technique is used in tea tasting because it heightens our sense of smell by modifying the nasal cavity.

Sugar should not be added when tasting a "grand cru" tea, but is sometimes useful for sweetening a liquor that has been infused for too long, as is shown here in Sri Lanka at a harvesting location.

→ Retronasal olfaction (through the mouth)

As soon as the tea enters the mouth, another mechanism comes into play: the receptor zone receives odors and aromas retronasally.

Tea contains many aroma compounds: some of these are already in the gaseous state owing to the effect of heat, while others are about to enter that state under the action of saliva, movements of the tongue, and other more specific actions performed by tasters such as "slurping" or masticating.

In this scenario the gaseous molecules reach the receptor area by an internal route when we exhale. Exhalation takes place naturally when we swallow, although we can also produce it deliberately. In fact it is possible to enhance the retronasal perceptions by purposely breathing out deeply through the nostrils while retaining the tea in the mouth.

Exhaling through the nose creates a depression in the pharynx which directly causes air to be sucked from the mouth. This contains a gaseous stream of molecules which sweeps the receptor area where we sense smell resulting in 100 percent of the molecules being recognized.

We ought to make clear that the sensations of smell vary considerably according to whether they are apprehended internally or externally. This is notably due to the fact that the environment is different. In the mouth, temperature, mastication, and the action of enzymes present in saliva initiate a number of physical and chemical changes resulting in the appearance and disappearance of aroma compounds.

Note too that these compounds are largely insoluble and few of them enter the saliva and consequently the gaseous stream. Hence we perceive only a minimal amount of these compounds, which is one reason why tasters breathe in while sipping tea: the oxygen inhaled creates a certain "effervescence" in the liquid, favoring the migration of the aroma compounds to the gaseous state.

The receptor cells capture the aroma-bearing molecules and transmit their information to the brain, which then integrates it with other information already stored in the memory. As far as smell is concerned, an emotional dimension attached to personal memories is often linked

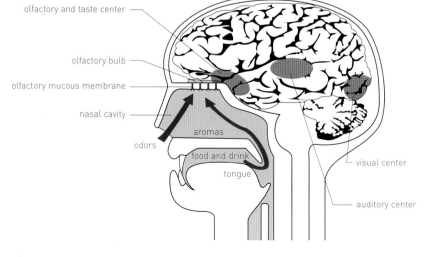

The external and internal olfactory passages. The most acutely sensitive area of our sense of smell is located high up within the nasal cavity. In contrast to those odors which reach it via the nasal passages, the aromas from food and drink are received retronasally.

olfactory and taste center

olfactory bulb

olfactory mucous membrane

nasal cavity

odors

aromas

food and drink

tongue

visual center

auditory center

to the stored information; it is filtered by our subjective experiences and infused with emotional connotations (such as pleasure, pain, distaste, etc.) that make it hard to describe verbally. It is this lack of common references and suitable vocabulary that leads to our difficulties in describing odors, as we will show.

An odor is never perceived in isolation but in contrast with those in the same environment. In the context of a comparative tasting, this has important consequences: to appreciate the subtle variations between the teas being tasted, rather than outright contrasts, the order of tasting needs to be varied constantly. Unlike our other senses, our sense of smell reaches saturation point rapidly (whereas a deafening noise remains deafening, even after several minutes), and to be able to perceive an odor to which you have become accustomed, even after several minutes, requires a considerable effort. Add to this the fact that when faced with two different smells, we are only able to distinguish the most powerful or intense of the two.

It is often the case that the proximity of the areas sensitive to taste and smell can confuse the mind: people speak of a "taste" of jasmine when, in reality, they mean the scent.

🌿 Anosmia and aguesia

In the matter of taste and smell, everyone has his own particular sensitivities and individual thresholds of perception. Some people find it impossible to sense a particular odor, a condition called *anosmia*, while others cannot sense a particular taste, a condition known as *aguesia*. These differences are in part inborn, since the sensory receptors vary between individuals. For example, 20 percent of us are unable to detect the flavor resulting from the presence of monosodium glutamate, while a third of the population cannot recognize eucalyptol, the chief aromatic constituent of the eucalyptus leaf. But anomalies may also be acquired, and the appreciation of sensory information is powerfully conditioned by each person's culture, environment, and personal experiences. This appears in its most obvious form as a craving or repulsion: the smell of durian (a large, pungent fruit) is highly appreciated by the Chinese, but anathema to many Westerners—yet few Asians can stand the whiff of French cheese. When associated with some form of trauma, the aversion inspired by a smell can sometimes lead to anosmia—the odor in question can no longer be perceived. However, unlike the genetic form of the condition, it is reversible.

Although sensitivity to odors varies between individuals (see text above), we all share the capacity to sense smell but don't make full use of it. On the other hand, we do not all share the same culture, educational background, or history. And since recognition of a smell depends upon associations with the information stored in our memory, our past experiences have an influence on the smells we perceive.

We hope that it is now becoming clear how the art of tasting—in which we must concentrate in particular on the process of retronasal olfaction—can lead to the enrichment of our sensory culture, something we shall explore further in the next chapter.

Aromatic aromas are transient—"volatile" is the technical term—and we do not perceive them all in the same way. We can distinguish three main groups which our sense of smell recognises as a kind of continuum:

- Top notes (or foreground flavor): responsible for our first olfactory impression; volatile, disappearing rapidly.
- Middle notes (or middle ground flavor): they follow in second place; less transient.
- Base notes (or background flavor): heavier and more resistant, they give an aroma its length and roundness.

The existence of a good range of these notes is one of the criteria by which an odor or aroma is judged, including those produced by tea. This range is termed an aromatic balance and a tea is said to be "harmonious" when the notes develop continuously and smoothly from top to base.

TOUCH AND TEXTURE

Closely associated with flavor, texture refers to the tactile sensations experienced on the lips, the lining of the cheeks, the palate, and the tongue. While we might expect this to be a factor when tasting foodstuffs, it may come as a surprise to learn that it also applies to tea, given that in the final analysis we are dealing with an aqueous solution of fixed viscosity.

Like his counterpart in the wine world, the tea taster draws on a large vocabulary associated with tactile sensation, to describe the variations in texture from one tea to another.

Tactile sensations in the mouth are described by tea specialists as "somesthesia" and primarily concern the perception of temperature, both heat and cold.

The temperature of the water may be vital to the preparation of tea, but it also plays an important part in tasting. When food or drink is too hot, our whole mouth contracts and battles against pain or discomfort; we are concentrated on this single sensation, and our remaining senses temporarily shut down. Professional tasters invariably let their tea cool a little, both to accentuate its characteristics and to optimize their perceptions of taste and smell.

Although all teas possess identical levels of viscosity, their textures vary owing to the presence of polyphenols (tannins). When we taste a tea, these substances create an impression of roundness, astringency, or indeed "depth" depending on their molecular structure. With both wine and tea, astringency—a sensation that causes living tissue to contract—is associated with the bitter sensation produced by the tannins in the drink. These do not act directly on the tactile receptors in the mouth, but on the saliva, modifying its composition and rendering it abrasive to a greater or lesser degree. These changes are what produce our perception of astringency. Saliva acts as a lubricant for the buccal mucosa which allows us to experience a whole spectrum of tactile sensations: bitterness, dryness, and bite, but also body, roundness, consistency, etc. Since tannins are also responsible for bitterness, the sensation of astringency is often associated with bitterness too and the one becomes confused with the other. Astringency is one of the properties of tea: it is a plus in the right amount but in excess it is extremely unpleasant.

SIGHT

Vision also plays a valid role in the art of tasting tea for two reasons. On the one hand, simply observing tea in its various forms (dry leaves, infused leaves, liquor) provides information about it, and on the other, even though we may be perfectly well aware of it and might try to make allowances for it, sight influences us and leads to preconceptions. Before we even take a bite of something, we have formed an idea about it, and this creates expectations. For example, numerous tests carried out on syrups for children have shown that as soon as we drink a green liquid we begin to perceive a taste of mint, even if it contains no mint whatsoever. Sight provides us with a mass of information that can influence us and corrupt our other perceptions, sometimes to the point of pure invention.

To prevent sight interfering with the process during tea tasting, they are often conducted "blind"—and preferably in a bare room with little or no decoration. Not only is all written information concerning the tea in question (name, price, grade, etc.) blanked out, but the leaves themselves are frequently not on view. If tasting a tea that you saw to be rich in buds you would be tempted to assume that the liquor must be delicious. So written information about the tea and the visual appearance of the leaves is only taken into consideration at a later stage. And when several tasters are working at the same time, it is accepted policy to ignore the expressions on the faces of the others—happy or otherwise.

Given that it enables us to describe the features of the dry leaf, the infusion, and the liquor, our sense of sight should be used to complement our evaluation of the tea when it is being tasted, not influence it.

HEARING

Just as with sight, hearing also leads to tasting preconceptions. It provides a great deal of information, verbal and non-verbal, which can easily sway our judgment when tasting tea. Take one scenario as an example: a buyer visiting a plantation is preparing to taste ten teas for comparison purposes. Just before he starts, the planter whispers in his ear that the tea on the far left is outstanding. The taster is bound to then pay more attention to that particular sample during his tasting, perhaps at the expense of the rest. To taste a tea properly, using calm and un-biased judgment, any such information from a third party should be viewed with skepticism and not be taken into account.

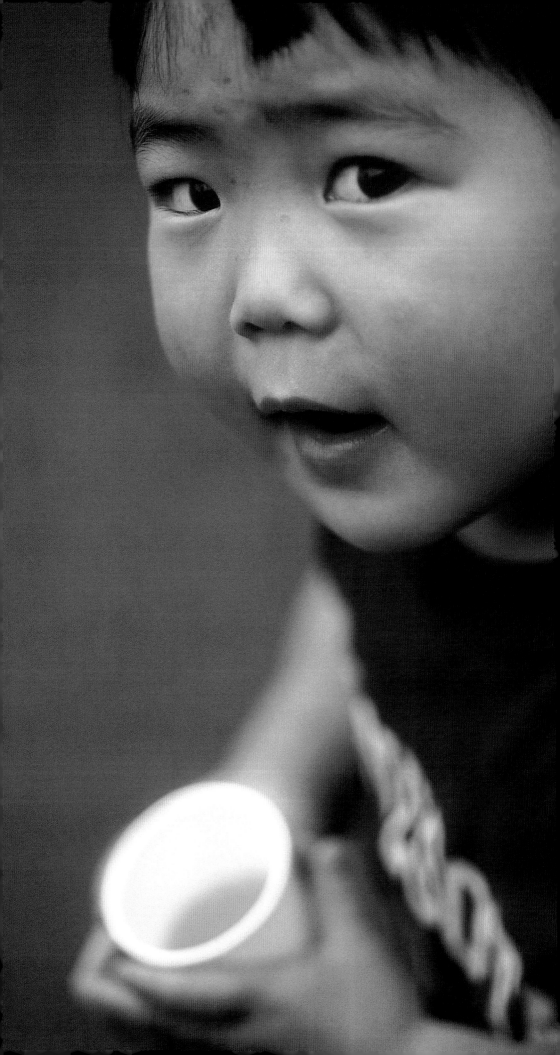

HOW WE EXPRESS
OUR SENSATIONS

We have just seen how our sense organs come into play when we taste a tea: they absorb small pieces of information and transmit them to the brain, which then interprets them. All these numerous pieces of information, especially as far as the sense of smell is concerned, mount up and combine to form a whole, a unique picture of the tea we have just tasted which our brains then feed back to us in the form of images, emotions, and words.

We also stated earlier that, to be a good taster, a person does not need to have an exceptional sense of taste and smell. On the other hand, training is absolutely indispensable, as dissecting and interpreting the image our brain feeds back to us is far from easy. The problem lies in isolating one sensation from another and determining what belongs to touch and what to taste. For example, we have a general tendency to confuse bitterness with astringency. Unraveling this tangle of sensations demands great powers of concentration and linguistic precision: in fact, it is by expressing the sensations we experience that we learn to differentiate between their various nuances and classify them at an earlier stage.

THE IMPORTANCE OF
VERBALIZATION

More than our other senses, taste and smell are rooted in our culture and our emotions. For instance, we are programmed to avoid bitter tastes and in nature bitterness is typical of poisonous plants; by tasting them, we have learned to eliminate them from our diet. As for smell, it has always been the poor relation in the education of the senses. Have we undertaken not to use our sense of smell to its fullest extent in order to underline our indisputable supremacy over the animal kingdom? Whatever the reason, our culture and upbringing results in our paying little attention to its full capabilities.

Children readily learn about colors, sounds, or even tastes as their senses develop—but rarely odors. Without a common vocabulary to describe what we smell, communicating the experience can be problematic.

When presented with a taste or odor, we say what we think of it quite spontaneously: "I like/don't like that," "that's good"/"that's awful," "that smells good"/"that smells horrid." Progressing beyond these knee-jerk reactions requires a definite and conscious effort. Granted, tasting basically revolves around the emotions it produces; nevertheless, if we are to analyze and describe each of the sensations we experience with any degree of accuracy, it is essential, at a certain point, to be able to dissociate ourselves from these emotions in order to focus on the sensations.

→ Refining our sensations

It is by expressing our sensations in a methodical fashion and by describing them in the most precise terms possible that progress in the art of tasting can be made. And, surprising as it may seem, the more exact and subtle our description of a sensation, the richer will be our perception of it and the greater the pleasure it produces: as we master the terminology, our sensations grow in subtlety and depth and our senses of smell and taste become ever more discerning.

→ Communication as a means to progress

In addition, perfecting our ability to classify sensations also teaches us to communicate them to others; in fact, we shall see that the ultimate challenge in tasting lies in the establishment of a common vocabulary. For the beginner, communication is a powerful aid to progress: in the context of group tastings, it is the interaction between our own sensations and those of others that leads us to explore the process in greater detail and enriches our own sensations.

Suppose, for example, three friends are tasting Dong Ding. Paul finds that the tea has a floral note, but cannot pin it down. This had not occurred to Joan, but now that her attention has been drawn to it, she agrees that the tea has a heavy, opulent bouquet reminding her of the scent of white flowers. Peter picks up on this last remark and is now aware of a powerful, heady scent of wisteria. Paul in turn suddenly notices this wisteria scent: it recalls his childhood and his grandmother's garden. He hasn't managed to identify it before, but as soon as it is given a name, he immediately experiences both the pleasure of old memories recalled and the satisfaction of being able to put the name on the tip of his tongue to this familiar sensation.

Nevertheless, a group tasting should always begin in silence to allow each taster to concentrate on his own sensations. We stressed earlier that other people's opinions can interfere with the tasting process by introducing preconceptions. If, during our imaginary session, Paul were to remark out loud that there was an aroma of honey in the tea samples, the other participants would also be tempted to look for it, with the risk of interfering with their own results. The tasting and the sharing of impressions would be corrupted, and Paul would have deprived his friends of the joy of their own sensations.

Of course, thrilled at having identified a certain sensation or aroma, beginners find it hard not to tell everyone else. To prevent this, group tasting is often carried out using special record sheets on which each member writes down his sensations. The information recorded is only shared later; the tasting then enters a secondary phase with everyone contributing to the pool of knowledge.

There is another advantage in writing down impressions rather than voicing them aloud: the physical act of doing so "purges" a sensation from the mind and allows the taster to concentrate on the next one.

So, when Paul is tasting Oriental Beauty, he experiences an infinite aromatic complexity and the final bouquet reminds him of a firework. He tries to classify the aromas on his tasting sheet: plums, wood and wax polish, roses, apricot jam, vanilla. This makes sure he will not forget them; having recorded them safely, he can concentrate on the remaining ones.

For these reasons the best progress in tasting is made when you work as a small group, especially with someone more experienced in the art—a sort of mentor who will, for instance, be able to draw the participants' attention to the aromatic complexity of a Spring Darjeeling and describe it in the best way possible using the accepted vocabulary of tasting.

In fact, this is where the ultimate challenge for the apprentice taster lies: the mastering of an arsenal of terms in universal use but which, without training, do not readily occur to us when trying to classify and describe our sensory perceptions. Just as it is not enough to recognize letters of the alphabet to be able to read, the beginner can only progress with the assistance of a more experienced colleague.

CLASSIFYING AROMAS AND ODORS

Recognizing and naming tastes, which are limited in number, is fairly straightforward; with a little training we can readily differentiate between the various textures of tea or any foodstuff, and, thanks to our developed visual culture, it is not hard to describe what we see. Dealing with odors, however, is another matter altogether.

Our memories retain traces of smells and every other form of sensation. When we smell something, our brains "replay" whatever is associated with that sensation. With other perceptions a word rapidly comes to mind to describe them—red, sweet, cold, sparkling, etc. But where smell is concerned our memories frequently fail to prompt us for a name. Instead, they conjure up a memory or an emotion. A certain smell will remind us of a person, a place, a journey. More than all our other senses, smell is subject to associations that make us happy or sad or transport us back to the past. Anything based on personal and subjective experiences is hard to express to others and thus smell, to a certain extent at least, is incommunicable. The situation is aggravated by

Following pages: one bud and two leaves. This is a top quality, delicate pluck destined to make a Chinese green tea of the highest standard.

the fact that no one has taught us to give a name to an odor in the way that, since earliest childhood, we are taught to recognize the spectrum of colors or define temperature on a scale from freezing to burning.

The difficulty, in terms of tea or any other drink, lies in being able to use a universal language of smell that will allow us to communicate, exchange, and transcend personal images and memories. Many professional tasters and perfume experts have looked into the way that odors are classified. By consensus, there are two major forms of vocabulary in use:

- The vocabulary of organic chemistry, which consists of describing the compounds responsible for odors. Obviously, this is very technical, and virtually impenetrable to anyone who has not studied it. And as it is of most concern to the perfume industry and scientific research, we can safely ignore this aspect.
- A more image-based approach, inspired by nature. Although not the answer to every problem—our experiences of nature are not all identical—this approach does have the advantage of starting from common ground by using nouns and adjectives in everyday use.

THE TEA-TASTER'S VOCABULARY

→ The odors, scents, and aromas

Let's start with the hardest part, the vocabulary of odors, which helps us describe those characteristics linked to the sense of smell that can be detected both in the dry leaf and the infusion, and also the characteristics of the liquor, perceived by retronasal olfaction.

Like many professional tasters, we begin with families of odors, rather than the molecules or groups of molecules that create the odors. Our objective in assembling this vocabulary is to define a certain number of the major aromatic "families" encountered in the course of tea tasting.

This approach allows us to pass from general sensations to specific ones and fits in well with the way the odors enrich one another. It is important to understand that these families do not stand in isolation and there are no strict barriers between them. So, an iodized note suggesting fish, like that found in Japanese Sencha teas, often also has floral accents of the rose type. The note of hay that can be detected in many dry tea leaves may lead on towards the vanilla and woody groups.

HERBACEOUS, GREEN
Fresh herbaceous: green stems, privet, freshly mown grass, sap, sorrel, watercress, cultivated mushrooms
Aromatic herbs: basil, mint, bay leaves, coriander, sage, dill
Cooked vegetable: artichoke, spinach, French beans, zucchini, cooked vegetables, raw vegetables
Dried herbaceous: hay, wicker, straw, tobacco, malty, coumarin (resembling new-mown hay)

MARINE

Shellfish: winkles, mussels, oysters, whelks
Crustaceans: crab, velvet crab, crab claws
Fish: salmon meat, fish skin
Others: iodine, seaweed, kelp

FLORAL

Fresh floral: fresh roses, orange blossom, peony, geranium, hyacinth, freesia, lily of the valley, lilac, narcissus
White flowers: jasmine, daisy, marguerite, mimosa, wisteria, lily, osmanthus (a native Chinese species)
Exotic flowers: frangipani (the Temple tree of Hawaii), orchid, Tahitian gardenia, magnolia, ylang-ylang (from the *Cananga odorata* tree), Rose absolute (*Rosa damascena*)

FRUITY

Orchard fruits: pear, apple, quince, grape, plum, mirabelle, cherry, grape, peach, apricot
Berries: strawberry, raspberry, blackcurrant, blackberry, black fruit, red fruit
Exotic fruit: mango, passion fruit, lychee, kiwi
Citrus fruit: zest, lemon, orange, mandarin orange, bergamot orange
Cooked fruit: prune, date, fruit jam, stewed fruit, fig, raisin, currant, cherry stone
Nuts: green almonds, bitter almonds, chestnuts, hazelnuts, walnuts, horse chestnuts

SPICY

Mild spices: cinnamon, licorice, vanilla, anise, nutmeg
Hot spices: clove, cardamom, pepper

BUTTERY, DAIRY PRODUCE

Fresh butter, melted butter, cream, milk, condensed milk

SWEET, VANILLA

Vanilla sugar, honey, wax, pollen

RICH

Chocolate, cocoa, mocha, sweetened chestnut purée, frangipane, caramelized apple, caramel, jam

UNDERGROWTH

Humus, damp leaves, moss, patchouli

EARTHY

Damp soil, cellar, mushroom, mold, dust, stony, wet earth after a storm, peat, saltpeter

WOODY

Waxed wood, dry wood, cedar, sandalwood, vetiver (a relative of lemon grass), balsa wood, pine, arnica
Woody with gamy notes: holly, blackcurrant leaves

GAMY

Leather, saddlery, horse

Big cat, musk, damp wool, sweat

Manure, stable, tannery, menagerie

Cat urine, indole (chemical present in some plant oils and tar, also in feces)

Truffle

BURNT

Roasting coffee

Breadcrumbs, bread crusts, brioche

Toasted hazelnuts, peanuts, popcorn

SMOKED

Bacon, juniper, tar, hydrocarbons

MINERAL

Metallic, hot metal, silica, flint

→ A reminder of flavors

Salty

Sweet

Acid

Bitter

Umami (Japanese word meaning "savory" or "meaty")

→ Words describing texture

Astringency: a bitterness in the mouth, of varying degrees, caused by tannin. Sometimes a sensation of dryness.

Body: characteristic of a liquor combining good structure with a certain thickness. Adjective: full-bodied.

Flowing: describes a liquor that is supple, without asperity. Used to describe teas with low tannic content.

Mouth-filling: gives a sensation of fullness in the mouth. See also roundness.

Oily: reminiscent of oil in texture, with a varying degree of delicacy.

Powdery: describes a very slight astringency on the palate that leaves an impression of a fine powder in the mouth.

Rasping: is said of very astringent teas, often of poor quality or infused for too long.

Robust: describes a very full-bodied tea.

Roundness: characteristic of a liquor that fills the mouth in a rounded way. Adjective: rounded in the mouth.

Silky: describes a supple and slightly oily liquor, reminiscent of silk.

Smooth: describes a liquor lacking harsh tannins and therefore without asperity.

Japanese Matcha is beaten with a very fine bamboo whisk, the *chasen*.

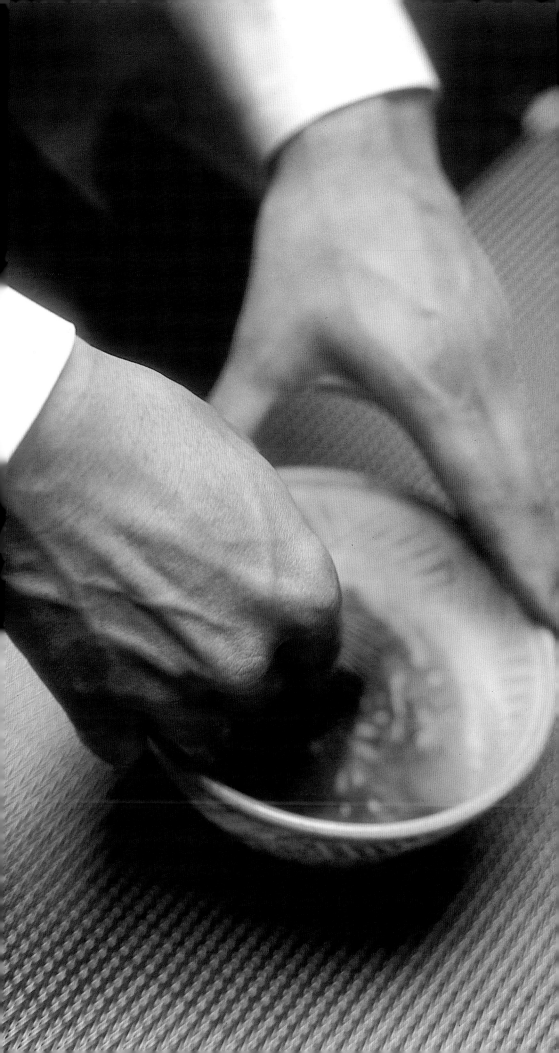

Structured: describes a predominantly tannic, "mouth-filling" liquor.

Supple: is said of a liquor that is more velvety than astringent.

Thick: describes a liquor with a viscosity not like water but more reminiscent of oil or cream.

Unctuous: is said of a tea that is rounded in the mouth and slightly oily.

Velvety: describes a slightly thick liquor, reminiscent of velvet.

Watery: describes a liquor without astringency or sense of texture.

→ Additional tasting terms

Ample: a liquor that is full and round, with flavors that fill the mouth.

Aromatic: describes a rich liquor with plenty of flavor.

Aromatic palette: the entirety of the notes perceived in a liquor.

Aromatic profile: the whole of the aromatic characteristics of tea. It takes account of the transience of the notes (initial-main-background) and often of the impact of the texture and flavors on the balance.

Ascending: often used to describe very volatile and direct initial aromas.

Attack: describes the first notes perceived, either by direct inhalation or retro-olfaction.

Balanced: describes a liquor in which the aromas succeed each other smoothly, well highlighted by the flavors and texture.

Bouquet: the whole of the aromatic characteristics sensed by the nose.

Complex: describes a bouquet that is very rich in clearly defined aromas.

Dominant: describes those families of aromas most strongly present in the liquor or infusion.

Final: describes the last notes picked up either by inhalation or retro-olfaction.

Finesse: a liquor with subtle and precise aromas.

Frank: describes a tea with well-defined characteristics (texture, flavors, aromas, etc.) without defect or ambiguity.

Frivolous: a tea that is both rich in aromas and short in the mouth—an impression of elusiveness.

Fullness: sensation offered by a tea which fills the mouth, without acidity and with rather sweet aromas.

Generous: rich in aromas.

Harmony: when flavor, texture, and aromas are well balanced, with a fine succession of notes.

Heavy: refers to a background aroma.

Infusion: this means both the act of infusing and the wet leaves that are recovered after infusion. In the case of tea, the product of the infusion is always referred to as the liquor.

Intense: having strength and duration.

Liquor: the liquid obtained by infusing tea leaves.

Lively: a liquor that is fresh and light with a dominant note that is slightly, but not excessively, acid. Very agreeable in general.

Long in the mouth: is said of a tea with aromas that leave a pleasant and lasting impression in the mouth and at the back of the mouth, after tasting.

Monolithic: describes a narrow aromatic palette, the individual notes being inseparable from each other.

Mouth: the entirety of the sensations perceived by the palate.

Nose: see bouquet.

Note: synonymous with aroma.

Opulent: describes a rich, heavy, and often heady aroma.

Peak: initial notes expressed in fits and starts.

Persistence: characteristic of aromas that linger long in the mouth.

Presence: the way the tea presents itself in the mouth.

Short in the mouth: leaves little trace in the mouth or at the back of the mouth after tasting.

Strong: rather vague term that is generally applied to a full-bodied, dark-colored liquor.

Sustained: describes an aroma that remains a long time in the mouth.

Sweet: is said of teas having a slightly sweet flavor, with no astringency—associated with sweet, vanilla-flavored aromas.

Tannic: describes a liquor that is rich in tannins.

The world's 50 best teas

- CHINA
- TAIWAN
- JAPAN
- INDIA
- NEPAL
- SRI LANKA

CHINA

HISTORY

From the story of its accidental discovery by the emperor and father of Chinese medicine Shen Nong, in 2737 BC, to its proven use as a drink during the reign of Emperor Wen, founder of the Zhou Dynasty (1122–256 BC), China is acknowledged as being the home of tea, with a history extending back almost five thousand years.

For centuries, the Chinese character *tu* was used to denote tea leaves in written script, the same character that was used for all bitter-tasting plants. It was not until the eighth century that a Tang Dynasty emperor made a distinction by giving it a specific name, by removing the upper stroke from the character *tu*, creating the new character *cha*.

Up to that time, tea was used either as a medicine or a stimulant, generally in the monasteries. Under the Tang Dynasty (AD 618–907) it gained in popularity as a drink and tea drinking in everyday life came to be seen as an activity of refinement. Teahouses appeared and tea's popularity spread as, for the first time, it helped to inspire artistic creation—painters, potters, and poets extolled its virtures—creating around it a sophisticated world full of symbolism. One of the artists inspired by tea, Lu Yu (AD 733–804), wrote the first treatise on it, *Cha Jing* (*The Classic of Tea*)—a poetic work in which he described the nature of the plant and codified its system of preparation and tasting. At that time, tea was compressed into bricks which were first roasted, then reduced to a powder and mixed with boiling water.

Under the Song Dynasty (960–1279) a second school of tea drinking grew up which, with its poetic ceremonies and the importance it placed on respecting the rules of tea preparation, was a precursor of the Japanese Cha No Yu. The teas drunk on these occasions—always green—became more and more refined and the fine china associated with them took on a role of great importance. The leaves were ground to a fine powder, which was then added to simmering water and whipped to a frothy consistency with a bamboo whisk.

Under the Ming Dynasty (1368–1644), the manufacture of tea in compressed cake form was banned by imperial decree and tea began to

The best Chinese teas often come from mountainous regions where harvesting has to be done by hand. To guarantee the finest quality pluck, only experienced workers are recruited.

be consumed the way it still is today, infused in a pot or bowl. This new school exercised an important influence over the objects and accessories used in tea's preparation. The kettle replaced the tea bottles used in the Tang era and teapots and the zhong (a lidded cup) became the ideal utensils in which to infuse tea—the more correct term for the zhong is *gaiwan* (see page 110). Tea became universally popular and a whole new economic sector grew up around its export.

From the end of the sixteenth century, a whole range of manufacturing methods came into use. Up to that date, green tea had been the only kind that was manufactured, but from then on teas of different colors began to make their appearance, most notably with the development of black tea (1590–1600), semi-oxidized teas (1725), and white teas (1796).

The Chinese successfully guarded the secrets of tea manufacture during the Qing Dynasty (1644–1911) and right up to the 1850s. This enabled them to maintain a flourishing trade with the West, but from the mid-1850s, now a victim of the Opium Wars and the Taiping rebellion, the Chinese economy went into recession. Also affected by the fact that the British had finally managed to discover the secrets of tea production (see page 21), exports fell into an irreparable decline from 1886 onwards. It was not until much later, in 1984, that Chinese production rose again to the level it had enjoyed before 1886, and it took a further two years before China could supplant Sri Lanka as the second largest tea producer in the world.

CHINESE TEA AND ITS CONSUMPTION

The Chinese can be justly proud not only of offering the widest and richest range of teas in the world—running into thousands—but also of excelling with their "grand cru" teas. These are highly regarded in gastronomic circles, and give great pleasure to the most demanding of tea connoisseurs year after year.

While all colors of tea are made in China (see page 60), it is green tea that is sold the most there. Two thirds of China's tea production, almost 75 percent of which is green tea, is consumed by the home market. The remaining 25 percent is divided between black and dark teas (20 percent) and Wu Long (5 percent). Local production of white and yellow teas is marginal.

At 13 ounces (370 g) per head per year, consumption may, at first, seem relatively low and might appear to indicate that tea drinking is the prerogative of a small number of people, or that it is drunk only occasionally, but this is not the case. In China, tea occupies an essential place in everyday life and these few ounces per head are less surprising when the way the Chinese prepare tea is taken into account. They use the same leaves throughout the day, every morning throwing a handful of leaves into a vacuum flask that they take to work and refill with hot water regularly as the day progresses.

For many years the drinking of other teas, particularly Wu Long and Pu Er, was confined to the inhabitants of the towns in the south (Guangzhou) and the Chinese who lived in Hong Kong and overseas. During the last thirty years, with the re-opening of the teahouses that were closed down during the Cultural Revolution (1966–76) and especially with the increasing emergence of middle and upper classes in China, interest in these teas has been renewed in the affluent coastal provinces, leading to some extraordinary surges in price (see pages 167–168 and 177).

ZONES UNDER CULTIVATION

2,380,000 acres (952,000 hectares) under cultivation
1,000,000 tons of tea produced
A yield of 2,165 pounds per 2½ acres (982 kilos per hectare)
(Source: FAO statistics 2006, including production from Taiwan)

Tea cultivation is concentrated in the southeastern provinces, in particular Fujian, Zhejiang, Yunnan, Szechuan, Hunan, Hubei, and Anhui. More than twenty provinces in all produce tea in areas with widely differing weather conditions—some of them are able to harvest all the year round, while in others harvesting is more seasonal.

The best-quality teas often originate from plantations cultivated at moderate altitudes—between 1,640 to 4,000 feet (500–1,200 m)—but on some of the high plateaux in Yunnan, there are plantations at over 6,560 feet (2,000 m). In China, these mountains are famous and many have given their names to the teas grown there, rather like the *appellation* system in the French wine industry, as have many of the villages in which they are expertly processed.

→ Fujian

As well as being the largest tea-producing region, accounting for almost one fifth of Chinese tea manufacture, Fujian Province also makes the widest range of teas. All the different manufacturing methods originated in this region, with the exception of those for green and yellow teas.

Tea is grown throughout the province, but three areas are particularly renowned: the area surrounding the town of Fuding, where the best white, green, and jasmine teas are produced; the mountainous area of Wu Yi, which separates Fujian from Jiangxi, legendary for its Wu Long or "Cliff Teas," and its smoked teas; and the Anxi district, which produces the best Tie Guan Yin teas.

→ Zhejiang

With 17 percent of the country's tea production, Zhejiang is the second largest producer. The best teas rub shoulders with the most ordinary in this province where only green teas are made. Gunpowder, a tea that is often mediocre, is destined uniquely for export and is produced in industrial quantities. It originated in Zhejiang, as did Long Jing, the excellent traditional green tea that the Chinese prize above all others.

→ Yunnan

Home to the forest bordering on Laos and Myanmar (Burma), Yunnan is the acknowledged home of the earliest tea plants and still contains a huge number of wild specimens (see page 25). The departure point for the first tea and horse trading routes, the region remains true to its history. It still produces green tea compressed into flat cakes, convenient for transportation, just as it did 1,500 years ago (see page 67)—and in recent years in spectacular quantities. The two principal regions producing teas in this form—named after the town of Pu Er through which the tea-brick trade passed—are the prefecture of Xishuangbanna and the district of Lincang on the banks of the Mekong.

For the past sixty years, Yunnan has also been one of the two largest producers of black tea in China.

→ Anhui

A region of lesser importance with regard to the quantity it manufactures (6 percent), Anhui is nevertheless one of the foremost producers of quality teas. This province includes the famous mountain range, the Huang Shan, the source of a great number of the best "new season" green teas and also of Qimen—a black tea with a worldwide reputation.

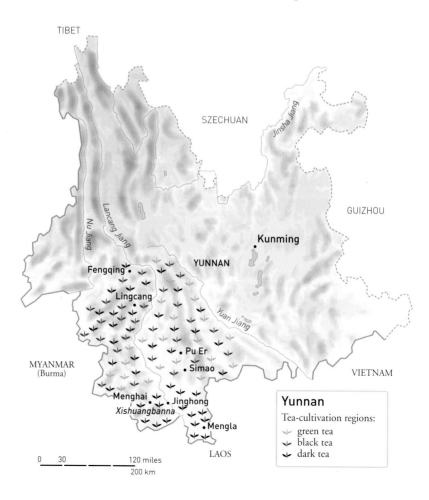

TIBET

SZECHUAN

Jinsha Jiang

GUIZHOU

Nu Jiang

Lancang Jiang

Kunming

YUNNAN

Fengqing

Lingcang

Yuan Jiang

MYANMAR
(Burma)

Pu Er

Simao

VIETNAM

Menghai
Xishuangbanna
Jinghong

Mengla

LAOS

0   30   120 miles
        200 km

Yunnan

Tea-cultivation regions:

⤵ green tea
⤵ black tea
⤵ dark tea

Anhui, Zhejiang and Fujian

⚓ Tea dispatch port

Tea-cultivation regions:
- green tea
- black tea/smoked tea
- Wu Long
- white tea

QIMEN

Other names or spellings: Keemun, Qi Hong Gong Fu
Black tea from Anhui Province
Harvested in spring and summer

Qimen, a small town in Anhui Province, is situated in the south
of the Huang Shan (Yellow Mountains), an area thought to offer
the most perfect weather conditions for tea growing. This region is
famous for its green teas, which are among the finest in China, but
the production of black tea is relatively recent. In 1876, Yu Ganchen,
an important government official from Qimen, retired to his native
village after spending his career in Fujian, the main region for black
tea production at that time. He had had plenty of time to become
familiar with the manufacturing techniques used in the making of
black tea and decided to launch a venture in Qimen. The result was
original and delicious; the Qimen teas he produced offered a unique
aromatic bouquet combining gamy notes with richness.

Qimen is what in China is known as a "refined" tea (as against the
"unrefined" teas which are manufactured using the leaves in the just-
plucked state, then cutting, grading, and sorting them into different
categories at the end of the manufacturing process). The very regular
appearance of the leaves of the beautiful Qimen tea is striking. The
standard grade of Qimen tea is used as the basis for a number of
blends and scented teas.

Tasting notes

Dry leaf
Appearance: almost black in color, the
leaves are tightly rolled, short and even,
slightly shiny, with few buds visible.
Scent: a note of intense leather.

Infusion
Color: dark red.
Scent: a note of intense leather.

Liquor
Color: dark copper.
Texture: a lot of sweetness, powdery
sensation.
Taste: no bitterness.
Aromas: two typical groups, leather and
cocoa, enriched with small woody and
malted notes, and occasionally arnica.
Aromatic profile: a powdery texture and
rich aromas that are perfectly balanced;
the note is sustained for several minutes
at a time.

Method of preparation
Ideally, in a tasting set: 3–5 minutes in a YiXing teapot holding 10 fluid ounces (300 ml),
in water heated to 185°F (85°C).

QIMEN MAO FENG
Black tea from Anhui Province
Harvested in April

This grade of Qimen tea is very different from the others. The leaves used for Qimen Mao Feng are not plucked from the tea bushes that produce the Qimen teas already described, but from cultivars normally used for the green Huang Shan Mao Feng (one of the famous Anhui green teas, see page 163), which have very tender leaves and very downy buds—hence the name Mao Feng, "downy tip" or fine hair.

Qimen Mao Feng is also notable for the method of manufacture, which is very similar to that of Huang Shan Mao Feng: after withering, the leaves are rolled lengthwise by hand into needles, which gives them their long, slender appearance. They are then sent to the oxidation hall, after which they are dried. Qimen Mao Feng must be classed as an "unrefined" tea as its leaves are not graded or sorted into categories.

These two unique features produce a tea of great delicacy, with very fragile leaves almost as fine as hair and an aromatic bouquet that, in addition to the leather and cocoa notes typical of the Qimen teas, offers added fruity and fresh aromas.

In China, along with the "Yunnan Buds," Qimen Mao Feng teas are produced only rarely and are considered to be the *nec plus ultra* of unrefined tea.

Tasting notes

Dry leaf
Appearance: long, dark, fragile leaves, delicately rolled into needles; small golden-tipped buds.
Scent: woody and rich, with a fresh note of apple.

Infusion
Appearance: the delicacy of the leaves used in the preparation of this tea is all the more apparent once they are unfurled.
Scent: a fruity note (stewed apple, cooked orange) is superimposed on the usual leather and cocoa aromas.

Liquor
Color: dark red.
Texture: rounded and full, with an astringency which becomes apparent in the second instance.
Taste: slightly bitter.
Aromas: floral in attack (honey, pollen) then a leather note, lighter than that in the other Qimen grades, together with cocoa and fruit.
Aromatic profile: great complexity of aromas which are revealed progressively; plenty of presence and length in the cocoa note, very woody (cedar).

Method of preparation
Ideally, in a tasting set: 4–5 minutes in water heated to 185°F (85°C).
For everyday use: in the same way as the other Qimen teas.

YUNNAN

Other names: Dian Hong Gong Fu, Black Congou

Black tea from Yunnan Province

Harvested from March to November (the best crops are harvested in spring)

Yunnan began producing black tea in the 1940s, at the instigation of the government, who hoped to develop black tea production for export. The region offers ideal geological and weather conditions for growing tea: red, fertile soil, a misty and humid climate, and a constant average daily temperature from 59 to 73°F (15–23°C) all year round, which gave Kunming, the provincial capital, built at an altitude of 6,560 feet (2,000 m), the nickname of "The City of Four Springs." Tea growing takes up the whole of the south and southwest of the province. The principal variety of tea bush grown is Da Ye, a bush with large leaves used to make Pu Er. Until recently, Yunnan produced mostly black tea (which the Chinese call red, hence the name Dian Hong, "Red from Yunnan"), but because of the great popularity of Pu Er (see page 175), production is now primarily dedicated to the manufacture of dark teas.

Together with Qimen, Yunnan black tea is among the best in China. Easily appreciated, since it is very scented and with scarcely any bitterness thanks to the delicacy of the leaf and the number of buds it contains, it is available in a great many grades.

Tasting notes

Dry leaf

Appearance: well-rolled and very regular leaves. Brown-black in color with a number of tawny buds according to the grade.

Scent: powerful and rich (honey, wax, undergrowth).

Infusion

Color: chocolate.

Scent: the same notes as in the dry leaf but more intense.

Liquor

Color: brown with red highlights.

Texture: rounded with light astringency.

Taste: neither bitterness nor acidity.

Aromas: the notes open out with plenty of depth; a heavy flowery note, honeyed, waxed wood.

Aromatic profile: the soft, honeyed notes give an impression of fullness, greatly complementing the roundness in the mouth.

Method of preparation

In a tasting set: 3 to 4 minutes in a YiXing teapot holding 10 fluid ounces (300 ml), in water heated to 185°F (85°C). If you are a fan of Yunnan teas, be sure to keep a teapot for their exclusive preparation; it will gradually become seasoned adding greatly to the tasting experience.

YUNNAN BUDS
Black tea from Yunnan Province
Harvested at the start of spring

Like the other black teas of the province, this tea is made solely for
export and even though destined for "barbarians" it is manufactured
with the same expertise habitually employed for the best green and
white teas. But unlike the other Yunnan grades, often graded and
refined in large quantities (in Yunnan, the tea trade is organized
historically around large state factories manufacturing leaves bought
from farmers in the surrounding area), the buds are divided into small
lots and are processed entirely by hand, right through to the final
grading.

Like Silver Needles or the Jun Shan Yin Zen, Yunnan Buds are
made up almost entirely of downy buds which take on a beautiful
tawny color in oxidizing.

Yunnan Buds is unquestionably the finest tea of this family. While
not drawn from a Chinese tradition, it is no less exciting on the
tasting level and counts as one of the finest achievements of Chinese
tea production. It is worth noting that it also displays some similarity
to the very rare bud harvests in Assam, a region not too distant from
it geographically (see page 216).

Tasting notes

Dry leaf
Appearance: a spectacular pluck
composed entirely of very long,
golden buds.
Scent: a gamy note is added to the
Yunnan honey and flower scents.

Infusion
Color: very dark brown.
Scent: dominated by undergrowth and
gamy notes (damp wicker, leather).

Liquor
Color: almost black.
Texture: evocative of velvet, with a fine
astringency.
Taste: a touch of bitterness.
Aromas: an amazing variety. Wicker,
mushroom, truffle, tobacco, mocha,
beeswax, and leather are just a few
of the notes this type of tea offers.
Aromatic profile: full and balanced,
the flavors remain on the palate long
after the last mouthful.

Method of preparation
Ideally made in a tasting set: 4 minutes in water heated to 185°F (85°C).
For everyday use: prepare in the same way as for other Yunnan teas (see page 156).

BLACK NEEDLES
Other names or spellings: Golden Needles, Jin Zen
Black tea from Fujian Province
Harvested beginning May

It is quite likely that the manufacture of black tea was perfected in
Fujian in the sixteenth century, but nowadays the amount produced
there is insignificant, the main production long having passed to
Yunnan Province and, to a lesser extent, Anhui.

The producers of Fujian nevertheless still possess considerable
expertise (as the history of Qimen shows) and in the 1990s a few
producers in the regions around Fuding and Zhenghe made use of
this ancient knowledge once again to produce teas for the modern
palate. The production of high-quality black tea has resumed in
moderate quantities and two teas in particular have come to the
fore: Black Monkey and Black Needles.

Black Needles is manufactured at the beginning of May from leaves
of the famous "Great White" tea bush, also used in the manufacture
of white teas and some green teas (see pages 165, 172, and 173). The
method of manufacture is exactly the same as that for black tea except
for the rolling. This is done by a machine which flattens and twists
the leaves lengthwise, so that they take the form of needles. The down
which covers the buds does not survive this process and at the end
of it the leaves are shiny and look not unlike a fine Japanese Sencha.

Tasting notes

Dry leaf
Appearance: very long, fine, flat leaves,
shiny and black. An occasional tawny
sparkle from the buds where the down
has not been completely eliminated
during the rolling.
Scent: cocoa and spiced, the nose tends
towards dry wood, wicker.

Infusion
Color: brown.
Scent: an ample and complex bouquet.
A buttery note emphasizes the scent of
cocoa and evokes melting chocolate.
Delicate notes of cooked apple, vanilla,
and mild spices.

Liquor
Color: dark, with great clarity.
Texture: supple, with a fine astringency
(powdery sensation).
Taste: no bitterness but a touch of acidity.
Aromas: the scent of cocoa dominates
the whole with spicy (cinnamon, nutmeg)
and woody (tobacco) facets.
Aromatic profile: the attack is generous,
leading up to a sensation of tasting cocoa
powder. The more woody and spicy scents
leave a long-lasting impression in the
mouth.

Method of preparation
Ideally made in a tasting set: 3 to 4 minutes in water heated to 185°F (85°C).
Or 3 to 5 minutes in a YiXing teapot holding 10 fluid ounces (300 ml), in water heated
to 185°F (85°C).

LAPSANG SOUCHONG
Other name: Zheng Shan Xiao Zhong
Smoked black tea from Fujian Province
Harvested from April to November

Renowned the world over, this smoked tea is often considered to be the Chinese tea *par excellence*, but in the eyes of the Chinese, who do not drink it, it is "tea for Westerners."

Originally made on Mount Zheng, in the Wu Yi Shan range (Fujian), a region with a great deal of experience in drying leaves over coal-fueled fires (see also Shui Xian and Da Hong Pao), nowadays it is produced all over Fujian.

Unlike Shui Xian and Da Hong Pao, Lapsang Souchong is a black tea that is withered over fires fueled by conifers (usually spruce or cedar). Like the "taste of fire" Wu Long teas, it is also dried in bamboo baskets over heated charcoal.

Several qualities of Lapsang Souchong are available, according to the quality of the pluck and the amount of smoking, which totally eclipses the aromatic compounds present in the leaf. For this reason it is generally made from the lower leaves, or "souchong," which contain less theine.

This is a tea to which the palate can become accustomed, so lovers of Lapsang Souchong might find themselves seeking out teas that have been smoked to an increasing degree in order to produce the same sensation. To help re-sensitize a jaded palate, try drinking a different tea for a few weeks.

Tasting notes

Dry leaf
Appearance: large leaves, very matte, the color of charcoal.
Scent: smoky (bacon) with a hint of wet leaves on a forest floor.

Infusion
Color: brown bordering on khaki.
Scent: the same as the dry leaf.

Liquor
Appearance: limpid amber.
Texture: completely smooth.
Taste: a faint bitterness.
Aromas: a fairly uniform smoky note which should not, however, mask the herbaceous, almost undergrowth notes offered by a good Lapsang Souchong.
Aromatic profile: frank and heavy, a powerful attack, and lingering presence in the mouth (up to 15 minutes!).

Method of preparation
3–5 minutes in a teapot holding 10 fluid ounces (300 ml) in water heated to 185°F (85ºC).
Note: This tea leaves a lasting stain in the pot so it is best to keep a pot exclusively for its preparation.
Lapsang Souchong goes well with brunch or savory dishes. Used in the kitchen as a condiment, it is one of the rare ingredients able to impart a smoky aroma.

LONG JING / DRAGON WELL

Old name: Lung ching
Green tea from Zhejiang Province
Harvested once a year in spring

Long Jing—the most common of China's green teas and the favorite
of the Chinese people—comes originally from the hills around the
town of Hangzhou and the Lake in the West, a region with a long
tradition of tea growing. (The "Lake in the West" was mentioned by
Lu Yu in his *The Classic of Tea*.) Due to its success, its manufacture
has gradually spread to many other provinces and today it is one of
the most copied green teas in all China.

The harvest begins on or around the first week of April and goes
on for several weeks. Tea made from the first three days' pluck is never
sold but given to government officials.

The Long Jing leaf is the same shape as the young bud. Processing
this "Buddha's eyelid" needs an expert hand—the leaves are tossed in a
wok for about twenty minutes, with slow, precise, regular movements.

Long Jing is divided into seven grades, of which Shi Feng (or Lion
Peak) is the the finest. The name Shi Feng was initially reserved for
the crop taken from the eighteen tea trees that grew on the mountain
of the same name and that had been selected by an emperor of the
Qing Dynasty. These plants, now under guard, still produce a harvest,
but the name Shi Feng is now applied to all high-quality crops from
this mountain.

Tasting notes

Dry leaf
Appearance: flat leaf, yellow-green in
color; well shaped, it resembles a tea
leaf still on the tree.
Scent: herbaceous and burnt-vanilla,
sometimes almost rich (chocolate).

Infusion
Color: the young buds used in the
best grades are bright green, almost
fluorescent. The bud and two leaves of
the pluck are revealed during infusion.
Scent: herbaceous then nutty (chestnut,
horse chestnut).

Liquor
Color: golden, pale and shiny.
Texture: very full, thick, and supple.
Tastes: a touch of bitterness and acidity;
can be slightly sweet.
Aromas: accurately reflect the dry leaf—
burnt-vanilla background, supporting
the fresh herbaceous and mineral center
often found in Chinese green teas.
Aromatic profile: good length in the
mouth and good balance of flavors
and aromas. The best Long Jing offer
complex aromatic bouquets: green notes
(zucchini, artichoke hearts), iodized (fish),
amino acids, licorice, and toast.

Method of preparation
In a tasting set: 4 minutes in water heated to 167°F (75°C).
Or 3 pinches of leaves in a small zhong, either infused for up to 4 times successively
for 30–40 seconds each time, or for a single period of 3–4 minutes, according to taste.

The world's 50 best teas → China

BI LUO CHUN

Other names or spellings: Dong Ting, Bi Luo Chun, Pi Lo Chun
Green tea from Jiangsu Province
Harvested once a year at the end of March

Already in existence under the Ming Dynasty, for centuries this tea
was known as Xia Sha Ren Xiang, which translates as "Astounding
fragrance" or "Fragrance to cause fear and trembling." Legend has
it that in ancient times, reluctant to stop work that was going well
though their baskets were full, the workers carried on plucking and
stuffed the leaves into their tunics. Warmed by their body heat, the
leaves produced a strong smell.

This name continued to be associated with the tea until the
eighteenth century and the Qing Dynasty, when Emperor Kangxi
tasted Xia Sha Ren Xiang while visiting the shores of the lake where
it was grown and enjoyed it enormously. Put off by a name that he
felt was not fit for an imperial drink, he renamed it Bi Luo Chun,
or "Green Snail Spring," a name inspired by the way the leaf was
rolled into small, intense green spirals.

Several provinces have turned to producing Bi Luo Chun, which
is very popular in China, but only the tea from Dong Ting lake in
the Jiangsu province is entitled to be sold under a certificate of origin.

Tasting notes

Dry leaf
Appearance: very small, very delicate
and extremely downy—almost curly—
leaf. The silvery color of the bud contrasts
with the jade green of the leaves.
Scent: herbaceous, both fresh and
cooked (vegetables, artichoke).

Infusion
Appearance: the pale green buds are tiny.
Scent: generous and ascending, intensely
herbaceous against a mineral, almost
tar, background.

Liquor
Color: very pale yellowish-green.
Texture: a touch astringent.
Taste: a little more bitterness than in
other "new season" green teas, because
of the rolling of the leaf.
Aromas: three families of powerful notes,
marine (fish), cooked herbaceous, and
dry fruity (dried fruit, chestnut).
Aromatic profile: instant presence on the
palate, explained notably by the texture-
flavor association. A perfectly smooth
and balanced sequence of notes.

Method of preparation
In a tasting set: 4 minutes in water heated to 167°F (75°C).
Or 3 pinches of leaves in a small zhong, either infused for up to 4 times successively
for 30–40 seconds each time, or for a single period of 3–4 minutes, according to taste.

The world's 50 best teas → China

161

TAI PING HOU KUI

Green tea from Anhui Province
Harvested once a year in spring

This very famous tea, often mentioned in the works of the poets, is produced in the Tai Ping region, in the south of the Huang Shan mountains (Anhui Province).

There are many legends that have grown up around it. According to one of these, the slopes on which the tea bushes were planted were far too steep for people to work on, so the locals trained monkeys to climb the trees and pick the leaves in their place.

This legend would explain the tea's name, which means "Monkey King from Tai Ping." However, according to another legend, it is the Taiping Rebellion of the 1850s, a tragic episode in Chinese history that ended in a bloody repression, which is linked with its name. A special feature of Tai Ping Hou Kui is revealed during the infusion when the veins in the leaves turn bright red—some claim in tribute to the blood spilled by the rebels during the revolt.

The uniqueness of this tea comes from the very special shape of its leaf: a stem of a deep, intense green, comprising a bud and two flattened leaves. During infusion, it opens out to resemble a flower floating on the surface of the zhong. Tai Ping Hou Kui derives its reputation from the flowery note of its scent that sometimes resembles that of orchids.

Tasting notes

Dry leaf

Appearance: stems measuring 1¼ to 2 inches (3–5 cm) in length, flattened with a wooden hammer; intensely green leaves.
Scent: fresh herbaceous note on a roasting background, also reminiscent of the "damp earth after a storm" so beloved of Chinese poets.

Infusion

Color: fresh, pale green, veined with red.
Scent: predominantly herbaceous and mineral with, depending on the harvest, occasional floral (orchid), fruity (blackcurrant), or iodized peaks.

Liquor

Appearance: crystalline clarity.
Texture: very rounded with occasional touches of astringency.
Taste: slight bitterness.
Aromas: on a par with the scents of the infusion. The rich and complex herbaceous notes are peculiar to very fine Chinese green teas.
Aromatic profile: it is the well-sustained mineral note that leaves the final impression.

Method of preparation

In a tasting set: 3½ minutes in water heated to 158°F (70°C).
Or one-third fill a good-sized zhong and infuse for 30–40 seconds, several times consecutively.

HUANG SHAN MAO FENG / DOWNY TIPS FROM THE YELLOW MOUNTAINS

Green tea from Anhui Province
Harvested once a year in spring

Recognized throughout China as a high-quality tea, rich in buds, many green and black Mao Feng teas are produced, all originating from different provinces. Huang Shan Mao Feng is an exceptional tea that is considered by the Chinese to be the very finest of its type. Its reputation for excellence derives partly from its provenance in the Huang Shan (Yellow Mountains) range. One of the most famous of the mountain ranges in China to produce green teas, all the plantations are situated at altitudes of between 885 and 2,625 feet (300–800 m) with ideal climatic and geological conditions, but the highest summit is 6,115 feet (1,864 m). With peaks disappearing in and out of the clouds, the tea bushes that grow in this region are frequently described as "Yun Wu," or "cloudy and foggy."

Huang Shan Mao Feng's reputation is based on the delicacy both of the pluck and the way it is manufactured. Only the mature bud and the first adjacent leaf are picked. They are rolled by hand into the shape that is the most recognizable of all the leaf shapes—the "sparrow's tongue," with its pale green and gilded color.

Tasting notes

Dry leaf
Appearance: the bud and the first leaf, slightly curved, are clearly recognizable.
Scent: herbaceous and floral, together with a heavier dry-roasted note (as in peanuts, coffee beans, etc.).

Infusion
Color: green tending towards yellow.
Scent: an ample and quite distinct sequence of the notes found in the dry leaf, together with the scent of exotic fruits.

Liquor
Color: pale gold.
Texture: more astringent than other Chinese green teas, it gives a great deal of presence in the mouth, without being at all rasping.
Taste: acidity and light *umami*.
Aromas: a very good, dense herbaceous note, rich and many-faceted, often punctuated with more discreet notes—nutty (horse chestnut, chestnut, hazelnut), exotic fruit (mango), marine, and iodized notes, spices, etc.
Aromatic profile: these teas are generally remarkably well balanced; the notes follow each other against a continuous background of greenery together with astringency.

Method of preparation

In a tasting set: 4 minutes in water heated to 167°F (75°C).
Or 3 pinches of leaves in a small zhong, infused for 30–40 seconds, up to 4 times successively, or for a single period of 3–4 minutes according to taste.
Note: The Huang Shan range produces another very highly regarded tea, Huang Hua Yun Jian. Harvested at a very high altitude on plots planted on the north-facing slopes of the mountains, where the sunlight is weaker, the late-produced tea is darker in color.

HUANG SHAN MU DAN /
PEONY OF THE YELLOW MOUNTAINS

"Hand-tied" green tea from Anhui Province
Harvested once a year in spring

Chinese tea manufacturers have been producing a number of hand-tied teas for some years now — the tea leaves are bound together in a small bouquet which unfolds slowly in the cup.

Huang Shan Mu Dan, the traditional hand-tied tea from Anhui Province, owes its excellent reputation to the high quality of the leaves selected and, in the case of this particular tea, the very interesting flavor that accompanies its attractive appearance. Unfortunately, this cannot be said for most hand-tied teas, which are nearly always made with leaves of mediocre quality.

Producing small hand-tied bunches is very labor-intensive, but despite their high prices, these teas generally come from regions that produce only inferior-quality harvests. In an effort to improve the profit margin on these mediocre teas, the manufacturers have turned to hand-tied teas as a more lucrative outlet. The latest fashion is for tying a flower in the center of the bunch. When infused in a glass pot the flower looks striking as it unfolds and "blossoms," but the final result in the cup is not always very rewarding.

Huang Shan Mu Dan is, therefore, one of the rare teas to combine aesthetic appeal with gastronomic quality, and occasionally the infusion develops a note of fresh peony and delicate rose, which adds to the poetic nature of this tea.

Tasting notes

Dry leaf
Appearance: around 100 young buds are tied together in a star-shaped bunch.
Scent: herbaceous and toasted notes.

Infusion
Appearance: during infusion the star shape turns into a flower like a chrysanthemum or a peony.
Scent: the typical cooked chestnut note of fine Chinese green teas that is also reminiscent of artichoke, on a vanilla background.

Liquor
Appearance: pale and limpid.
Texture: unctuous, with some traces of astringency.
Tastes: acid and very slightly sweet.
Aromas: a fine balance between mineral-herbaceous and roasted, against a very soft background (licorice).
Aromatic profile: the licorice note can be very long lasting.

Method of preparation

To appreciate the visual aspect of this tea, choose a pretty glass holding about 5 fluid ounces (150 ml) and infuse the "tea-flower" in it for 4 minutes in water heated to 175°F (80°C).
It may also be prepared in a zhong.

BAI MAO HOU

Green tea from Fujian Province
Harvested once a year in the spring

Relatively rare and much less well known than the legendary Long Jing, Bi Luo Chun, or Tai Ping Hou Kui, Bai Mao Hou shares with the latter the distinction of being connected with monkeys! There are a number of Chinese teas with picturesque names recalling the fact that trained monkeys were occasionally used to reach the inaccessible summits of wild tea trees. Bai Mao Hou, however, owes it name (White Hairy Monkey) to the appearance of its leaf, which is covered in down resembling the long white hair that grows on the backs of old monkeys.

For the most part, this tea is produced near to Fuding, in the province of Fujian, a region that specializes in white teas and jasmine teas. Manufactured from the famous Great White tea bushes, it is worthy of inclusion among the best new-season teas produced in China.

Tasting notes

Dry leaf
Appearance: an imperial pluck containing a surprising amount of large-sized buds. Flashes of silver among the fine dark-green leaves.
Scent: toasted and freshness, almost citrus zest.

Infusion
Color: pale green.
Scent: very herbaceous, with great freshness (peaks of floral-citrus zest and aromatic herbs often occur), and in the background, roasted chestnuts, and a slight gamy note.

Liquor
Color: pale gold.
Texture: smooth and light.
Tastes: sweet and *umami*.
Aromas: a fresh floral attack (peony) against a background of cooked vegetable (zucchini, artichoke), almost vanilla.
Aromatic profile: complex in its aromas, well-balanced, Bai Mao Hou often leaves a strong impression of minty freshness in the mouth.

Method of preparation
In a tasting set: 4 minutes in water heated to 167°F (75°C).
Or one third fill a good-sized zhong with leaves and infuse for 30–40 seconds, several times.

GUNPOWDER

Other names: Zhu Cha (Pearl Tea), Gong Xi Cha (Splendid Tribute)
Green tea from Zhejiang Province
Harvested and manufactured throughout the year

The origin of Gunpowder tea, today produced in industrial quantities in the Zhejiang region and also in a number of other provinces, is ancient and rather vague. According to some sources, it was first made under the Tang Dynasty. There is no doubt, however, that it was one of the first teas to be exported to Britain in the eighteenth century.

Its arrival in North Africa was, in a way, accidental. At the start of the 1850s, the Crimean War deprived the British of some of their traditional markets and in searching for new commercial openings for their stocks, they looked towards Morocco where, as in most North African countries, an infusion made of mint leaves was the most common drink, or sometimes absinthe. Gunpowder tea, which had the capacity to lessen the bitterness of these infusions without robbing them either of their flavor or color, was well received.

Nowadays Gunpowder is the tea most often used in mint tea. Shunned by the Chinese on account of its mediocre quality, this tea, in the form of tiny pellets or pearls, nevertheless occupies the top position in Chinese green tea production. And, as always with teas destined for export, the Chinese state has put its stamp on it. Gunpowder is made in huge, entirely mechanized factories which supply it in different categories (there are sixteen official grades).

Tasting notes

Dry leaf

Appearance: the leaves are rolled into very small, shiny pellets varying from pale to dark green, depending on the quality.
Scent: dry herbaceous, straw, wicker.

Infusion

Color: dark green, rather like artichoke leaves.
Scent: also artichoke (cooked herbaceous and vanilla).

Liquor

Appearance: orangey-yellow, a little cloudy due to the tightly rolled leaf.
Texture: very astringent, spicy.
Taste: a very evident bitterness and sometimes slightly sweet.
Aromas: like those of the dry leaf (herbaceous, wicker) with a gamy background.
Aromatic profile: the aromas are present from the initial attack and remain rather uniform until the note is finally extinguished.

Method of preparation

Best drunk with fresh mint, Moroccan fashion: use 1 tablespoonful of tea for 17 fluid ounces (500 ml) boiling water, a little bunch of mint and a few large lumps of sugar. Leave to infuse for 4 minutes before serving in tall glasses.

TIE GUAN YIN / IRON GODDESS OF MERCY

Other names: Ti Kwan Yin, Tieh Kuan Yin
Semi-oxidized tea from Fujian Province
30–40 percent partial oxidation
Harvested and manufactured twice a year (April to May; October
to November)

Produced in the district of Anxi, Tie Guan Yin is one of China's
most popular Wu Long teas. Its name refers both to the tea and to its
cultivar—a tea bush with fleshy, oval leaves, also known as Guan Yin
with the Red Heart because of the violet-red color of the young buds.

In terms of oxidation, there are two types of Tie Guan Yin: in
the first, oxidation is carried out according to a traditional Chinese
method, while in the second it is closer to the very light oxidation
processes used for the Taiwanese Bao Zhong and produces teas that are
often marketed under the name of Anxi Tie Guan Yin (see page 168).

A traditional Tie Guan Yin must have a "taste of fire"—the mineral
and roasted notes that come both from the oxidation, pushed as far as
30 percent (30 percent of the leaf surface is blackened, mostly around
the edges, while 70 percent remains green), and the quite protracted
firing at the end of the manufacturing process.

Unlike the Tie Guan Yin from Anxi, while this traditional Tie Guan
Yin is the one most appreciated by Chinese connoisseurs, it is no longer
affected by fashion, which often pushes up prices to such an extent.

Tasting notes

Dry leaf
Appearance: the tightly rolled leaf is
dark green verging on black and brown.
Scent: fresh herbaceous and woody-
burnt nose.

Infusion
Color: olive green.
Scent: floral and marine notes are added
to the herbaceous-woody bouquet.

Liquor
Color: golden.
Texture: slightly astringent.
Taste: a touch of acidity.
Aromas: fresh, woody with iodized and
mineral accents. Seaweed, salmon,
wicker, dry wood, artichoke, breadcrumbs, and flint are some of the notes
that build up in the cup.
Aromatic profile: the notes are all
expressed very intensely and simultaneously, the end of the palate remains
fresh, supported by the acidity of the tea.

Method of preparation
By the Gong Fu Cha method: 5–8 successive infusions each lasting 20–40 seconds.
In a tasting set: 6–7 minutes in water heated to 203°F (95°C).

The world's 50 best teas → China

ANXI TIE GUAN YIN

Other name: Jade Tie Guan Yin
Semi-oxidized tea from Fujian Province
10 percent partial oxidation
Harvested and manufactured twice a year (April to May; October
   to November)

Tie Guan Yin from the Anxi district, is made from the same tea
bushes as the traditional Tie Guan Yin (see page 167), but undergoes
a much lesser degree of oxidation of around 10 percent—say one hour
of gentle brewing during sweating, as against the six to seven hours
needed for the manufacture of traditional Tie Guan Yin. The final
firing is brief and done for the sole purpose of drying the leaves. The
resulting tea tends to be intensely floral, with fresh and herbaceous
notes—the opposite of the dark and roasted bouquet of the classic
Tie Guan Yin

For some years now, these scented and lightly oxidized Wu Long
teas (and especially the Tie Guan Yin from the Anxi district) have
been achieving a great deal of popularity in China. While the growers
have certainly increased production in an effort to meet the demand,
the tea is now so fashionable that its cost is utterly prohibitive—
priced for its rarity rather than for its intrinsic value. As happened
with Long Jing thirty years ago, this tea's success has induced many
farmers to plant varieties of Tie Guan Yin on their own plantations,
some of them well outside the Anxi district.

Tasting notes

Dry leaf
Appearance: very compact small pearls, deep green in color.
Scent: a very promising nose. A real bouquet of white flowers.

Infusion
Appearance: a bright green color; the size of the leaves is revealed in the infusion.
Scent: the same floral notes as in the dry leaf, supported by a buttery, vanilla note.

Liquor
Color: golden yellow.
Texture: velvety.
Taste: touch of bitterness.
Aromas: keeps its promise—all the freshness of the bouquet (daisy, lily of the valley, hyacinth, wisteria, mimosa) enriched with a very soft gamy note recalling the scent of jasmine (indol).
Aromatic profile: a simultaneous explosion of very rich floral aromas, with extreme length in the mouth, tailing off in a finish that is both herbaceous and opulently floral.

Method of preparation
By the Gong Fu Cha method: 5–8 successive infusions each lasting 20–40 seconds.
In a tasting set: 6–7 minutes in water heated to 203°F (95°C).

HUANG JIN GUI / GOLDEN OSMANTHUS

Other names or spellings: Huang Jing Kwei, Yellow and Gold Wu Long
Semi-oxidized tea from Fujian Province
10 percent partial oxidation
Harvested and manufactured twice a year (April to May; October
   to November)

Less well known than its rival, Tie Guan Yin, Huang Jin Gui also
originated in the Anxi region. The leaves come from a variety of
tea bush called Huang Dan (Golden Dawn) and are manufactured
according to the same process as Tie Guan Yin. Lightly oxidized like
the latter, Huang Jin Gui develops the same family of scents in the
cup—intensely floral, often with very buttery notes. This ancient
tea was first produced during the Qing Dynasty—though since the
Qing (1644–1911) spanned more than 250 years, there is a great deal
of scope for the exact date of its creation—and had been virtually
forgotten. However, it has been rediscovered in recent years,
particularly since trade in the Tie Guan Yin harvests has become
subject to considerable speculation.

   Its name reflects both the scent of the osmanthus flower produced
by the leaves and the golden, limpid color of its liquor.

Tasting notes

Dry leaf
Appearance: a single, pretty pale-green, rolled leaf.
Scent: powerfully floral and buttery.

Infusion
Color: bright green.
Scent: like that of the dry leaf but even fuller.

Liquor
Color: a sustained golden yellow.
Texture: like very light oil.
Taste: slight acidity.
Aromas: an opulent floral attack (lily, osmanthus, white blossom) on a soft, buttery, and vanilla background.
Aromatic profile: a tea with great intensity; the aromas are generous, starting with the attack and remain long on the palate, well beyond the last mouthful.

Method of preparation
By the Gong Fu Cha method: 5–8 successive infusions lasting 20–40 seconds.
In a tasting set: 6–7 minutes in water heated to 203°F (95°C).

DA HONG PAO / BIG RED ROBE

Other names or spellings: Bohea, Ta Hong Pao
Semi-oxidized tea from Fujian Province
40–50 percent partial oxidation
Harvested mid-May

Originating in the north of the Wu Yi Shan, the Fujian mountain range, Da Hong Pao is one of the legendary Chinese teas. Four exceptional Wu Long teas are produced in these mountains: Tie Luo Han (Old Man of Iron), Bai Ji Guan (Crest of the White Cockerel), Shui Jin Gui (Golden Turtle), and Da Hong Pao. These teas—all made from a specific variety of tea bush—are also called Si Da Ming Cong (Four Great Tea Bushes), or Yan Cha (Cliff Tea). Da Hong Pao is reputed to be the best of the four.

Originally made from leaves plucked from tea trees dating from the Ming Dynasty, there are now only four of these trees remaining, guarded by the army. The few ounces of tea that they produce inevitably add to the legend and are prohibitively expensive. The bulk of the rare crops used to manufacture Da Hong Pao comes from clones taken from old these historic plants and cultivated nearby. It derives its name from the red color of the bushes. Xiao Hong Pao (Little Red Robe) is made from the smaller leaves of the same tea bushes, which undergo a special process—they are spread in a thin layer on plaited bamboo trays, shaken with a rotating movement that requires great dexterity.

Tasting notes

Dry leaf
Appearance: a large leaf, slightly crumpled lengthwise, color verging on charcoal.
Scent: complex and intense—notes of burning, black fruit, roasting.

Infusion
Color: during infusion the leaf turns first red, then brown, then black.
Scent: a powerful roasting note, not unlike coffee, set off by fruity, floral, and sometimes gamy or woody peaks.

Liquor
Color: mahogany.
Texture: rounded and velvety; a delicate astringency appears gradually.
Taste: none.
Aromas: black fruits (blackberries), dried fruit (apricot), spices (cinnamon, licorice), flowers (osmanthus), tobacco, leather, sandalwood, undergrowth, and hydrocarbons are a few of the amazing notes which enhance the roasted background.
Aromatic profile: very balanced with notes that are closely linked, giving the impression of a scent of complexity rather than a series of clearly identifiable aromas.

Method of preparation
By the Gong Fu Cha method: successive infusions lasting 30–60 seconds, almost as many as you want.
In a tasting set: 6–7 minutes in water heated to 203°F (95°C).

SHUI XIAN / WATER SPRITE

Other names or spellings: Min Bei Shui Xian, Shui Hsien
Semi-oxidized tea from Fujian Province
40–50 percent partial oxidation
Harvested and manufactured from April to November

Shui Xian is sometimes considered by the Chinese to be the fifth
Yan Cha (Cliff Tea) because, like the other Four Great Tea Bushes of
the previous entry, it is also grown on the slopes of the Wu Yi Shan
mountains and is the product of a specific variety of tea bush. It is
the most popular of the Wu Long teas from Wu Yi Shan and, while
it is grown and manufactured in a number of areas in the province,
the very best Shui Xian comes from this mountain range.

This tea is often served in restaurants to accompany dim sum.
Like the other Yan Cha, it is a very dark Wu Long, 50 percent
oxidized. Its final firing over heated charcoal leads to strong roasted
notes—sometimes even burnt—in mediocre quality teas, of which
there are a number.

Tasting notes

Dry leaf

Appearance: a very long leaf, barely
crumpled, the color of anthracite.
Scent: predominantly roasted and
charcoal.

Infusion

Appearance: infusion reveals a low-grade
leaf with a harsh texture.
Scent: two extremes; charred notes
(coffee, pyrazine, blackberry) and wood
(patchouli).

Liquor

Color: bronze.
Texture: astringent.
Tastes: acid and bitter at the same time.
Aromas: firing introduces a number
of notes that differ from one Shui Xian
to another—marine (grilled salmon,
smoked fish), smoky (juniper berry,
bacon, tar), woody (dry wood, cedar),
fruity (blackcurrant, prune).
Aromatic profile: good Shui Xian teas
are well-balanced; texture and flavor
are not sharply defined, but they support
the aromas and bring sparkle (acidity)
and length in the mouth (bitterness
coupled with astringency).

Method of preparation

By the Gong Fu Cha method: successive infusions of 30–60 seconds, repeated 5 times.
In a tasting set: 6–7 minutes in water heated to 203°F (95°C).

YIN ZEN / SILVER NEEDLES

Other names: Bai Hao Yin Zen
White tea from Fujian Province
Harvested once a year in late March or early April

Yin Zen became famous during the Song Dynasty and as a result, a number of legends arose around it, including that it was only harvested on nights of a full moon, or only by naked young girls or virgins, or even that it was harvested with scissors of gold. One of the beliefs held, however, is quite true—like all the best green teas, Yin Zen was deemed suitable as tribute for the emperor and part of the crop was reserved for imperial use.

The Yin Zen tea made today, however, is more recent in origin, having been created at the end of the eighteenth century. In 1796, in the town of Fuding, the farmers decided that they would pluck only the buds from their tea trees. One hundred years later, a variety of very large tea trees was discovered in the region, which produced particularly downy buds, highly suited to the manufacture of white teas. Given the name of Da Bai (Great White), this variety is still used in the manufacture of Yin Zen and also Bai Mu Dan.

Yin Zen enjoys a prestigous reputation across the globe and is often thought to be the finest in the world, because of the selectivity of the pluck and the delicacy of its scents. Its extremely subtle appeal is not instantly obvious to the uninitiated and it can be very disappointing if badly prepared or if the consumer has no experience of white teas.

Tasting notes

Dry leaf
Appearance: magnificent! Long, pale green buds covered in a delicate silver down.
Scent: delicate note of wicker.

Infusion
Color: light green.
Scent: a rich and honeyed note, cocoa butter, also a musky, gamy note.

Liquor
Color: very pale yellow.
Texture: slight astringency, powdery sweetness.
Taste: none.
Aromas: soft and rich—waxed wood, honey, damp wicker, very ripe fruit.
Aromatic profile: a miracle of subtlety and balance; a small number of very delicate aromas, occurring in harmonious continuity, set off by the velvety liquor.

Method of preparation
This is best prepared in a zhong, one-third filled with leaves, using short but numerous infusions of 15 seconds or so rather than the 5–10 minutes traditionally recommended.
Note: Yin Zen (Silver Needles) is sometimes confused with Lu Yin Zen (Green Needles), manufactured from the same Da Bai buds but according to a method used for green tea. The down may be left on the Silver Needles—they serve as the basis for the best jasmine teas (Jasmine Pearls and Silver Needles with Jasmine)—or may be removed by an extra manufacturing stage, the tea then being marketed as a new season green tea.

The world's 50 best teas → China

BAI MU DAN / WHITE PEONY

Other name: Pai Mu Tan
White tea from Fujian Province
Harvested once a year in late March or early April

Like Silver Needles, Bai Mu Dan is manufactured from the Da Bai (Great White) tea bush (see Yin Zen, page 172) and takes its name from the bud and first leaves, which are similar in length and appearance to the petals of the peony.

This white tea is a recent innovation: traditionally only the bud was used in the production of Yin Zen, a rare and expensive white tea, and it is only since 1922 that the two or three leaves immediately below the bud have been included in its manufacture.

Harvested in spring over a very short period of time, Bai Mu Dan is mainly produced in the area surrounding the town of Fuding. It is popular with Chinese consumers, especially in the hottest regions of the country, because of its great thirst-quenching properties. It is an ideal initiation to white tea.

Tasting notes

Dry leaf

Appearance: a large dark-green, downy bud, with flashes of brighter green and silver. For the best grades of Bai Mu Dan, the pluck is limited to the bud plus two leaves.
Scent: very pronounced note of wicker and mown hay.

Infusion

Appearance: the leaves regain their green color while revealing their fragility.
Scent: evocative of freshly baked bread, with herbaceous peaks of dried grass.

Liquor

Color: straw.
Texture: slight astringency appears if infused for a little too long.
Tastes: very slightly sweet and acid; very noticeable *umami*.
Aromas: a floral attack (rose) which develops on a note reminiscent both of damp wicker and aromatic herbs (mint, thyme). Often the background evokes vanilla and cocoa.
Aromatic profile: a few notes in common with Silver Needles, but with more power and personality. The notes are more intense and longer-lasting.

Method of preparation

Our favorite way: half-fill a zhong with leaves, without packing them down, and pour on water heated to 158°F (70°C). Infuse for 10 seconds before discarding this first water, then continue infusing for successive periods, starting at 10 seconds and becoming progressively longer.
For a more classic way: see page 230.
Note: the same type of harvest is sometimes manufactured by a process similar to that used for Wu Long, and sold under the name of White Downy, a delicious tea with fruity and cocoa notes.

JUN SHAN YIN ZEN / SILVER NEEDLES FROM THE EMPEROR'S MOUNT

Yellow tea from Hunan Province
Harvested once a year, around April 20

Jun Shan Yin Zen was originally from Jun Shan, a tiny island covered with tea bushes in the middle of Lake Dongting. Though only produced in tiny quantities, this is the best known representative of yellow tea—another of the Chinese tea families. As explained on page 73, the term "yellow tea" frequently causes confusion. Yellow is the name given to very high-quality green teas that are deemed worthy of being drunk by the emperor (*huang*, meaning yellow, is the imperial color).

Yellow teas are very similar to green teas. After firing and a light rolling, the buds are wrapped in a piece of cloth and left to rest for twenty-four hours, at the end of which time they will have turned faintly yellow (the more prosaic reason for the name yellow). A brief drying completes the process.

This tea has another special quality that endears it to the poetic Chinese: sometimes during infusion the buds begin a kind of dance in the zhong. They gradually rise up on end, float to the surface then sink back down three times in a row. However, in our opinion Jun Shan Yin Zen is an overrated tea. Although its delicacy is impressive and, when it happens, the dance of the buds is enchanting, from a tasting point of view its high price is not justified.

Tasting notes

Dry leaf
Appearance: a beautiful long, regularly-shaped leaf, rolled into a fine, brownish-yellow needle.
Scent: a combination of toast and damp undergrowth.

Infusion
Appearance: once the leaf has unfurled, the bud and one leaf of the imperial pluck can be seen quite clearly.
Scent: powerful nose with a herbaceous-marine attack on a background that is both fruity-vanilla (dried fruit, horse chestnut) and toasted-burnt (popcorn, peanuts, breadcrumbs).

Liquor
Color: pale yellow.
Texture: silky.
Taste: a touch of bitterness.
Aromas: reproduces the scents of the infusion, with a reinforced fruity note.
Aromatic profile: when it is well-controlled, the bitterness offers delicate support to the aromatic notes. Be careful, however; the bitterness can develop too quickly and mask the aromas.

Method of preparation
In a tasting set: 4 minutes in water heated to 167°F (75°C).
Or 3 pinches of leaves in a small zhong, infused successively in short bursts (30–40 seconds) repeated 4 times, or for a longer single period (4–5 minutes), according to taste.

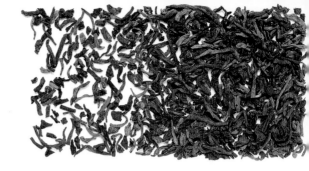

LOOSE BLACK PU ER FROM THE YEAR'S PRODUCTION

Other names or spellings: Cooked Pu Er, Pu Erh
Dark tea from Yunnan Province (post-fermentation artificially induced)
Manufactured all year round

The manufacture of black Pu Er is a recent development. First made in the early 1970s at Kunming, the techniques used in Guandong Province are also used to produce this tea. The initial aim was to accelerate the post-fermentation process that occurs in compressed tea cakes, but since it works equally well when the leaves are loose (see page 75), the manufacturer realized that there was no need to compress the entire production. From this we can deduce that there were no black Pu Er nor loose Pu Er teas produced before 1973 and that all the authentic Pu Er teas produced prior to this date were fermented naturally and compressed.

From 1970 to 1990, only the best grades of black Pu Er were stored in loose form, but since the 1990s, all grades of both categories may be either compressed or stored loose. In the case of loose teas, Pu Er comes in ten different grades: the finest are graded and the leaves have a very regular appearance. Note, however, that unlike the raw Pu Er (that is, those which have fermented naturally), aging has only limited effect on black Pu Er.

Tasting notes

Dry leaf
Appearance: a very regular, well-graded leaf, chocolate colored with a powdery appearance.
Scent: woody and gamy.

Infusion
Color: black.
Scent: a group of gamy components, ranging from leather to notes of the stable and passing on via more marine notes (oily salmon) to another component group featuring undergrowth and damp earth.

Liquor
Appearance: very dark with red glints, very limpid indeed.
Texture: soft and watery.
Taste: none.
Aromas: the gamy notes are much weaker than in the infusion, undergrowth and damp cellar being the most predominant (mushroom, tree moss, mold). An iodized note is often detectable.
Aromatic profile: the heaviest of the undergrowth notes are often exceptionally long-lasting in the mouth.

Method of preparation
In a YiXing teapot holding around 10 fluid ounces (300 ml): infuse for 3–4 minutes, using water heated to 203°F (95°C).
Note: This tea leaves a lasting stain, so it is preferable to keep a pot for its exclusive

VINTAGE QI ZI BING CHA (15 YEARS OLD)

Other name: Pu Er Been Cha
Dark tea from Yunnan Province (post-fermentation artificially induced)
Manufactured throughout the year

Qi Zi Bing Cha, meaning "Seven Cakes of Tea," harks back to the traditional way it was packed in stacks of seven compressed cakes, strapped together with bamboo shoots. Their production has long been restricted to a handful of factories in Yunnan (Kunming, Lancang, Menghai, Haiwan, and Xiaguan). Information about the tea is printed on the wrapping paper and must comply with strict regulations. You can even buy a guide to help you decode them.

Until the end of the 1980s, the consumption of Pu Er was largely limited to Hong Kong and Taiwan, but since the early 1990s there has been a spectacular increase in consumption in mainland China, due to a number of studies claiming health benefits derived from drinking it. As a result, there has been an increase in the number of factories producing it and today many are producing mainly Pu Er teas, compressed in different forms. Compressed into cakes of tea weighing 3½ ounces (100 g), 12 ounces (357 g), or 14 ounces (400 g), they are formed into the shape of birds' nests, bricks, mushrooms, and melons (sometimes wrapped in citrus peel). The shape does not appear to have much impact on the taste.

Tasting notes

Dry leaf

Appearance: the surface is made up of fine grade leaves, those at the center of the cake being coarser. As it ages, the cake gives the impression of turning stale and becomes increasingly crumbly.
Scent: a damp note (saltpeter) is added to the usual woody and gamy scent of black Pu Er.

Infusion

Appearance: the black leaf feels as if it is close to decomposing and clings to the fingers.
Scent: woody and undergrowth notes are predominent—damp wood, mildewed moss, musty notes.

Liquor

Appearance: dark with copper highlights, limpid and bright.
Texture: velvety and powdery at the same time; abundant content in the mouth.
Taste: sweet initially.
Aromas: as with the dry leaf, the damp component group is the richest—earthy notes, dusty notes coupled with mineral (flint). A note of licorice and vanilla that is missing from the un-aged Qi Zi Bing Cha makes its appearance here; this is one of the notes the Chinese look for most eagerly in vintage Pu Er.
Aromatic profile: an ample and very rounded mouth; the licorice note lingers most elegantly.

Method of preparation

In a tasting set: 4 minutes in water heated to 203°F (95°C).
By the Gong Fu Cha method: one-third fill the teapot with leaves, without tamping them down, and infuse 5–10 times depending on the quality of the Pu Er.
Note: A piece should never be broken off the cake of tea and put into the teapot whole—it would be too compacted to infuse properly. The best method is to chip away the required quantity of leaves with a knife.

FLAT GREEN TEA CAKE
FROM THE YEAR'S PRODUCTION

Green tea from Yunnan Province
Manufactured throughout the year

Though flat cakes of tea—and compressed green teas in general—
had been produced for centuries, their manufacture had become
marginalized, largely due to their minimal appeal in terms of taste
and smell. While very aromatic, the "new season" crop harvested from
Da Ye tea bushes, produces a rather astringent liquor and a slightly
brutal metallic bouquet.

The recent passion for Pu Er, however, whether "raw" or "cooked,"
soon focused the attention of connoisseurs on the vintage green
tea cakes stored in certain high-class teahouses in Hong Kong and
Guangzhou. Given the rarity value, the price of these green tea cakes
naturally soared sky high and, quickly identifying a lucrative niche,
a few resourceful businessmen promptly resurrected the manufacture
of compacted green tea cakes.

Today speculation in tea powers ahead and a great many people
have gone into the business of buying and storing green tea in
compressed form in the hope of making a rich profit in twenty years'
time. Only the future will tell whether the gamble has paid off; at
present there is an abundance of green tea cakes available on the
market at widely differing prices, in categories ranging from wild and
semi-wild teas to teas from hundred-year-old trees, and older. Since
their aging potential is unknown, it might be best to remain prudent.

Tasting notes

Dry leaf
Appearance: the cake is gray-green in
color, with buds visible on the surface;
lower quality leaves in the center.
Scent: gamy (saddlery) and mineral.

Infusion
Color: khaki-green.
Scent: a strong gamy and floral note
(horse, daisy) together with a mineral-
metallic component.

Liquor
Appearance: beige-yellow, slightly cloudy.
Texture: strongly astringent.
Taste: occasionally bitter.
Aromas: a combination of metallic
(hot metal), very herbaceous (cooked
vegetables, artichoke), and the occasional
gamy note which disappears early in the
aging process.
Aromatic profile: the texture and flavor
tend to overshadow the aromas and only
the mineral note lingers in the mouth at
the finish.

Method of preparation

In a tasting set: 4 minutes in water heated to 203°F (95°C).
Note: It is difficult to assess the potential of these teas and the Chinese are far from
unanimous in agreement about the criteria for evaluating them. In the meantime,
we should not forget that the aging of these cakes is also important, or is even the
most important factor in producing the fermentation aromas typical of Pu Er.

The world's 50 best teas   → China

VINTAGE BIRDS' NEST (20 YEARS OLD)

Dark tea from Yunnan Province (natural post-fermentation)
Tea stored in "cellars," manufactured using compressed green teas

This is the "real" Pu Er for purists—or rather, the original Pu Er—
tea which starts off as green and is transformed into what the Chinese
call "black tea" by natural fermentation. It is always compressed and
needs to age for at least five years in suitable conditions in order to
shed its astringency and metallic flavor in the cup.

The ideal conditions for storing these cakes are hotly debated
among tea lovers in China. According to one school of thought,
it is best done in an atmosphere that reproduces the climatic
conditions of the traditional Pu Er–consuming regions (Hong Kong
and Guangdong). However, stored in an atmosphere of 82 to 84°F
(28–29°C) and 70 percent humidity, there is a risk of the cakes
developing mold so conditions need to be monitored constantly.
Others recommend that the tea be stored in more temperate
conditions, in cool, dry and well-ventilated store rooms, away
from strong odors. Given the complexity of the post-fermentation
process and the risks involved in its control, while more fermentation
would take place in hotter and more humid conditions, storing
cakes in more temperate conditions undoubtedly better suits our
own climatic conditions.

Tasting notes

Dry leaf

Appearance: a dark leaf, deep brown;
small white specks appear on the surface
of the compressed cake shaped in a bird's
nest.
Scent: very ascending, typical of
mildewed moss.

Infusion

Appearance: black in color. Unlike
the cooked Pu Er, the leaf is neither
completely degraded nor sticky, but
rather tough and resistant.
Scent: echoes the notes of the dry leaf,
with more of the licorice notes. Complete
absence of gamy notes.

Liquor

Appearance: dark, almost black, but
bright and limpid.
Texture: very supple, with fine
astringency.
Taste: slightly sweet.
Aromas: an abundance of earthy,
damp aromas, also woody—peat,
mushroom, damp wood, tree moss,
camphor, patchouli, sandalwood, etc. A
pronounced background note of licorice.
Aromatic profile: the best Pu Er teas
offer an immensely rich aromatic palette,
with the notes following one after the
other, often sustained by their association
with the sweetness and note of licorice.

Method of preparation

In a tasting set: 4 minutes in water heated to 203°F (95°C).
By the Gong Fu Cha method: fill the teapot one-third with leaves without tamping them
down, and infuse 5–10 times according to the quality of the Pu Er.
Note: A piece should never be broken off the cake of tea and put into the teapot
whole—it would be too compacted to infuse properly. The best method is to chip
away the required quantity of leaves with a knife.

JASMINE PEARLS

Other names: Jade Pearls, Dragon Pearls, Phoenix Pearls
Jasmine scented tea from Fujian Province
Harvested once a year in April and scented in August

Extremely highly scented, Jasmine Pearls are among the best teas in this category. As with many hand-formed tea leaves, their shape evokes the extremely rounded and velvety texture of the liquor in the mouth.

The pearls are rolled individually by hand requiring great dexterity, each worker producing around 3½ ounces (100 g) an hour. As with the jasmine teas described on page 79, there are two stages in their manufacture. The pearls are made in April, at the same time as the leaves for the Green Needles tea are harvested. The worker chooses two or three downy buds, dampens them, and rolls them between the fingers, then uses a scrap of cloth or plastic to form the pearl shape. The pearls are dried on shelves in a dryer, then stored until August, when the jasmine is picked.

The next stage, the same as for the manufacture of all jasmine teas, involves scenting the pearls by exposing them repeatedly to contact with large quantities of fresh flowers. At least 790 pounds (360 kg) of flowers are needed to scent 220 pounds (100 kg) of pearls. The flowers and tea are placed in alternate layers, left for a time and then the flowers are picked out one by one. The process is repeated seven times.

Fake Jasmine Pearls, produced in other Chinese provinces and, in particular, in Vietnam, frequently appear on the market, but they are of a lower quality.

Tasting notes

Dry leaf
Appearance: pearls the size of garden peas, made from long silver buds.
Scent: dominated by the intense and ascending note of jasmine.

Infusion
Appearance: the three buds that make up each pearl unfurl.
Scent: still the jasmine, rich and complex, with no gamy note.

Liquor
Color: straw.
Texture: no trace of astringency, even after infusing for several minutes. An impression of very velvety roundness.
Taste: none.
Aromas: the floral note of the jasmine is both opulent and rich. Accents of red fruit (wild strawberry), sometimes stewed fruit. Green tea sap fills the background.
Aromatic profile: an intense attack, the floral note lingers a long time in the mouth and leaves an impression of flowery freshness long after the last mouthful.

Method of preparation
In a tasting set: 4 minutes in water heated to 167°F (75°C).
Or 3–4 pearls in a small zhong, infused for 2–3 minutes—the leaf needs time to unfold—repeated 3 times.

TAIWAN

HISTORY

The name might have changed, but for much of the tea world, Taiwan is still Formosa (The Beautiful), the name given to it by the Portuguese in the sixteenth century. Tea has been grown there for more than two centuries. While there is some written evidence of native tea trees being found in the center of the island during the second half of the eighteenth century, these have never been exploited. Based on purely physical criteria, they were classified scientifically as belonging to the *assamica* variety.

The first tea to be cultivated in Taiwan came from plants brought in from Fujian in 1796. Initial acclimatization experiments were carried out in the north of the island, where rainfall is more abundant and geological conditions more favorable. Several attempts were made to cultivate these first plants until other cultivars from Fujian were introduced in 1820. However, all the attempts at cultivation were carried out on a small scale and were not serious attempts at commercial production.

It was only in the 1860s, with the ratification of the Treaty of Tientsin between China and Great Britain, that tea growing became a commercial proposition and a regular export trade began.

From the start, almost all tea grown in Taiwan was sent for export. Coupled with the expertise and manufacturing methods imported from the mainland, the plants that had been brought in and acclimatized produced excellent results, especially for Wu Long teas. However, the export trade was initially concerned mostly with black and green teas, which were destined for the most part for the United States and Japan.

Until 1980, Taiwan exported 80 percent of its production. But from the middle of the 1970s, during a period of very strong competition from the Chinese mainland for the export market in green and black "standard" teas, the Taiwanese government decided to reorient the trade in quality and "grands cru" teas towards the home market. This was a move aimed at shaking off the yoke of competition and at the same time freeing the island's market of its dependence on exports and inviting the Taiwanese to reappropriate "their" teas. Nationalist ambitions and dreams of breaking with mainland China no doubt played a part in this desire to see a true Taiwanese tea culture emerging.

A commercial street in Beipu. A tea-seller stands at the entrance to her shop, inviting passers-by to sample a brew of Bai Hao Wu Long prepared by the Gong Fu Cha method.

These economic, cultural, and agricultural changes met with great success and exports were gradually reduced until today 85 percent of production is consumed locally on the island. Green and black tea production is now marginal and Taiwan is the proud producer of some of the best Wu Long teas in the world, while their "grands crus" also make up a dynamic economic sector. Tea production is organized around farmers' associations, which strive to promote their tea at festivals and shows, etc.

Finally, tea drinking as an art form has also sprung up in Taiwan. The Taiwanese have appropriated and refined the Gong Fu Cha preparation method, which in China is a simple method open to variations. In the hands of the Taiwanese it has taken on more ritual, particularly with the addition of a special cup for inhaling the aromas—the aroma or sniffer cup.

TAIWANESE TEA AND ITS CONSUMPTION

Nowadays, the tea drunk in Taiwan is for the most part home grown, mainly of the type the Chinese call "blue-green" teas, but also green and jasmine teas, which are served especially in restaurants. Nor have the Taiwanese escaped the great craze for Pu Er teas. They have been drinking them for a dozen years or so now and the appreciation of Pu Er is no longer confined to a narrow circle of enlightened connoisseurs. Since 1991, the island has imported more tea than it exports, the overwhelming majority of imported teas coming from mainland China.

Tea is an integral part of daily life for the Taiwanese, just as it is for the Chinese. Both at home and in the workplace a table specially devoted to tea is always set aside, where discussions and social interaction can take place. The tea is prepared according to the Gong Fu Cha method, art of tea here is more elaborate than on the mainland and takes the form of a ritual. It is quite possible that this ritualization has come about because of the strong Japanese influence on the culture of the island. Perhaps the Taiwanese have developed their own ritual as a way of marking themselves out from the culture of the mainland, like the Japanese with their Cha No Yu.

It is often possible to taste teas of very high quality in the teahouses, which play an important role in everyday life. They are places of contrasts—both havens of serenity cut off from the outside world and meeting places for cultural, intellectual, artistic, commercial, and often political life. The teahouses are also home to many of the activities and passionate discussions that accompany the pleasure of tea tasting.

ZONES UNDER CULTIVATION

49,420 acres (20,000 hectares) under cultivation
25,353 metric tons of tea produced
A yield of 2,534 pounds per 2½ acres (1,150 kilos per hectare)
(Source: statistics of the Taiwanese Tea Experiment Station 2005)

Situated on the Tropic of Cancer, the conditions on the island are ideal for the cultivation of tea. More than half of the island is over 650 feet (200 m) in elevation and the many mountain ranges (the highest summit is mount Yu Shan, at 12,967 feet/3,952 m) offer cool, damp conditions that favor the production of high-quality teas. The most highly regarded Taiwanese teas are the "blue-green" or semi-oxidized teas that are divided into three categories: Bao, Zhong, lightly oxidized; Wu Long, shaped into pearls (Dong Ding, Jin Xuan, Gao Shan Cha, etc.); and Bai Hao Wu Long.

→ Nantou district

The main tea-producing region on the island, providing half the harvest, Nantou is home to the village of Lu Gu and its lake, the birthplace of Dong Ding, situated at an altitude of between 1,640 to 2,625 feet (500–800 m). In the southwest of the district, the Shan Lin Xi mountain range, rising to 5,900 feet (1,800 m), produces some of the high mountain teas (Gao Shan Cha). Nantou and its region produce mainly Wu Long teas in dense pearls that the Taiwanese commonly refer to, confusingly, as Wu Long.

→ Taipei district

Many of the Taiwanese green teas come from this region. Though their quality is basic, this district also produces some well known and highly regarded Bao Zhong teas, but only on a modest scale. For the last hundred years, the lightly-oxidized Bao Zhong have been made in the area around Pinglin, a village to the south-east of Taipei.

→ Hsin Zhu district

To the north of the island, at an altitude of between 328 and 656 feet (100–200 m), this region of plains produced the first teas oxidized at 60 percent and over—a characteristic unique to Taiwan. These include the Bai Hao Wu Long teas and their finest examples, often known as Oriental Beauty. The best plantations are in the villages of Beipu and Emei.

→ Chia Yi district

This district, which includes the Ali Shan mountain range, is one of the most renowned regions in Taiwan for high mountain teas and represents about ten percent of the island's production. The plantations lie at an altitude of between 3,280 and 4,920 feet (1,000–1,500 m).

Tea is also grown in significant quantities in the districts of Taitung, Tao Yuan, and Miaoli.

Taiwan

⚓ Tea dispatch port

Tea-cultivation regions:
🌾 Wu Long

CHINA

Taiwan Strait

• Keelung ⚓

Taipei •

Tao Yuan •

Wen Shan

Hsin Zhu •

Pinglin •

• Beipu-Emei

Miaoli •

TAIWAN

Li Shan

Nantou •

Lu Gu •

Shan Lin Xi

Chia Yi •

Ali Shan

▲ Yu Shan
(12,966 ft /
3,952 m)

• Taitung

⚓ •
Kaohsiung

0   12   60 miles
                         100 km

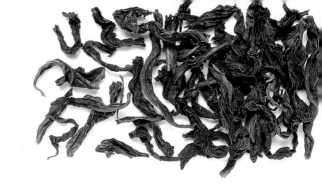

BAO ZHONG

Other names: Wen Shan Bao Zhong, Pouchong, Paochong
Semi-oxidized tea from the Taipei district
10–20 percent partial oxidation
Harvested twice a year, in spring and winter

Bao Zhong is the specialty of the region around Pinglin, a village situated in the Wen Shan mountains, in the north of Taiwan. The plantations that produce this tea lie at an altitude of between 820 and 2,132 feet (250–650 m). Covering about 4,500 acres (2,000 hectares), they produce less than 772 tons of tea per year. The name Bao Zhong, meaning literally "wrapped in paper," is a reminder that under the Qing Dynasty, just before firing, the fresh leaves destined for the imperial tea tribute were wrapped in a square of paper made from odorless cotton.

On account of its low degree of oxidation (in the region of 10 to 20 percent), this is very close to a green tea, but offers radically different aromas. Its leaves, ripe and well-opened, are slightly crumpled lengthwise, or sometimes—though more rarely—rolled into a ball. Its consumption is on the increase due to the current preference among its customers—both Taiwanese and mainland Chinese—for teas with light and herbaceous flavors.

Tasting notes

Dry leaf
Appearance: a long, dark green leaf.
Scent: fresh herbaceous and buttery-vanilla.

Infusion
Color: the center of the leaf is spinach-green, the outside edge brown.
Scent: two well-balanced components, herbaceous (fresh almonds, new-mown grass) and buttery-vanilla (stewed fruit, light caramel). A third, floral-rose component group occasionally appears.

Liquor
Color: golden yellow.
Texture: unctuous; very lightly astringent.
Taste: acidity and delicate bitterness; slightly sweet (more rarely).
Aromas: complex fresh floral bouquet (rose, hyacinth, head note of jasmine) on a softer, slightly peppery background.
Aromatic profile: a good succession of notes gives the impression of traveling from flower to flower.

Method of preparation
By the Gong Fu Cha method: 4–6 successive infusions of 20–40 seconds.
In a tasting set: 6–7 minutes in water heated to 203°F (95°C).

DONG DING

Other names or spellings: Tung Ting, Wu Long Cha, Oolong Cha
Semi-oxidized tea from the Nantou district
30–40 percent partial oxidation
Five harvests per year, the winter and spring harvests being the best

The cultivation of tea was introduced to the Lu Gu region by Lin Feng Chi, a young man who left Taiwan in 1885 to study in Fujian Province in mainland China. He returned to Lu Gu with a diploma in his pocket and thirty-six tea plants from the Wu Yi mountains as a gift for a compatriot who had helped to pay for his studies. Duly planted with great care, these thirty-six plants acclimatized well to the local environment and began producing crops. The tea, named Dong Ding (Icy Peak), after the mountain that overshadowed the village of Lu Gu and its lake, met with such great success that the district of Nantou decided to give itself over gradually to growing and manufacturing it.

Dong Ding, which is 30 to 40 percent oxidized, is the principal example of tea rolled into large, very dense pearls.

Traditionally this tea is manufactured from the Chin-Shin Oolong cultivar, but it is now increasingly produced using Jin Xuan hybrids (Golden Lily, see the Jin Xuan page 189) and Cui Yu (Jade Green), hence the name Jade Wu Long that is given to certain Taiwanese teas).

Tasting notes

Dry leaf
Appearance: a tightly-rolled leaf, the size of a garden pea, an intense green in color.
Scent: floral, herbaceous and buttery, on a vanilla background.

Infusion
Appearance: the unfolded leaf appears resistant and tough—the sign of a certain maturity.
Scent: reproduces the scent of the dry leaf, with a very ample, sweet, milky note.

Liquor
Color: pale yellow.
Texture: like a very light oil; very rounded.
Taste: a touch of bitterness.
Aromas: floral notes very different from those of the Bao Zhong teas, plus sweetness, then opulence (gardenia, frangipani); generally set off very well by the very rich, buttery, and vanilla background.
Aromatic profile: the scale and power of the floral, herbaceous, and buttery notes are characteristic of this family of teas.

Method of preparation
By the Gong Fu Cha method: 5–8 successive infusions for 20–40 seconds.
In a tasting set: 6–7 minutes in water heated to 203°F (95°C).

GAO SHAN CHA / "HIGH MOUNTAIN TEA"

Semi-oxidized tea from the Chia Yi district
20–30 percent partial oxidation
Harvested in spring

The name "High Mountain Tea" only applies to teas grown and harvested at an altitude of more than 3,280 feet (1,000 m). The principal production regions are in the mountain ranges of Shan Lin Xi, Ali Shan and Lishan. The mountains in Li Shan are home to the highest plantation in the world, rising to 8,038 feet (2,450 m) at Da Yu Ling.

At this altitude, and in a sub-tropical climate, the mountains are enveloped in mist morning and evening, and often for much of the day. The tea bushes in the high mountains are therefore deprived of much of the sun's rays and this low level of exposure, with the accompanying lower temperatures, naturally has an effect on the bushes. The leaves contain less catechin but more amino acids and nitrogenous compounds. They are an intense green in color, rather like a well-kept lawn.

Gao Shan Cha can be made from any of the different varieties of tea bush grown for the production of Dong Ding teas.

Tasting notes

Dry leaf

Appearance: larger and much brighter green pearls than those of Dong Ding. Very compact.
Scent: buttery vanilla together with a fresh herbaceous note.

Infusion

Appearance: this is not a leaf but a stem made up of three, or even four leaves, which unfold during successive infusions by the Gong Fu Cha method.
Scent: a fresh and floral (rose) attack, followed by notes of more opulent white flowers. A warm vanilla and very buttery base.

Liquor

Color: golden yellow.
Texture: very smooth and unctuous.
Taste: a touch of sweetness.
Aromas: complex floral and herbaceous—white flowers (daisies), fennel, cut fresh herbs—supported by a vanilla and coumarin note (resembling new-mown hay).
Aromatic profile: a fine scope to the floral note, with many herbaceous and rose (hyacinth) peaks. The buttery vanilla note lingers unusually long in the mouth.

Method of preparation

By the Gong Fu Cha method: 5–8 successive infusions of 20–40 seconds each time.
In a tasting set: 6–7 minutes in water heated to 203°F (95°C).

ANTIQUE DONG DING

Other names or spellings: Tung Ting, Wu Long Cha, Oolong Cha
Semi-oxidized tea from the Nantou district
20–30 percent partial oxidation

The best of the Taiwanese "grands crus" are always stored with particular care, packed in containers that are completely airtight, or sometimes even frozen, since teas which are kept for lengthy periods have a tendency to soak up moisture in the island's humid climate. In order to combat this problem, the stored leaves undergo re-firing every two or three years. This repeated firing causes the development of fruity and charcoal notes that add considerable interest to the taste.

In view of the recent craze for these super-roasted teas that are aged for several decades and are only available in very small quantities, some growers decided to develop a method aimed at imitating the taste of these "aged" teas, using repeated firings.

The Chinese liken these so-called "antique teas" to time machines. The leaves gradually become lighter in color until they almost return to their original green during the repeated infusions using the Gong Fu Cha method. Rather like going backwards in time, the process of repeated infusions gradually reveals the successive firings that the leaves have previously undergone. It would still be quite a leap from here to claiming that these teas have a rejuvenating effect, but there are probably some merchants who would be prepared to make it!

Tasting notes

Dry leaf
Appearance: ebonized Dong Ding pearls.
Scent: very roasted and fruity (cooked fruit, blackberry).

Infusion
Appearance: even after repeated infusions, the leaf does not unfurl to any extent. Its color, on the other hand, gets steadily lighter, verging on khaki.
Scent: very like that of the dry leaf; the coffee bean and cooked fruit notes, typically produced by firing, are very much in evidence.

Liquor
Appearance: light mahogany and, above all, clear and bright.
Texture: watery.
Taste: sweet.
Aromas: fruity, of course (prune, black-berry, blackcurrant), sometimes a little spicy (cinnamon) on a roasted and woody background (dry wood, cedar).
Aromatic profile: rich and generous, these repeatedly-roasted teas have plenty of reserves (they can be infused many times) and always offer well-sustained aromas.

Method of preparation
By the Gong Fu Cha method: 7–10 successive infusions, each of 20–40 seconds.
In a tasting set: 6–7 minutes in water heated to 203°F (95°C).

JIN XUAN / GOLDEN LILY

Other names or spellings: Jin Shuen, Jin Shen, Chinshuan,
Milky Wu Long
Semi-oxidized tea from the Nantou district
20–30 percent partial oxidation
Harvested in spring

Jin Xuan was originally the name of the cultivar TTES12, developed
by the Taiwanese Tea Experiment Station. This hybrid came from
the main variety grown on the plantations producing Dong Ding,
and was specifically developed for the production of Jin Xuan.

Manufactured by the same method as Dong Ding, the leaves from
this cultivar give tea that is richly scented with unusually intense
buttery, milky notes, much more marked than in the normal Dong
Ding. It is because of these typical characteristics that Jin Xuan
gradually came to be sold under the name of its variety, or as Milky
Wu Long.

Generous both in its aromas and its yield, with its great ability to
adapt to the soil conditions, the hardy Jin Xuan cultivar has gained
ground progressively throughout the Nantou district, and has also
been introduced into other tea-growing regions. The manufacture
of Bao Zhong teas from this variety is notably beginning to take
place at Pinglin.

Tasting notes

Dry leaf
Appearance: Dong Ding type pearls,
yellowish-green in color.
Scent: very rich. Buttery, vanilla, and
fruity on a herbaceous background.

Infusion
Color: pale green.
Scent: the rich note loses intensity and
fades on a floral, rose note.

Liquor
Appearance: orangey-yellow, limpid.
Texture: velvety.
Taste: none.
Aromas: custard, caramelized apple,
fresh caramel, condensed milk are a
few of the surprisingly rich notes that
these teas evoke. Generally, they are
linked with floral (white flowers) and
herbaceous (new-mown grass) notes.
Aromatic profile: the supple and
"creamy" texture particularly sets off the
unusual milky aromas found in this tea
and gives it good length in the mouth.

Method of preparation
By the Gong Fu Cha method: 7–10 successive infusions, each of 20–40 seconds.
In a tasting set: 6–7 minutes in water heated to 203°F (95°C).

BAI HAO WU LONG / BLACK DRAGON

Other names: Oriental Beauty, Wu Long Fancy
Semi-oxidized tea from the Hsin Zhu district
50–70 percent partial oxidation
Harvested in summer

Cultivated on a very small area (about 370 acres/150 hectares) around the village of Beipu, Bai Hao Wu Long is one of the most symbolic and representative of Taiwanese teas. It owes its unique aroma in part to a natural accident: its leaves are eaten by an insect—the paoli (*Jacobiasca formosana*), a small leafhopper also known as "green fly." When the insects bite into the leaves, it stems the growth of the young shoots and changes their color, which takes on a blotchy, parma-violet tint, and distorts and shrivels the branch. If a leaf attacked by this insect is not plucked it will drop off by itself. The paoli's bite upsets the chemical composition of the leaf, giving rise to very original notes after oxidation, both fruity and woody at the same time.

The leaves are plucked only in summer, from the end of June to the end of August, the period when the paoli is active. All use of insecticides in this region is prohibited because in the process of getting rid of other pests capable of damaging the bushes, the precious paoli itself would be at serious risk.

The tea is oxidized to a particularly high degree—as much as 50 to 70 percent.

Tasting notes

Dry leaf
Appearance: a very large leaf, black and brown at the same time, with silver highlights marking out the buds.
Scent: woody, spicy, and vanilla-burnt; unusually intense in a dry leaf.

Infusion
Color: some leaves the color of tobacco, others greener, some tending towards red.
Scent: three types of notes, fruity, woody-damp (wicker), and spicy-vanilla.

Liquor
Color: bronze.
Texture: smooth, with no astringency.
Taste: delicate bitterness.
Aromas: those of the infusion, but with greater complexity. Dried fruit (prune, dried apricot) and a mild spiciness (licorice, cinnamon).
Aromatic profile: a tea that takes its time, its aromatic elements follow on from each other harmoniously, to an ever-increasing extent.

Method of preparation
By the Gong Fu Cha method: 5 successive infusions, each of 20–40 seconds.
In a tasting set: 6–7 minutes in water heated to 203°F (95°C).

ORIENTAL BEAUTY

Other name: Bai Hao Wu Long
Semi-oxidized tea from the Hsin Zhu district
50–70 percent partial oxidation
Harvested in summer

Oriental Beauty is the poetic name frequently given to this fine Bai Hao Wu Long, though the name itself is not a guarantee of quality—the great disparity in price should prompt caution.

In the last thirty years the value of these exceptional teas has increased greatly. In the 1970s, at the instigation of the government, competitions to find the best "grands crus" were held in all the tea-growing regions on the island. At a time when the bulk of tea was exported and local consumption was relatively low, its aim was to persuade the farmers to produce better quality teas and for the Taiwanese people to reclaim their excellent local teas.

Nowadays, the best of the Beipu production is entered in these competitions. Each farmer offers a sample of his tea and the "best tea of the year" is sold by auction, often at a staggering price. In 2006, an Oriental Beauty sold for almost €50,000 a Jin (21 ounces/600 g). Since these lots are mostly bought by businesses or wealthy Taiwanese, it is rare to find an Oriental Beauty outside the island and tasting one is an experience every tea connoisseur would be thrilled to have at least once in his life.

Tasting notes

Dry leaf
Appearance: a magnificent leaf, intact and richly endowed with buds; very fragile as it is so large.
Scent: fruity, flowery, and woody; the richness of the notes heralds the explosion of aromas in the cup.

Infusion
Appearance: the mark on the leaf left by the insect is visible, the leaf is shrivelled up on itself and looks almost atrophied.
Scent: the three aromatic component groups of the dry leaf are all there, perfectly balanced.

Liquor
Color: coppery.
Texture: completely without astringency.
Taste: none.
Aromas: a succession (not necessarily in this order) of well-related notes—floral (rose, hyacinth), aromatic herbs, cooked fruit (fig, prune, cherry stone) all against a woody-vanilla background, and then gamy leather. Their aromatic potential is so great that it is possible to count dozens of these notes.
Aromatic profile: unusually lengthy persistance of each scent, which fades on a woody, floral, and herbaceous background.

Method of preparation
By the Gong Fu Cha method: 7 successive infusions, each of 20–40 seconds.
In a tasting set: 6–7 minutes in water heated to 203°F (95°C).

The world's 50 best teas → Taiwan

191

JAPAN

HISTORY

While there are records of tea having being consumed in Japan since the eighth century—notably during Buddhist ceremonies—it seems to have suffered something of a 400-year eclipse. It was only in the twelfth century that Eisai, a Buddhist monk returning from a voyage to China, brought with him some tea seeds that were duly planted on Kyushu, Honshu, and most notably in the Uji region—areas which are now reputed to produce the best teas throughout the whole of the Japanese archipelago. Eisai was, in a way, the father of the Japanese tea industry—he also brought with him from China the custom of preparing the drink by grinding the tea to a fine powder (Matcha) that was current under the reigning Song Dynasty. But the habit of tea drinking spread relatively slowly and for a long time was only indulged in by the highest stratum of society.

In the sixteenth century, the famous Zen priest Sen No Rikyu (1521–1591) codified the relationship between tea, Buddhism, and the different tea schools, and in so doing gave the Cha No Yu (tea ceremony) its ritualized form. From this time onwards, tea gained in popularity and was gradually adopted by all levels of Japanese society. The consumption of Matcha, which had long been the prerogative of the nobility, also became customary in the large towns (such as Edo—modern-day Tokyo—Kyoto, and Osaka), particularly among merchants and the well-to-do. It was not until the seventeenth century that a Chinese monk, Yin Yuan, introduced Japan to the latest fashion in tea preparation—infusing the leaves in hot water.

Two centuries later, in the Uji region once again, several farmers, notably Nagatani Soen (1681–1778), improved the technique of steaming and rolling the leaves that made it possible to infuse the scents in the cup almost instantaneously. This new tea, called Sencha and sold on the market at Edo, enjoyed resounding success among the Japanese people.

In 1859, with the opening up of the port of Yokohama and the signing of the Treaty of Commerce and Navigation with the United States, trade was on the increase and tea, together with silk, became the most exported commodities. In the latter years of the nineteenth cen-

In Japan, tea drinking punctuates the daily routine. With or without ceremony, the ritual is inseparable from the quest for harmony and serenity.

tury, the mechanization of harvesting and manufacture brought about a decisive acceleration in production.

Propagated solely from seed until the beginning of the 1960s, tea growing underwent a radical development when propagation from cuttings was introduced. In 1954—a very important date in the history of Japanese tea—Hikosaburo Sugiyama developed a Yabukita hybrid tea bush at Shizuoka. This very hardy cultivar of excellent quality adapted well to the different climates of the Japanese islands and was soon being planted throughout Japan. It did so well that, today, 90 percent of Japanese tea plantations are planted with bushes grown from cuttings and 85 percent of these are Yabukita. This does not mean that Japanese tea cultivation is exactly problem-free. In the first place, all the Japanese plantations are potentially exposed to pest infestation or disease, and in the second, at the end of its vegetative growth cycle, the Yabukita tea bush tends to suffer a drop in quality. The farmers need to be very vigilant with regard to the dates of the pluck and start the harvest without delay when the time is right.

JAPANESE TEA AND ITS CONSUMPTION

A real institution in Japanese society, tea is served in restaurants every day (Bancha, Hojicha). It can also be enjoyed in small groups as a convivial and sophisticated drink (Gyokuro, Sencha), or can play a central part in the Zen philosophy and aesthetic that is embodied in the Cha No Yu (Matcha).

In fact, tea is such an integral part of Japanese culture that there is a specific name—*o cha*—for Japanese tea, which is always green, as opposed to the term *ko cha*, which describes any teas which are not Japanese—that is, black teas, Wu Long, or scented teas. *Ko cha* are very popular in Japan, which is one of the main importers of high quality Darjeeling and the very fine Chinese and Taiwanese teas.

Along with Taiwan, Japan is the only tea-growing country to consume the bulk of its own production, yet even then it does not have enough to satisfy demand. As a result, the Japanese have made investments in China, Indonesia, and Vietnam, where Sencha-type teas produced by methods identical to their own are then exported to Japan, though their origin is not always specified. Much Japanese tea, including the teas for the home market, is not, in fact, produced in Japan.

ZONES UNDER CULTIVATION

49,000 hectares (122,500 acres) under cultivation
110,231 tons of tea produced
A yield of 4,497 pounds per 2½ acres (2,040 kilos per hectare)
(Source: FAO 2006 statistics)

THE JAPANESE TEA CEREMONY: THE CHA NO YU

The act of drinking tea in Japan transcends lifestyle and the preoccupations of aesthetics to reach a philosophical dimension, as expressed in the highly ritualized Japanese tea ceremony. The Cha No Yu (meaning literally, "hot water for the tea") teaches the way of *chado* ("the path of tea"), and is "a cult founded on the adoration of beauty even in the most trivial daily pursuits." (Okakura Kakuzo, *Le livre du thé*, Éditions Philippe Picquier, Paris 1996.)

Developed towards the end of the sixteenth century by Sen No Rikyu, under the influence of Zen Buddhism, the Cha No Yu takes place in a simply decorated pavilion reserved for the purpose, generally situated in the shaded corner of a garden. A maximum of five people may participate in the ceremony.

It begins with a light meal (*kaiseki*) then, after a short pause, continues with the *goza iri*, the central part of the ceremony, which starts with the serving of a thick tea (*koicha*) then another, lighter one (*usucha*). The ceremony often ends after the *usucha* and takes about an hour, but some tea ceremonies can last as long as four hours.

After various purifications and the usual polite civilities, the host strikes the gong five times, and at the end of a sequence of carefully executed gestures, he pours three spoonfuls of Matcha into a bowl (*chawan*), adds a ladleful of hot water and beats the mixture with a bamboo whisk until it forms a thick consistency. He places the bowl beside the hearth and the guest of honor approaches it on his knees, drinks three mouthfuls and compliments the host. He then takes a piece of paper (*kaichi*) that he brought with him, wipes the bowl where his lips have touched it and passes it to the next guest, who proceeds in the same way, and so on. The last guest gives the bowl back to the first one, who offers it to the host.

As well as having played an important role in the development of architecture and the arts of landscape gardening and floral arrangement, the meticulously observed rituals of the tea ceremony have had a fundamental influence on Japanese etiquette, and today the Cha No Yu remains one of the keys to understanding Japanese society.

The plantations are situated on the plain or on the valley slopes in the southern part of the Japanese archipelago, mostly on Honshu and Kyushu. The climate is relatively cool, with an annual average temperature of between 52 and 64°F (11–18°C), depending on the latitude—the temperature and rainfall levels are fairly similar across Japan. Production is focused almost exclusively on green teas that are stabilized by steaming. Another feature of Japanese tea production is the heavy reliance on a single cultivar—the Yabukita—despite the existence of fifty-four other cultivars that are recognized officially. The harvests take place four times a year, the first harvest of the year being the most highly prized. The tea is rarely plucked manually—other than for the best Tencha (the raw material for Matcha), Gyokuro, and Sencha—but even though the harvest is, technically speaking, mechanized, hand shears are just as likely to be used as mechanical harvesters.

→ Prefecture of Shizuoka

Together with the tea plantations in Turkey and Georgia, the plantations of Shizuoka are the most northerly in the world. The climatic conditions are harsh, even severe, for a large part of the year and in some seasons the plants have to be guarded against frost, but the climate also has an effect on the quality of the Shizuoka teas.

Sencha is the most important tea from this region, which processes the leaves grown in the prefectures of Honshu and Kyushu as well as its own. Tea processing, Japanese style, is carried out in two quite distinct stages. The first stage is the production of the raw tea, or Aracha, while the second stage involves the refining of the tea and giving it its final shape. With about 52,000 acres (21,000 hectares) of plantations producing 45 percent of Japanese tea, Shizuoka sees 70 percent of all the leaves harvested in Japan enter its factories to be processed.

→ Prefecture of Kyoto

Less important in terms of size and production (it represents only a little over 3 percent of Japanese production), this region is both the birthplace of Japanese tea production and the producer of the most prestigious Matcha, Gyokuro, and Sencha teas. The best plantations are located in the area surrounding the town of Uji, to the southwest of Kyoto.

→ Prefectures of Kagoshima and Kyushu

The second largest tea-growing region in Japan, Kagoshima produces 22 percent of its tea production, including all types of green tea. The other prefectures of Kyushu (Miyazaki, Fukuoka, Saga, and Kumamoto) are responsible for about 10 percent of the national harvest, and are the preferred location for the production of Tamaryokucha.

Tea-producing prefectures

Russia

China

Russia

North
Korea

Hokkaïdo

South
Korea

Sea of Japan

Japan

Honshu

*Pacific
Ocean*

Kyoto

Gifu

Ibaraki — Saitama

Shizuoka

Tokyo

Aichi
Mie
Nara

Saga

Fukuoka

Kouchi

Shikoku

Nagasaki
Kumamoto

Kyushu

Miyazaki

Kagoshima

186 miles / 300 km

Prefecture of Shizuoka
Tea-cultivation regions:
green tea

NAGANO

YAMANASHI

KANAGAWA

*Mount Fuji
(12,388 ft /
3,776 m)*

SHIZUOKA

• **Fuji**

AICHI

• **Shizuoka**

• Hamamatsu

Pacific Ocean

0   3   12 miles
            20 km

Sea of Japan

• **Maizuru**

FUKUI

Fukuchiyama

• Ayabe

• Miyama

KYOTO

SHIGA

HYOGO

• Kyoto

• Uji

Prefecture of Kyoto
Tea-cultivation regions:
green tea

• Joyo

OSAKA

0   3   12 miles
            60 km

NARA

SENCHA
Green tea
Harvested three times a year, from April to September

There are a great many types of Sencha teas, and prices vary according to the place where it was harvested, the quality and the time of year of the pluck. The Uji region has the reputation for producing the best Sencha teas, but the bulk of them come from Shizuoka and the Fukuoka region on the island of Kyushu.

Sencha teas represent about 80 percent of the country's production. They enjoy great popularity in the home market where they are highly appreciated for their refreshing scents. Their special characteristics come from the method used to dry them—a period of steaming after which the leaves are formed into very fine needles. The process is repeated three times. There are two types of steaming: one light and the other lasting for a longer period, known as Sencha Fukamushicha.

The better quality the Sencha, the lower the temperature of the water used for the infusion should be. The best Sencha contain a greater proportion of amino acids (notably theanine), which are destroyed by too strong a heat.

The first harvest of the year, carried out in April, is very sought after, like everything else in Japan that touches on the renewal of the seasons, and is sold under the name Shincha (New Tea). The tea world awaits it anxiously, especially as the first lots to come up for auction provide essential information about the quality of the lots to follow and the market tendencies.

Tasting notes

Dry leaf
Appearance: the leaf is rolled into long, well-flattened needles of dark and brilliant green.
Scent: very fresh herbaceous note coupled with a marine note.

Infusion
Appearance: the leaf appears to be very tender, like cooked spinach.
Scent: many fresh notes (iodine, herbaceous, aromatic herbs, citrus zest) on a softer background (cooked vegetable).

Liquor
Appearance: pale green, slightly cloudy.
Texture: smooth and slightly oily.
Taste: slight bitterness.
Aromas: the same notes detected in the infusion are also found in the cup—the sweetness of zucchini and spinach, enhanced by the marine freshness of shellfish.
Aromatic profile: the best Sencha are both lively and ample, sustaining the herbaceous notes nicely.

Method of preparation
In a Japanese teapot: according to the method described on page 118.
In a tasting set: 2 minutes in water heated to 167°F (75°C).

GYOKURO
Green tea grown under shade
Harvested once a year in April

Gyokuro (Dew Pearls) is among the best of Japanese teas. Much sought after, it is made by a process introduced in 1835 at Uji by Kahei Yamamoto. Three weeks before the harvest, the leaves are shielded from the light with straw (the traditional method), or with loosely woven cloth. This allows the leaves, known as Tencha, to develop some very characteristic notes.

This shading process, which filters 80 percent of the sun's rays, produces several results:

- it inhibits photosynthesis in the leaf
- it forces the tree to draw up a large amount of nutrients
- it increases the proportions of sugars, amino acids, and caffeine, decreases the amount of catechins and modifies the aromatic compounds of the leaf, which darkens in color

The taste gains in softness and delicacy and develops less bitterness. A good Gyokuro can be distinguished by its dark green, very delicate and shiny leaves.

In the tea boutiques in Japan, Gyokuro is often sold before it even reaches the shop; the customers buy the harvest by subscription to make sure they don't miss out on tasting the best product of the year.

Tasting notes

Dry leaf
Appearance: long, dark green, very shiny leaves, as fine as needles.
Scent: herbaceous nose, floral and iodized.

Infusion
Appearance: young, very tender shoots, of a very bright green.
Scent: floral (rose) notes and milky-marine notes with their typical oily and fruity tendencies (crustaceans, winkles).

Liquor
Appearance: pale greenish-yellow, slightly cloudy.
Texture: slight thickness but no astringency.
Taste: lightly *umami*.
Aromas: very rich in crustacean notes: whelk, crab, "oily" shellfish are some of the aromas evoked, all accompanied by herbaceous and flowery scents.
Aromatic profile: the herbaceous notes of these teas are very sustained and sometimes set off by fresh peaks (mint, aromatic herbs) at the back of the mouth.

Method of preparation
In a Japanese teapot: according to the method described on page 118.
In a tasting set: 1–2 minutes in water heated to 140°F (60°C).

The world's 50 best teas → Japan

MATCHA
Powdered green tea
Harvested and manufactured once a year, in April

It was in the twelfth century, on his return from China where he had been studying, that the Buddhist monk Eisai and his disciples introduced tea to Japan. At that time in China, the leaves were powdered and whisked in hot water in a bowl. The Japanese adopted the same method and Matcha came to form the center of the Cha No Yu, the tea ceremony whose elaborate ritual was established in the sixteenth century by the monk Sen No Rikyu.

Matcha is also made from the Tencha leaves but instead of being formed into needles, as for Gyokuro, they are ground to a fine powder that is a beautiful jade color.

Two types of Matcha are used for the Cha No Yu: *usucha*, the most common, made from the leaves of young tea bushes, which give a light tea; *koicha*, made with leaves from bushes that are at least thirty years old and produce a strong tea.

Matcha is also used in cooking, especially in pastry where it is one of the components of *wagashi* (a cake made from red bean paste).

The quality of Matcha teas varies greatly: some are made from Aracha, rather than Tencha. The best are sold in vacuum-packed boxes holding 1¼ ounces (40 g), which corresponds to an ancient Japanese unit of measurement. They deteriorate rapidly and must be used quickly.

Tasting notes

Dry leaf
Appearance: a fine, beautiful jade green powder, like flour.
Scent: subtle, simultaneously herbaceous and new-mown hay.

Infusion/Liquor
Appearance: intense dark green, cloudy.
Texture: muddy.
Taste: bitter.
Aromas: powerful herbaceous notes (watercress, sorrel, spinach), sometimes iodized (seaweed), but generally with few if any top notes.
Aromatic profile: the overwhelming presence of bitterness means the green note is extremely long in the mouth.

Method of preparation
This ceremonial tea can also be prepared in a less elaborate manner as an everyday drink for pleasure (though it does require a Matcha whisk). Place a teaspoonful of Matcha in a large, dry bowl, pour over 5 fluid ounces (150 ml) of simmering water and beat with the whisk, briskly, to a thoroughly emulsified froth.

TAMARYOKUCHA

Other name: Guricha
Green tea
Harvested three times a year, from April to September

This tea accounts for 5 percent of Japanese tea production and comes mostly from the Miyazaki and Saga prefectures on the island of Kyushu.

Unlike the Sencha leaves, which are rolled lengthwise into long, green, shiny needles, after being steamed at around 212°F (100°C), the leaves destined to produce Tamaryokucha are shaken and rolled around in a special machine, which turns them into a shape like a comma.

Kamairicha is a tea that is sometimes classed as being in the Tamaryokucha family. While the shape of its leaves is similar, the firing method used is different. Instead of being steamed the leaves are fired in the open air, a method which is more similar to the one used for Chinese green tea. In fact, these two teas are quite different, especially in taste: the Kamairicha leaves are matte and of a less intense green and the fresh, herbaceous scents normally found in Japanese green teas are also lacking.

Tamaryokucha teas develop aromas very like those of Sencha, but which are softer and more rounded.

Tasting notes

Dry leaf
Appearance: very small, dark green leaves formed into a "comma" shape.
Scent: fresh and burnt nose (toasted hazelnut).

Infusion
Color: dark green.
Scent: the notes take on depth and a full roundness; they tend towards cooked vegetable, on a milky-creamy background. Marine and iodized peaks.

Liquor
Appearance: yellowish-green, cloudy.
Texture: silky.
Tastes: *umami*, bitterness.
Aromas: a combination of original notes—spinach, zucchini, butter, cream, fish, salmon, etc. A tea with strong evocative powers!
Aromatic profile: extremely delicate notes following each other harmoniously to a fresh, pleasant finish.

Method of preparation
In a Japanese teapot: according to the method described on page 118.
In a tasting set: 2 minutes in water heated to 158°F (70°C).

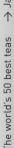

The world's 50 best teas → Japan

201

BANCHA HOJICHA
Other name: Houjicha
Roasted green tea
Manufactured from the autumn harvest (Yonbancha)

Bancha (which can be translated as "common tea") is made from the last harvest of the year, known as the "equalization" harvest, as it also serves to level out the plucking surface. The leaves are plucked mechanically, lower down the tree, taking in a number of stems, together with thick and often damaged leaves.

If tasted as an introduction to Japanese green teas, the roasted version of Bancha, known as Hojicha, is the most interesting. The firing, or roasting, of tea in the style of coffee was first tried in the 1920s at Kyoto, exposing it to temperatures of around 392°F (200°C) for several minutes. Even today, in some tea retail outlets, you can still see the merchant roasting Bancha amid the heady, fruity, and toasty aromas given off by the dense smoke escaping from the roasting oven's tiny chimney.

This tea enjoys great popularity in Japan and is the variety that is almost always served in restaurants specializing in raw fish, for which it makes a good accompaniment.

The caffeine content of Bancha leaves is relatively low.

Tasting notes

Dry leaf

Appearance: a long and wide brown leaf, rather irregular, the color ranges from chocolate to khaki, depending on the degree of roasting.
Scent: woody and fruity on a roasted background.

Infusion

Color: from bronze-green to black.
Scent: the woody-fruity note is the most predominant, with occasional marine (grilled fish) and spicy (cinnamon) notes.

Liquor

Appearance: a fine mahogany color, very clear.
Texture: watery.
Taste: slightly sweet.
Aromas: blackberry, dry wood, and vanilla are the three component groups of this tea, sometimes set off by marine and herbaceous accents.
Aromatic profile: the woody-toasty note is agreeably long in the mouth.

Method of preparation
Japanese fashion, in a large teapot holding 10 fluid ounces (300 ml): ½ ounce (15 grams) of tea is infused for 30 seconds in water heated to 185°F (85°C).
In a tasting set: 4–5 minutes in water heated to 185°F (85°C).
Note: makes an excellent iced tea (recipe page 94).

GENMAICHA

Green tea, corn, and rice
Made from the autumn "equalization" harvest (Yonbancha)

Genmaicha is a mixture of standard quality green tea (Bancha), popcorn, and roasted brown rice, it is very popular in Japan and often drunk with meals.

According to legend, Genmaicha had an interesting if rather tragic beginning. In the fifteenth century, at Hakone, on the Izu peninsula, on the island of Honshu, a samurai was drinking a bowl of tea while drawing up a battle plan for his troops. His servant, a certain Genmai, unfortunately let a few grains of rice fall into the bowl. Infuriated by the servant's clumsiness, the samurai immediately cut off his head, but drank the bowl of tea nevertheless and enjoyed it—the aromas of the rice combined with those of the tea produced a very harmonious drink. So, in memory of his dead servant, the samurai insisted on being served a bowl of tea with rice daily, which he named Genmaicha.

A more prosaic explanation for the origin of Genmaicha probably lies in the fact that the inhabitants of provinces far from the tea-producing regions, took to mixing cereals with the tea leaves to make them go further. Whatever the reason, it is now a popular drink all over Japan.

This tea can sometimes be found ground and mixed with Matcha powder, which gives it a slightly bitter flavor (Matcha-Genmaicha).

Tasting notes

Dry leaf
Appearance: a mixture of fairly coarse leaves, popcorn, and toasted brown rice.
Scent: intensely toasted (toasted bread crusts, cereals) with a few herbaceous notes in the background.

Infusion
Color: khaki, white, and brown.
Scent: the same as the dry leaf; the herbaceous notes are more evident.

Liquor
Appearance: pale green, rather clear.
Texture: a touch of astringency.
Taste: *umami.*
Aromas: tea aromas (seaweed, peas, zucchini) mingled with roasted cereals (hot bread, peanut, dried fruit, nuts).
Aromatic profile: good harmony between the two component groups which respond to each other, with a roasted, burnt finish.

Method of preparation
Japanese fashion, in a large teapot holding 10 fluid ounces (300 ml): ½ ounce (15 grams) of tea infused for 30 seconds in water heated to 185°F (85°C).
In a tasting set: 4–5 minutes in water heated to 185°F (85°C).
Note: makes an excellent iced tea (recipe page 94).

INDIA

HISTORY

The history of tea in India only really began in the nineteenth century.

From the end of the eighteenth century the British had been looking into the possibility of cultivating tea in India by acclimatizing seed harvested from Chinese tea trees. But, as well as being on a small scale, their trials came up against the problems of too little raw material and a total lack of expertise. Projects and studies continued over the next few decades, without ever getting beyond the experimental stage.

In 1823, when Robert Bruce noticed the local tribesmen in the Assam jungle chewing leaves from trees that bore a close resemblance to the tea trees the British had seen in China, he was convinced that he had located a native tea tree. Bruce reported his discovery to the British authorities, but it aroused little interest in Calcutta, despite the fact that the increasingly intolerable (to the British) monopoly that the Chinese exercised over the supply of black tea meant that developing tea cultivation was high on the British agenda.

It was not until ten years later, after the death of Robert Bruce, that his brother Charles was given the task of developing the native tree's cultivation. He created the first tea plantation in Assam, but the first batch of tea it produced, sold in Calcutta in 1836, was not at all convincing, having little in common with the tea produced in China.

For the British, the obvious solution was to send spies to China to uncover the secrets of tea production and to bring back sufficient seed to set up cultivation in their colonies on a grand scale. The most famous of these spies, Robert Fortune (see page 21), was sent on a mission to China in 1848. He returned several years later with a wealth of information, 20,000 sapling tea trees and a trained workforce of eighty-five Chinese workers with all the skill and expertise needed to launch the project.

From this moment on the cultivation of tea in India really took off. Contrary to expectations, the first Assam teas were well received in London, and the systematic clearing of the Assam jungle so that the indigenous tea trees might be planted on a large scale, was soon begun. In 1840, in a parallel development, Chinese seeds and saplings were

As here in Kolkata (Calcutta), strolling tea-sellers (*chai-wallahs*) are ubiquitous in India. At every street corner they peddle a delicious blend of black tea and spices infused in milk and known simply as *chai*.

→ India

The world's 50 best teas

planted in the Nilgiri Hills and left to acclimatize there, becoming commercially viable in 1854. In 1859, further plantations were founded in the foothills of the Himalayas, at Darjeeling.

From 1887 onwards, the importation of Indian tea into the United Kingdom outstripped Chinese tea. In a little less than three decades, the production of black tea saw a spectacular increase, rising from a few hundred tons in 1860 to 35,000 tons in 1885, and reaching more than 200,000 tons in 1914.

During the 1930s in Assam, the invention of the CTC method (see page 61), enabling tea to be manufactured from the lower quality leaves which had rarely been used until then, was in turn responsible for significantly speeding up production in India. The more so because this type of tea—of mediocre quality but with an even granular texture, was particularly suited to the teabag industry which was rapidly expanding at that time.

India is now the foremost tea producer in the world and the tea industry, which is an essential part of the national economy, directly employs more than a million people.

INDIAN TEA
AND ITS CONSUMPTION

While it became interested in producing green teas in the 1990s, India produces almost exclusively black tea of two specific types: orthodox teas, manufactured by the process described on page 60, and the CTC black teas.

The statistics for the production of tea for the home market in India deserve special mention. Introduced by the British colonials as a crop for export, it is now drunk by the whole population. This was not always the case however; from virtually nothing in 1850, consumption on the home market has risen so that it now accounts for almost 80 percent of the country's production.

Tea drinking is extremely popular at all levels of Indian society. While some people still prepare it according to the typical English method, the majority of Indians now drink *chai* every day (pronounced to rhyme with "high")—a delicious mixture of black tea, spices, and sugar, infused in boiling whole milk. The spices used vary according to the region, but the most usual are cardamom, cinnamon, ginger, cloves, pepper, mace, and nutmeg. The *chai-wallahs*, or roving tea-sellers, can be seen everywhere, in the streets, on trains, etc.

On the other hand, the best teas that India produces (the Darjeelings, in particular, and also the finest harvests of Assam) are beyond the means of local people and are exported.

ZONES UNDER CULTIVATION

1,235,000 acres cultivated (500,000 hectares)
1,022,945 tons of tea produced
A yield of 4,092 pounds per 2½ acres (1,856 kilos per hectare)
(Source: FAO statistics 2006)

The three principal tea-growing regions are Darjeeling, Assam, and the Nilgiri Hills, but there are others that are less important in terms of quantity or quality. The Darjeeling region, which represents only a little more than one percent of national production, is the most prestigious and well-known name connected with the Indian tea industry.

→ Darjeeling

The area around Darjeeling—a relatively large town, well-known for the freshness of its climate and pure air—is situated at an altitude of between 1,312 and 8,200 feet (400–2,500 m), and today contains eighty-seven tea plantations, sixty-one of which are subdivided into three different categories, according to altitude.

These categories were once a significant guide to the reputation of the tea produced, but have little meaning now since the quality of the harvest has improved on all the plantations, due as much to the competence of the planter as to the altitude. Darjeeling produces orthodox black teas and a marginal amount of Wu Long and green teas. The quality of this production varies greatly, as does the price. The price for the finest "grand cru" can be a hundred times greater than that for the lowest of the standard teas.

On account of their high prices, most Darjeeling teas are sent for export (to Germany, Japan, France, the United Kingdom, the United States, Russia, and the Netherlands for the most part) and—the price of success—are the most widely counterfeited teas in the world: each year around 40,000 tons are sold, which is four times the total production declared by the manufacturers.

There are four annual harvests—spring (March to April), summer (May to June), monsoon (July to August), and autumn (October to November)—with each offering its own typical flavor characteristics. The most sought-after crops are those of spring and summer. The monsoon crop is the most mediocre.

→ Assam

Situated in northeast India between Bangladesh, Myanmar (Burma), and China, Assam is relatively low-lying and very fertile. It is crossed by the Brahmaputra and its tributaries. A region covered with tropical forest until the nineteenth century, today this province produces almost half of all Indian tea. Its rainfall pattern is similar to that of Darjeeling (dry season from November to January and monsoon from May to September), but is much heavier. Four harvests are possible (spring, summer, monsoon, autumn), but the spring harvest takes place only rarely and is less sought after than the summer harvest. The bulk of production takes place between April and October. Alongside the very large plantations, which often cover more than 1,235 acres (500 hectares), there are some 40,000 independent farms which harvest their leaves and sell them on to the factories.

→ The Nilgiri Hills

The Nilgiri Hills in the south of India form the second largest tea-producing region. Unlike in Darjeeling and Assam, the leaves are harvested all year round without a break. Almost the entire region is dedicated to the production of black tea by the CTC method, but the teas produced are of only mediocre interest. Of the region's 173 factories, those producing orthodox teas can be counted on the fingers of one hand.

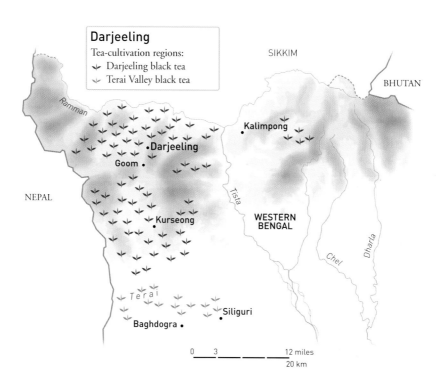

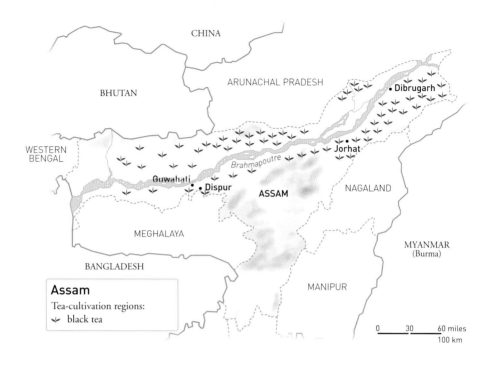

Assam
Tea-cultivation regions:
🌱 black tea

CHINA

ARUNACHAL PRADESH

BHUTAN

WESTERN
BENGAL

Dibrugarh

Jorhat

Brahmapoutre

Guwahati

Dispur

ASSAM

NAGALAND

MEGHALAYA

MYANMAR
(Burma)

BANGLADESH

MANIPUR

0   30   60 miles
100 km

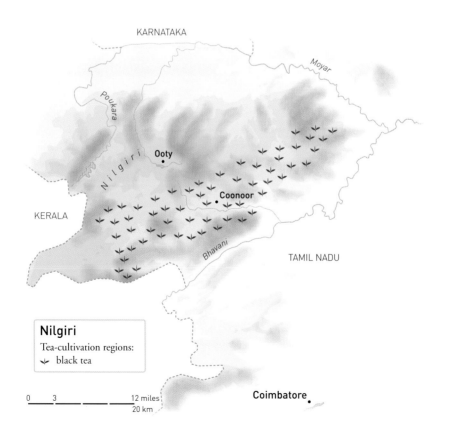

Nilgiri
Tea-cultivation regions:
🌱 black tea

KARNATAKA

Moyar

Poukara

N i l g i r i

Ooty

Coonoor

KERALA

Bhavani

TAMIL NADU

0   3   12 miles
20 km

Coimbatore

DARJEELING FIRST FLUSH "CLASSIC" (SINENSIS HYBRID)

Black tea

Harvested from March to April

The spring harvest (first flush) in Darjeeling is eagerly awaited by tea lovers all over the world. The first of the year, it takes place between the end of February and the end of April. Produced in very small quantities, the rare Darjeeling spring teas possess great aromatic qualities and a delicacy that has earned them the name "the champagne of tea." Throughout the winter, while the tea bushes are left to rest, their shoots store up essential oils. The first plucks of the year contain a large proportion of these high-quality young shoots, known as "golden tips." The spring Darjeeling teas are easily recognizable by the green color their leaves turn during infusion. The first harvests (flush) take place on the low-altitude plantations which benefit from an irrigation system.

Two thirds of the tea bushes on the Darjeeling plantations are of the *sinensis* variety, descended from Chinese varieties planted by the British during the second half of the nineteenth century. Many plantations still continue to maintain plots that were planted with these original tea plants, which are now over one hundred years old.

It is the *sinensis* tea bushes that produce the typical characteristic almond note that stands out among the others in the spring-harvested Darjeeling teas.

Tasting notes

Dry leaf

Appearance: a regular and well-formed leaf, rich in small green fragments and silvery buds.

Scent: a very ascending nose; herbaceous and toasted (breadcrumbs), often with a very typical almond note.

Infusion

Color: very green for a black tea—more of a khaki color.

Scent: rich and complex bouquet with floral notes (rose), herbaceous (fresh almond, grape), and sometimes exotic fruit.

Liquor

Color: amber.

Texture: a slight astringency distributed evenly throughout the mouth, a little thickness.

Taste: delicate acidity and bitterness.

Aromas: complex aromas, not always easily distinguished one from another—flowers (rose, freesia, etc.), fruit (mango, passion fruit, peach, apricot, etc.), aromatic plants (mint, eucalyptus, etc.)—all against a delicate almond note.

Aromatic profile: after the aromatic explosion of the attack, the fresher, almondy notes are sustained and long lasting.

Method of preparation

In a fine earthenware YiXing (non-granular) or porcelain teapot holding 10 fluid ounces (300 ml): infuse ⅓ ounce (8–10 g) of tea for 3 minutes in water heated to 185°F (85°C).
In a tasting set: 2–3 minutes in water heated to 185°F (85°C).

DARJEELING FIRST FLUSH "CLONAL"

Black tea
Harvested from March to April

Like all harvests, the spring crop is strongly influenced by the weather conditions prior to the pluck, but over the years better growing and processing techniques have improved quality control. The choice of plants has also played an important role. The development of new cultivars at the research stations and the gradual replanting of aging plots (a tea bush under cultivation has a normal life-expectancy of about fifty years) have enabled new varieties of tea bush to be introduced in Darjeeling. As a result of this stock renewal, new kinds of teas with large buds and rich and complex aromatic floral bouquets can be found in the tea markets of Darjeeling.

The three varieties most often found among the best, so-called "clonal" harvests are P312 (Phoobsering 312), T78 (Tukdah 78), and AV2. The first two varieties were the result of a selection process carried out on two Darjeeling plantations. The last, AV2—Ambari vegetative 2—originated on a plantation in the Terai region. Cultivated in various tea-growing regions in India, it produced quite spectacular results in Darjeeling, notably in taste and aroma.

Tasting notes

Dry leaf
Appearance: a large greenish-yellow leaf, thick—almost puffy; a good number of silvery buds.
Scent: citrus zest (rare in a dry leaf) and slightly toasted (bread crusts).

Infusion
Color: very light, veering towards beige.
Scent: very powerful: the intense, fresh rose note is almost always accompanied by a rich note evoking freshly baked bread.

Liquor
Color: gold with pink highlights.
Texture: a great deal of roundness in the mouth; a delicate astringency plays its part in sustaining the aromas.
Taste: a slight acidity and always a delicate bitterness.
Aromas: these play on the contrast between fresh flowers and the burnt-vanilla notes in "clonal" type teas. Orange-flower, peony, rose, lychee all combine delicately with brioche-type scents which may also evoke almonds, but in the frangipane, almond milk, cherry stone category.
Aromatic profile: the multiple notes in the best Darjeeling teas are delicate and lingering, and follow each other in a distinct sequence.

Method of preparation
In a fine earthenware YiXing (non-granular) or porcelain teapot holding 10 fluid ounces (300 ml): infuse ⅓ ounce (8–10 g) of tea for 3 minutes in water heated to 185°F (85°C).
In a tasting set: 2–3 minutes in water heated to 185°F (85°C).

DARJEELING SECOND FLUSH "CLASSIC" (SINENSIS HYBRID)

Black tea
Harvested from May to June

Taking place in May and June during the hot season that precedes the monsoon, the summer harvest (second flush) happens at the time of the year when production reaches its highest level.

The processing of the leaves is similar to that carried out in spring, except that they are subject to greater oxidation which, combined with the effect of the climate, produces a brown liquor in the cup, with opulent woody, fruity scents.

While most of the summer-harvested Darjeeling teas are mixed and sold under the generic name "Darjeeling," the best of them are bought direct from the plantations and, like the fine, spring-harvest Darjeeling teas, are not mixed. They can be identified by their name of origin, together with their grade and sometimes additional information, such as the name of the main cultivar and plot number.

Tasting notes

Dry leaf
Appearance: a small, dark, regular leaf; a great many buds.
Scent: burnt-vanilla nose.

Infusion
Color: coppery.
Scent: two component groups emerge—woody and fruity (stewed fruit)—after an often quite opulent floral attack.

Liquor
Appearance: coppery and shiny.
Texture: astringency well to the fore; a summer-harvested (second flush) Darjeeling should "grab" the mouth.
Taste: slight bitterness.
Aromas: woody aromas, sometimes green, sometimes dry (cedar), are combined with a vast palette of mostly cooked or preserved fruit—plum, peach, apricot, dried fruit, quince jam—tending towards vanilla, sometimes caramel.
Aromatic profile: well-balanced astringency and bitterness offer good support for the notes.

Method of preparation

In a fine earthenware YiXing (non-granular) or porcelain teapot holding 10 fluid ounces (300 ml): infuse ⅓ ounce (8–10 g) of tea for 3 minutes in water heated to 185°F (85°C).
In a tasting set: 2–3 minutes in water heated to 185°F (85°C).

The world's 50 best teas → India

212

DARJEELING SECOND FLUSH "MUSCATEL"

Black tea
Harvested from May to June

In Darjeeling, "Muscatel" is applied to a tea with an aromatic bouquet that evokes the fruity sweetness of the muscat grape. The characteristics of this very rare bouquet are due to an insect—the jassid.

As with the paoli that attacks the leaves that produce the Bai Hao Wu Long tea of Taiwan, this green fly from the *cicadellides* family attacks the plantations in summer and causes serious damage to both young and old trees. When it bites into the tender leaves the jassid causes similar changes in the leaf to the paoli (see page 190). Unlike the Taiwanese species, however, it is not regarded as having a beneficial effect on the tea and many Darjeeling planters prefer to protect their trees against its attack rather than sacrifice a part of their harvest. Only some of the very best plantations, which have mastered the process for capturing the special bouquet the jassid produces and which are consequently sure of being able to sell their teas at the best price, are prepared to take the risk of letting the insect do its work.

Tasting notes

Dry leaf
Appearance: a classically made Darjeeling, well-rolled and regular; any number of buds, which are not always evident on account of their dark color.
Scent: a waxed wood note with floral and fruity peaks.

Infusion
Appearance: despite oxidation, the damage to the leaf caused by the insect is clearly discernible.
Scent: very rich and ascending nose. Predominantly floral, fruity and woody-spicy.

Liquor
Appearance: coppery and shiny.
Texture: slight astringency gives a good presence in the mouth.
Taste: slight acidity and slight bitterness.
Aromas: like those of the Bai Hao Wu Long teas, the aromas are numerous and very distinctive; flowery (geranium, rose, orange flower), fruity (prune, stewed fruit, mirabelle, black fruits), and woody (dry wood) notes are well sustained against a background of toast and roasting, reminiscent of coffee beans.
Aromatic profile: while the aromas are due to an insect, the balance between flavor, texture, and scents are definitely the work of the planter. These rare "Muscatel" teas are always remarkably harmonious.

Method of preparation

In a fine earthenware YiXing (non-granular) or porcelain teapot holding 10 fluid ounces (300 ml): infuse ⅓ ounce (8–10 g) of tea for 4–5 minutes in water heated to 185°F (85°C).
In a tasting set: 4 minutes in water heated to 185°F (85°C).

DARJEELING THIRD FLUSH
Black tea
Harvested from September to mid-November

After the monsoon is over, which lasts from July to September and only results in the most mediocre of the plucks, autumn sees the last harvests of the year. The temperature drops below 59°F (15°C) and the volume of the yield diminishes rapidly. The tea bushes then enter a dormant state for about three and a half months.

Apart from the "equalization" harvests (see page 202), careful attention is usually paid to the autumn plucks in order to guarantee vigorous vegetative growth once the winter is over.

Since they are tougher at this time of the year, the leaves need to wilt for a longer period. The degree of oxidation they undergo is somewhere between those from the spring and summer harvests.

Considered—sometimes wrongly—to have been produced from a harvest of inevitably mediocre quality, some of the autumn batches possess a fine aromatic balance and a character that is quite distinct from the other two harvests.

Autumn-harvested Darjeeling is recognizable by the color of its liquor, which is copper, tending towards orange.

Tasting notes

Dry leaf
Appearance: regular and dark, with buds ranging from gilded to silvery.
Scent: a spicy, woody-burnt nose. An impression of gingerbread.

Infusion
Color: brown, going towards red.
Scent: the scents are precise—waxed wood, nutmeg, and stewed fruit.

Liquor
Color: orange.
Texture: delicately astringent.
Taste: bitter.
Aromas: those of the infusion, together with a note of cooked vegetable on the slightly gamy (cooked chicory) attack.
Aromatic profile: very pronounced presence of the background note (woody, beeswax, pollen, honey, cooked fruit) and a good length in the mouth.

Method of preparation
In a fine earthenware YiXing (non-granular) or porcelain teapot holding 10 fluid ounces (300 ml): infuse ⅓ ounce (8–10 g) of tea for 4–5 minutes in water heated to 185°F (85°C).
In a tasting set: 4 minutes in water heated to 185°F (85°C).

ASSAM SECOND FLUSH OP

Black tea
Harvested from May to June

The Assam teas found great favor with the British when they first appeared on the London market in the mid-nineteenth century and are typical of what is known in the industry as the "British taste"— they are vigorous, spicy, tannic, and astringent, and well able to support the addition of milk. They are traditionally included in the blends that were created to suit tea drinking at different times of day, adding both body and structure.

Since the second half of the twentieth century, Assam teas have been struggling against competition from their African and Indonesian cousins, whose products have gradually replaced theirs in the composition of these blends. Today almost 50 percent of the tea sold in the United Kingdom comes from Kenya and Malawi.

While the overwhelming majority of teas produced today in Assam are CTCs, a few plantations still offer teas made by orthodox methods. With a good number of buds and easily recognizable for their golden color, these teas are graded by the same system as used in Darjeeling or Sri Lanka (see page 66).

Tasting notes

Dry leaf
Appearance: a long, well-worked leaf, rich in buds of a good size.
Scent: honeyed, spicy nose.

Infusion
Color: chocolate.
Scent: very ascendant; fresh fruit (green apple), on a soft spicy background.

Liquor
Color: coppery, going towards red.
Texture: well-presented astringency.
Taste: a touch of bitterness.
Aromas: green apple is very evident, supported by warmer notes, spicy and woody (vanilla, honey, mild tobacco, cinnamon).
Aromatic profile: generous aromas to which astringency and bitterness, essential in this type of tea, bring control and persistence.

Method of preparation
In a fine earthenware YiXing (non-granular) or porcelain teapot holding 10 fluid ounces (300 ml): infuse ⅓ ounce (8–10 g) of tea for 4 minutes in water heated to 185°F (85°C).
In a tasting set: 4 minutes in water heated to 185°F (85°C).

ASSAM GOLDEN TIPS
Black tea
Harvested from May to June

The Indian tea industry's grading system is pushed to the limit with this tea. Consisting entirely of buds, it is the very highest grade and most costly of all Assam teas. As soon as the pluck is finished the buds are separated manually from the leaves and then processed, being rolled with great care to ensure that they remain intact.

It was still possible to find these teas on the market twenty years ago. The planters readily processed the finest of their crops in this manner and despite their high prices they found buyers quickly. Nowadays, however, Golden Tips has completely dropped out of sight and it is impossible to buy these teas at the auctions in Guwahati or Kolkata (Calcutta).

Delicate and very expensive to produce, Golden Tips is now only made to order, and then the planters need to be coerced into producing even a few pounds of it. The problem is that it is impossible to judge the quality until the tea has been made. If the final product does not come up to scratch and the buyer will not confirm his order, the planter will have wasted his time and material, which is why it is rare to find a planter who will agree to produce Golden Tips.

Tasting notes

Dry leaf
Appearance: small, gilded buds rolled tightly lengthwise; tobacco-colored.
Scent: gamy and wet wicker.

Infusion
Color: chocolate.
Scent: three very typical and closely-linked component groups, leather, cocoa, and jasmine; sometimes citrus zest peaks.

Liquor
Color: ebony.
Texture: very little astringency for an Assam.
Taste: very little bitterness.
Aromas: the cocoa note is very much to the fore but beside it fruit (apple, stewed fruit) and honey contribute richness and balance.
Aromatic profile: the very faint astringency of this tea is more like Qimen and the Yunnan Buds than Assam teas. It has all the fullness and roundness of the Chinese teas.

Method of preparation
In a fine earthenware YiXing (non-granular) or porcelain teapot holding 10 fluid ounces (300 ml): infuse ⅓ ounce (8–10 g) of tea for 3 minutes in water heated to 185°F (85°C).
In a tasting set: 2–3 minutes in water heated to 185°F (85°C).

NILGIRI THIASHOLA SFTGFOP

Black tea
Harvested in January

Covering almost 495 acres (200 hectares) and employing around 2,500 people, Thiashola is the highest plantation in Southern India. Like many plantations created in the nineteenth century, it was planted by Chinese prisoners captured by the British during the opium wars.

The overwhelming majority of tea in the region is produced by the CTC method and is used for the preparation of Chai, among other teas destined for the home market. Thiashola, along with a few other plantations, notably those at high altitude, is the exception, and produces black teas of varying quality of the orthodox type.

Although the grades they produce cannot compete with their equivalents from Darjeeling, some of these teas offer typical aromatic characteristics that are still very interesting. This is particularly so with teas from the Thiashola plantation, which succeeds in recreating in the cup all the aromatic sensations experienced during manufacture.

Plucking takes place all the year round, but the best crop is the one harvested in January.

Tasting notes

Dry leaf
Appearance: a regular, violet-brown leaf, few buds.
Scent: herbaceous nose against a burnt-vanilla background.

Infusion
Color: between green, red, and brown.
Scent: a very powerful herbaceous note (as if in the withering hall) evoking freshly cut privet.

Liquor
Color: dark amber.
Texture: the astringency gives it a great deal of body.
Taste: small touches of acidity and bitterness.
Aromas: predominantly intense—herbaceous notes (green herbs, sage), then light woody tending towards vanilla.
Aromatic profile: the bouquet is very long in the mouth because of the relatively strong astringency of the tea.

Method of preparation
In a fine earthenware YiXing (non-granular) or porcelain teapot holding 10 fluid ounces (300 ml): infuse ⅓ ounce (8–10 g) of tea for 3 minutes in water heated to 185°F (85°C).
In a tasting set: 2–3 minutes in water heated to 185°F (85°C).

NEPAL

HISTORY

Following a visit to the tea plantations of Darjeeling in the 1870s, Colonel Gajraj Singh Thapa, son-in-law of the then Nepalese Prime Minister Rana and governor of the eastern part of Nepal, wanted to recreate the experiment in his own region and persuaded Rana to sign some land over to him. The first two plantations were eventually created in 1920, at Ilam and Soktim, covering around 250 acres (100 hectares), but the first factories were not built until the 1960s. During the years that followed, the cultivation of tea expanded slowly but surely, and in the mid-1980s, the government declared five districts in East Nepal as officially designated tea-cultivation zones.

Since then, a number of plantations have been created and equipped with factories and in 1997 the whole tea sector was privatized and experienced rapid growth as a result. Today Nepal has eighty-five plantations and tea provides a livelihood for more than 7,500 small farmers who sell their leaves to the factories.

NEPALESE TEA

Nepal produces mostly CTC production teas (see page 61), about one sixth of them by orthodox methods. These black teas have managed to acquire a good reputation among tea connoisseurs. Manufactured mostly around the towns of Ilam and Dhankuta, they are exported systematically, often at very high prices. In the far east of the country, near Ilam, it is not unusual for a batch of harvested leaves to be smuggled into India rather than being manufactured *in situ*. Some less than scrupulous Darjeeling plantation owners on the Indian side of the frontier buy them and add them to their own harvest to increase their production.

In the high-altitude plantations of Nepal, where rugged slopes and uneven terrain are largely inaccessible to vehicles, the harvest has to be carried by the workers to the processing plant.

40,000 acres cultivated (16,000 hectares)
13,779 tons of tea produced
A yield of 1,722 pounds per 2½ acres (781 kilos per hectare)
(Source: FAO statistics 2006)

There are three tea-growing regions in Nepal: the terai (where tea is grown on the plain), Ilam and Dhankuta. Mostly producing CTC teas, few teas of real interest come out of the Terai plantations, while the teas from Ilam try to copy the Darjeeling production too often. The teas from Dhankuta, where the plantations are only fifteen to twenty years old, are more interesting. The tea bushes there were selected from among the best cultivars and are often grown at an altitude of between 3,940 and 7,220 feet (1,200–2,200 m).

At the high-altitude plantations of Ilam and Dhankuta, the tea bushes are exposed to a more rigorous climate than on the plantations of Darjeeling. However, the pattern of the seasons, and therefore the harvests, is identical: one harvest in spring; a second harvest called the "summer harvest," which takes place in June; one harvest during the monsoon which produces an abundant but bland crop; and, finally, an autumn harvest.

The small growers at Ilam and Dhankuta still play an important role as there are no large plantations along the British model, such as the ones found in India or in the Nepalese terai. It is also interesting to note that tea cultivation in the mountainous regions relies more on traditional "honest" farming methods and respects the integrity of the forested areas.

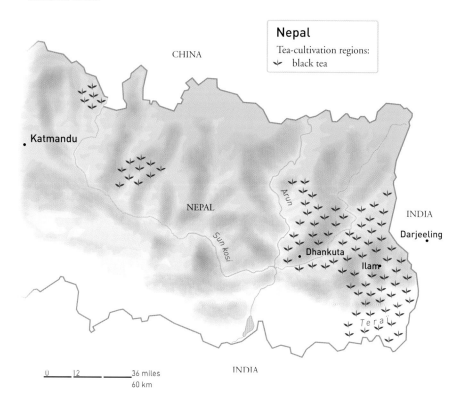

JUN CHIYABARI HIMALAYAN TIPS

Black tea

Harvested three times a year, from April to September

Created in 2001, the Jun Chiyabari plantation is situated at Hile, in the Dhankuta district, in the east of Nepal. Under the leadership of Andrew Gardner—a planter with both great passion and experience—it has acquired a reputation for producing the best tea in Nepal in just a few years. Gardner has concentrated essentially on improving the quality of the tea bushes and has gone back to such traditional production methods as hand-rolling the leaves.

Since this small plantation of 185 acres (75 hectares) cannot produce enough leaves itself, Gardner also buys from small local producers, paying them for their tea according to a minimum guaranteed rate. In return, Gardner also offers them tea bushes chosen from among the varieties cultivated on its own plots. Tea growing on the local farms is limited to 10 percent of the total area available for cultivation, so that the farmers do not become over-dependent on tea and suffer a serious loss of income in the event of a bad harvest.

Among the different teas produced by this plantation, this rolled Himalayan Tips is unlike any other black tea, and owes its characteristics to the fortunate combination of suitable "terroir," a rigorous choice of hybrid tea bushes, traditional manufacturing methods, and of course, all the human effort that helps to make it a success.

Tasting notes

Dry leaf

Appearance: a large pale leaf, with buds kept intact by being hand-rolled.
Scent: a generous nose, woody and burnt (breadcrumbs).

Infusion

Color: khaki green.
Scent: the same generosity comes to the fore; rosy floral attack giving way to a note of freshly baked bread.

Liquor

Appearance: color ranging from gold to orange, very limpid.
Texture: slight astringency.
Taste: slight bitterness.
Aromas: very original bouquet of three families of notes—rosy floral (geranium), dry herbaceous (twigs), and burnt (toasted bread, roasted coffee beans). This combination gives the tea its unique character.
Aromatic profile: powerfully aromatic; this tea is also valued for its structure, which is perfectly balanced among flavors, textures, and aromas.

Method of preparation

In a fine earthenware YiXing (non-granular) or porcelain teapot holding 10 fluid ounces (300 ml): infuse ⅓ ounce (8–10 g) of tea for 3 to 4 minutes in water heated to 185°F (85°C).
In a tasting set: 3½–4 minutes in water heated to 185°F (85°C).

SRI LANKA

HISTORY

Teas from Sri Lanka, known as Ceylon until 1972, and as the "Island of Tea" today, are still commonly referred to as "Ceylon" teas.

The island of Sri Lanka hardly seemed cut out to become one of the world's major tea producers when, in 1841, two hundred *assamica* tea plants from Bengal were introduced at Nuwara Eliya. At the time Sri Lanka was already given over to large-scale coffee production but the British were also keen to see it produce tea. The coffee growers did not, however, foresee the havoc that was to be wreaked by the parasite, *Hemileia vastatrix*, which struck the plantations in 1869 and, over the next twenty years, destroyed them completely.

The colonial authorities stepped in and developed tea as a substitute product. With their long experience in India, it soon became the most important crop in the country, turning Ceylon into the second largest tea producer in the world after just a few decades.

Independence in 1948 triggered political upheaval and in 1975 the government nationalized a great many of the plantations that had been in the hands of British companies until then—a policy that had disastrous consequences in terms of both yield and quality.

Confronted with a rapid decline in production and exports, and aware of its inability to manage the tea sector, the government launched a program of privatization towards the end of the twentieth century, but this further disrupted an already weakened industry.

This instability, together with the misguided policy, pursued for thirty years, of promoting yield at the expense of quality, damaged the Sri Lankan tea industry profoundly. Between the undeniable decline in the quality of its teas, now in free fall, and also of its expertise, Sri Lanka is now even more exposed to competition from countries that are new to the industry, whose harvests compare with the lower grades of Sri Lankan teas but are much more competitive in price.

Even today, elephants are employed in Sri Lanka to uproot tea bushes that need replacing.

SRI LANKAN TEA
AND ITS CONSUMPTION

Sri Lanka produces almost exclusively black tea, and most of it by the orthodox method. Introduced at the beginning of the 1990s, the CTC method (see page 61) accounts for only 10 percent of production.

Sri Lanka is one of the major tea-producing countries in the world and exports almost 95 percent of the tea it manufactures. However, paradoxically, while tea plants grow all over the island, tea plays a much less visible role in Sri Lankan society.

The amount of consumption per head—2½ pounds (1.2 kg)—certainly points to a genuine tea-drinking habit, but unlike in most other tea-growing countries, there are no traditions or customs associated with it. It is unusual to come across tea sellers in either the towns or the countryside and nobody drinks tea in the street.

ZONES UNDER CULTIVATION

525,000 acres cultivated (210,000 hectares)
339,512 tons of tea produced
A yield of 3,225 pounds per 2½ acres (1,463 kilos per hectare)
(Source: FAO statistics 2006)

Despite being relatively small in size, there is a surprising difference in climate across the regions of Sri Lanka and it is noted for experiencing two monsoons a year. Since the seasons vary greatly across the different regions, the harvest periods vary also.

Tea is grown in six principal regions: Galle, Ratnapura, Kandy, Nuwara Eliya, Dimbula, and Uva. However, rather than naming the island's teas after their place of origin, they are more often classified according to the altitude at which they are grown, which ranges from sea level to 7,220 feet (2,200 m). Teas grown at below 1,970 feet (600 m) are called "low grown;' those from between 1,970 and 3,940 feet (600–1,200 m), "mid grown;" and above 3,940 feet (1,200 m), "high grown."

INDIA

Sri Lanka

⚓ Tea dispatch port

Black tea-cultivation regions:
- ↘ low grown (below 1,969 ft / 600 m in altitude)
- ↘ mid grown (1,969 ft / 600 m to 3,937 ft / 1,200 m in altitude)
- ↘ high grown (above 3,937 ft / 1,200 m in altitude)

Palk

Strait

Bay of Bengal

SRI LANKA

Kandy

Colombo
⚓

Dimbula

Nuwara Eliya

Uva

Ratnapura

Galle

Indian Ocean

0   12   36 miles
                      60 km

HIGH GROWN: NELUWA
Black tea
Harvested from June to September

The most famous teas in the island, they are often used to wave the flag for the Sri Lankan tea industry and come principally from three regions: Nuwara Eliya, Dimbula, and Uva.

The best teas from Nuwara Eliya, the highest of the regions, are harvested from February to April. The Dimbula plantations are situated on the western slopes of the mountain range that runs down the center of the island to the south, while the Uva plantations are in the southeast of the same range.

Most of the high-grown teas suffer because they are processed using a machine called a Rotorvane, which has replaced the orthodox roller. While it can roll triple the amount of freshly wilted leaves at a time, the Rotorvane places excessive pressure on them. The leaf is kneaded to such an extent that the period of oxidation required can be reduced to just a few minutes.

No buds can survive this treatment, and in the case of most of the high-grown teas, little attention is paid to the appearance of the tea, and the three grades currently recognized (OP1, OPA, and OP) make no mention of any richness in buds but refer instead to the length of the leaf.

Inevitably, the best of the high-grown teas are those that are not processed by the Rotorvane.

Tasting notes

Dry leaf
Appearance: a tightly-rolled leaf, red-brown in color; no buds.
Scent: both woody and spicy.

Infusion
Color: brown.
Scent: a fruity-honeyed note is produced as well as the increasingly ample woody note.

Liquor
Color: bronze.
Texture: a touch of astringency.
Taste: slight bitterness.
Aromas: identical to the infusion, i.e., very woody; mild spices are also evident (especially cinnamon).
Aromatic profile: the astringency tends to last longer than the aromas.

Method of preparation
In a fine earthenware YiXing (non-granular) or porcelain teapot holding 10 fluid ounces (300 ml): infuse ⅓ ounce (8–10 g) of tea for 3 minutes in water heated to 185°F (85°C).
In a tasting set: 3 minutes in water heated to 185°F (85°C).

LOW GROWN: NEW VITHANAKANDE
Black tea
Harvested from May to November

While most of the growers of high-grown teas are convinced that they produce the country's best teas and live off their reputation, with scant regard for the changing markets, a number of low-altitude plantation managers are beginning to wonder what the future holds for their low-grown teas.

Concerned with improving the quality of their tea, and in order to produce tea for consumers who prefer to drink it without milk, some planters have realized that it would be worthwhile to change their production to less powerful, more aromatic teas. The New Vithana-kande plantation, which is one of the best known low-grown teas, looks like being one of the pioneers of change. Its famous "flowery broken orange pekoe finest extra special"—abbreviated to FBOPFEXS—is a good example of these new teas. Intense but made with great care, its leaves are rolled in such a way as to give body to the liquor without damaging the buds that guarantee a scent in the cup.

The FBOPFEXS has met with great success on the export market but accounts for just 1 percent of the crop at present. It is only produced during the best seasons—from May to November, excluding August, when the monsoon arrives.

The New Vithanakande estate is also different in that it buys fresh leaves from the 4,700 farmers who grow tea on smallholdings in the surrounding area.

Tasting notes

Dry leaf
Appearance: a dark leaf, long and well-rolled, with buds colored between gold and silver; also unbroken, contrary to what you would expect from the grade.
Scent: a fruity, gamy, and honeyed bouquet.

Infusion
Color: chocolate.
Scent: very typical—woody-fruity (apple) and spiced honey.

Liquor
Appearance: a mahogany color, very limpid.
Texture: slightly oily with a touch of astringency.
Taste: a hint of acidity.
Aromas: a gamy note comes to strengthen the usual honeyed aroma of the low-grown teas. Spices (nutmeg, cinnamon) and stewed fruit complete the picture.
Aromatic profile: ample but relatively short in the mouth.

Method of preparation
In a fine earthenware YiXing (non-granular) or porcelain teapot holding 10 fluid ounces (300 ml): infuse ⅓ ounce (8–10 g) of tea for 3 minutes in water heated to 185°F (85°C).
In a tasting set: 3 minutes in water heated to 185°F (85°C).

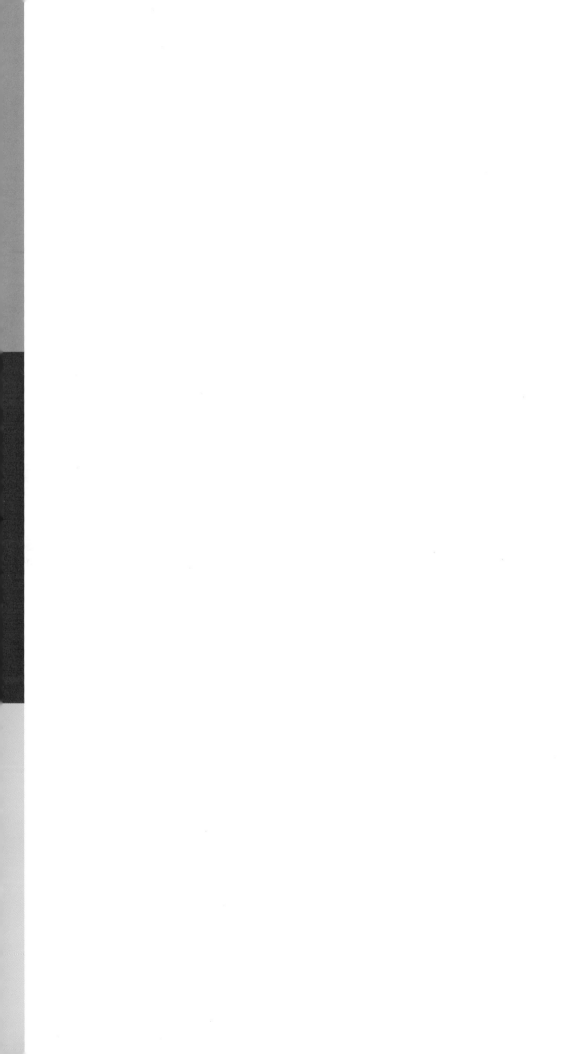

Appendices

TASTING TABLE

Preparation method	Length of infusion	Ideal quantities
BLACK TEAS		
In a Western teapot:		
Darjeeling first flush	2–4 mins	0.3–0.35 oz (8–10 g) for 10 fl oz (300 ml)
Darjeeling second/third flush	3–5 mins	0.3–0.35 oz (8–10 g) for 10 fl oz (300 ml)
Black China teas	3–5 mins	0.2 oz (6 g) for 10 fl oz (300 ml)
Other black teas	3–5 mins	0.2 oz (6 g) for 10 fl oz (300 ml)
CHINESE GREEN TEAS		
In a Western teapot:		
New Season Chinese green teas	2–4 mins	0.2 oz (6 g) for 10 fl oz (300 ml)
Other Chinese green teas	3–5 mins	0.2 oz (6 g) for 10 fl oz (300 ml)
In a zhong:		
Bulky teas	30 secs–4 mins acc. to taste	fill zhong to one-third
Denser teas	30 secs–4 mins acc. to taste	fill zhong to one-quarter
Fine jasmine green teas	30 secs–4 mins acc. to taste	fill zhong to one-quarter
JAPANESE GREEN TEAS		
In a Western teapot:		
Gyokuro	1–2 mins	0.2 oz (6 g) for 10 fl oz (300 ml)
Sencha	2–3 mins	0.2 oz (6 g) for 10 fl oz (300 ml)
Other Japanese green teas	2–3 mins	0.2 oz (6 g) for 10 fl oz (300 ml)
In a kyusu (see also p. 118):		
Gyokuro	2 mins 30 secs	0.35 oz (10 g) for 3½ fl oz (100 ml)
Sencha	2 mins	0.35 oz (10 g) for 7 fl oz (200 ml)
WU LONG		
In a Western teapot:	5–7 mins	0.2 oz (6 g) for 10 fl oz (300 ml)
Using Gong Fu Cha method:		
Pearled shape Wu Long	20 secs–1 min per refill	fill pot to one-third
Wu Long crumpled	20 secs–1 min per refill	fill pot to one-half
WHITE TEAS		
In a Western teapot:		
Silver Needles	5–10 mins	0.2 oz (6 g) for 10 fl oz (300 ml)
Bai Mu Dan	5–10 mins	0.2 oz (6 g) for 10 fl oz (300 ml)
In a zhong:	10 secs–1 min	fill zhong to at least one-third
DARK TEAS		
In a Western teapot:		
Raw Pu Er	3–4 mins	0.2 oz (6 g) for 10 fl oz (300 ml)
Black Pu Er	4–5 mins	0.2 oz (6 g) for 10 fl oz (300 ml)
Using Gong Fu Cha method:	30 secs–1 min per refill	fill pot to one-third
YELLOW TEAS		
In a zhong:	30 secs–4 mins acc. to taste	fill zhong to one-third
AROMATIC TEAS		
In a Western teapot:		
Jasmine teas	3–4 mins	0.2 oz (6 g) for 10 fl oz (300 ml)
Smoked teas	3–5 mins	0.2 oz (6 g) for 10 fl oz (300 ml)
Flavored black	4–5 mins	0.2 oz (6 g) for 10 fl oz (300 ml)
Flavored green	3–5 mins	0.2 oz (6 g) for 10 fl oz (300 ml)
Flavored Wu Long	5–7 mins	0.2 oz (6 g) for 10 fl oz (300 ml)

Temperature of infusion	Number of infusions
176–185°F (80–85°C)	1
176–185°F (80–85°C)	1
176–185°F (80–85°C)	1
176–185°F (80–85°C)	1
158–167°F (70–75°C)	1
158–167°F (70–75°C)	1
158–167°F (70–75°C)	Up to 4 refills for shortest infusions
158–167°F (70–75°C)	Up to 4 refills for shortest infusions
158–167°F (70–75°C)	Up to 4 refills for shortest infusions
104–140°F (40–60°C)	1
140–167°F (60–75°C)	1
158–176°F (70–80°C)	1
140°F (60°C) for infusion; 95°F (35°C) for drinking	Up to 3 water changes, reducing infusion time
176°F (80°C) for infusion; 149°F (65°C) for drinking	Up to 3 water changes, reducing infusion time
203°F (95°C)	1
203°F (95°C)	3–10, possibly 15–20 acc. to quality
203°F (95°C)	3–10, possibly 15–20 acc. to quality
158°F (70°C)	1
158°F (70°C)	1
158°F (70°C)	3 minimum
203°F (95°C)	1
203°F (95°C)	1
203°F (95°C)	3–10, possibly 15–20 acc. to quality
158–167°F (70–75°C)	Up to 4 refills for shortest infusions
158–167°F (70–75°C)	1
176–203°F (80–95°C)	1
176–185°F (80–85°C)	1
158–167°F (70–75°C)	1
203°F (95°C)	1

TEA CHRONOLOGY

2737 BC	China →	Semi-mythical discovery of tea by the emperor Shen Nong.
1122 BC–AD 220	China →	Zhou, Qin, Eastern, and Western Han Dynasties. The first mentions of tea in Chinese literature—in the *Shijing* (*Book of Songs*) and the *Erya* (*Dictionary of Objects*). The first tea-making utensils date from this era.
AD 618–907	China →	Tang Dynasty. The first tea "school:" boiled tea. At this time tea consisted of compressed and roasted bricks that were crumbled before being mixed with boiling water. Tea drinking becomes more widespread, especially under the influence of Buddhist monks.
c. 700	China →	The appearance of the ideogram *cha* to designate tea and distinguish it from other bitter plants.
8th C	Japan →	The first traces of tea drinking in Japan; tea is introduced from China by Buddhist monks.
c. 780	China →	Lu Yu (733–804) produces the first treatise on tea: *Cha Jing*, or *The Classic of Tea*.
960–1279	China →	Song Dynasty. The second tea "school": beaten tea. The leaves were pulverized using a quern; the fine powder obtained was dropped into boiling water, which was then beaten with a bamboo whisk to form a frothy mixture.
1191	Japan →	The monk Eisai (1141–1215) brings back tea seeds from a trip to China. Tea cultivation in Japan begins to spread.
1368–1644	China →	Ming Dynasty. The third tea "school": infused tea.
1391	China →	A decree forbidding the compression of tea destined for imperial tribute. The result was the first use of loose leaves and a new method of preparation: infusion.
1582	Japan →	Sen No Rikyu (1522–1591) codifies the relationship between tea, Buddhism, and various Japanese tea schools.
c. 1590	China →	The development of black tea in Fujian Province.
1599	England →	The founding by Elizabeth I of the East India Company, which will hold a quasi-monopoly on tea imports to England until 1834.
1606	Holland →	The first shipments of tea to Europe (Amsterdam).
1636	France →	The beginning of tea drinking in France.
1641–1853	Japan →	Japan is closed to foreigners (Sakoku period); for the next two hundred years the world supply of tea is in Chinese hands.
1644–1911	China →	Qing Dynasty.
1645	England →	The first shipments of black tea to London.
c. 1650	USA →	The beginning of tea drinking in the United States.
1658	England →	The first advertising of tea in England by Garraway.
1671	France →	The publication of the earliest European work entirely devoted to tea, coffee, and chocolate by Philippe Sylvestre Dufour.
1712	Germany →	Dr. Kaempfer publishes the first Western botanical description of the tea plant christened *Thea japonense*.
1715	England →	The first cargo of green tea arrives in England.
1721	England →	The East India Company's monopoly becomes absolute.
1725	China →	Wu Long is introduced.
1738	Japan →	Nagatani Soen (1681–1778) introduces improved techniques for steam-treating and rolling tea; Sencha is developed.
1753	Sweden →	Carl von Linné refines the botanical description of the tea plant, renaming it *Thea sinensis*.
1773	USA →	The East India Company obtains a monopoly on the sale of tea in the British colonies.
1773	USA →	With the Tea Act, London imposes a new tax on tea exported to the North American colonies.
1773	USA →	The Boston Tea party: in protest against the monopoly on tea, a group of men disguised as Indians throw the cargo from three ships overboard. The initial act of rebellion in what ultimately leads to the American War of Independence.
1788	India →	The earliest attempts to introduce tea plants to India.
1796	China →	The development of white teas.
1796	China →	Tea plants from Fujian are first acclimatized in Taiwan.

Late 18th–early 19th C	China →	Unhappy with the imbalance in their trading partnership with China and the notably ever-increasing imports of tea to the UK, the British introduce and develop the opium trade on Chinese soil. This leads to increasingly strained relations between the two countries and finally to two Opium Wars.
1823	India →	Robert Bruce discovers native tea trees in the Assam jungle.
1827	Java →	Tea cultivation is introduced by the Dutch.
c. 1830	England →	The recipe for Earl Grey is created.
1835	Japan →	Kahei Yamamoto develops Gyokuro at Uji.
1835	India →	The British annex Darjeeling.
1836	India →	The first sale of tea from Assam in Kolkata (Calcutta).
1839–1842	China →	The First Opium War. The Treaty of Nanking.
1839	England →	The first tea from Assam goes on sale in London.
1840	India →	The first plantations in the Nilgiris.
1841	Sri Lanka →	Tea is introduced to Ceylon (now Sri Lanka).
1848	India →	Robert Fortune is despatched by the Crown on an expedition to China, returning in 1851.
1853	Japan →	Commodore Perry lands in Japan. Direct relations between Japan and the USA are established, with decisive consequences on the tea trade between the two nations.
1856–1860	China →	The Second Opium War. The Treaty of Tientsin, following the Treaty of Nanking, establishes trade and tariff agreements that are strongly favorable to Western powers.
1859	India →	The first plantations in Darjeeling.
1866	England →	The most famous of the clipper races; the *Ariel* and the *Teaping*, en route from Fuzhou (China), both arrive in England within twenty minutes of each other after ninety-seven days at sea.
1868	Japan →	The start of tea cultivation at Shizuoka.
1869	Sri Lanka →	The first ravages of *Hemileia vastatrix* (leaf rust) on coffee plantations.
1869	Egypt →	The inauguration of the Suez Canal shortens the tea route.
1886	China →	Tea production in China starts to decline; in this year England imports more tea from her colonies than from China.
1903	Kenya →	The introduction of tea cultivation in Kenya.
c. 1910	USA →	The invention of the teabag by Thomas Sullivan.
1914	Malaysia →	The British introduce tea cultivation to Malaya.
c. 1920	Japan →	Tea shops begin to roast Bancha. The birth of Bancha Hojicha.
1920	Nepal →	The first tea gardens in Nepal.
c. 1930	India →	The CTC procedure is introduced.
1954	Japan →	The introduction of the Yabukita cultivar by Hikosaburo Sugiyama.
1959	West →	The International Code of Nomenclature for Botanical Species renames the tea plant as *Camellia sinensis*.
1960	Nepal →	The first tea-processing plants in Nepal.
c. 1970	China →	The introduction of the accelerated post-fermentation process at Kunming.
1972	Sri Lanka →	Ceylon becomes Sri Lanka.
1975	Taiwan →	The first tea competition in Taiwan.
1975	Sri Lanka →	The large number of plantations is nationalized in Sri Lanka.
1995–2000	Sri Lanka →	The tea trade is privatized.
1997	Nepal →	The tea trade is privatized.
1998	England →	London tea auctions are closed.

INDEX

Page numbers in bold refer to themes developed in the text; those in roman to individual occurrences; those in italics to names featured on the maps.

BIBLIOGRAPHY

Selected further reading:

- John Blofeld, *The Chinese Art of Tea*,
  Random House, 1985.

- Denis Bonheure, *Tea (The Tropical Agriculturalist)*,
  Macmillan Education Ltd., 1991.

- Catherine Bourzat, Laurence Mouton, *Voyages aux sources du thé*,
  Chêne, 2006.

- Paul Butel, *Histoire du thé*, Desjonquères, 2001.

- Michel Finkoff, *Mes jardins de thé: voyage dans les plantations de Ceylan et de Darjeeling*,
  Albin Michel, 1990.

- Robert Fortune, *A Journey to the Tea Countries of China*,
  Adamant Media Corporation, 2001.

- Okakura Kakuzo, *The Book of Tea*,
  Kodansha Europe, 2006.

- Sen Soshitsu, *Tea Life, Tea Mind*,
  Weatherhill Inc., 1991.

- Juliette Soutel-Gouiffes, *La Voie des quatre vertus*,
  La Table d'Émeraude, 1994.

- William H. Ukers, *All About Tea*,
  Hyperion Press, 1935 (republished 1999).

PHOTO CREDITS

- Photo archives of **Le Palais des Thés**. All photographs are by **François-Xavier Delmas**, except: **C. Baudry**: pp. 29 (top), 62 (left) / **Die Reise zum Tee**: pp. 20 (bottom right), 36 (left and center), 41 (right), 49 (top and center), 102 / **Formosa Tea Room/Halin International Group**: 43; **G. Wollenhaupt**: p. 81 / **Oikawa**: p. 115 (right) / **S. Haumuller**: p. 44.

- **Laurent Giraudou/Hemis.fr**: p. 218.

- **Laurence Mouton**: pp. 18, 26, 32, 39, 46, 55, 58, 61, 64–5, 67, 76-7, 91, 95, 98, 104–105, 107, 113, 117, 122, 125, 129, 134, 138–9, 143, 148, 180, 192, 204, 222.

- **Virginie Pérocheau**: pp. 103, 109, 111, 119, and all tea foliage photos pp. 154–227.

ACKNOWLEDGMENTS

The authors are deeply indebted to **Carine Baudry** for sharing her outstanding erudition and her extensive knowledge of aromas; also for the generosity with which she has enabled them to improve their tasting skills over the years.

Thanks also to:

Dr. Mridul Azarika
S. Basu
Amitava Datta
Anil Dharmapalan
Shao Fan Jun
Andrew Gardner
Timir Gupta
Xu He
Anil Jha
Bubul Katyal
Krishan Katyal
Peter Lee
Professeur Y. Liang
Ma Lin
Madame Ming
Hiro Okanaka
P. Pilapitiya
Katrin Rougeventre
Gary Song
G. Somani
Ye Yingkai

Editor: Nathalie Lefebvre assisted by Karine Hamelin
Art Editor: Sabine Houplain
Graphics: Ina Harsch
Maps: Cyrille Süss
Proofreader: Isabelle Macé
Production: Rémy Chauvière
English translation and layout: JMS Books LLP
Photogravure: Seleoffset, Turin (Italy)
Production Editor: Megan Malta
Production Manager: Louise Kurtz
Cover Design: Misha Beletsky

First published in France in 2007 by Hachette-Livre, Chêne

First published in the United States of America by Abbeville Press, 137 Varick Street,
New York, New York 10013

10 9 8 7 6 5 4 3 2 1

©Hachett-Livre, Chêne

Printed and bound in Hong Kong.

For bulk and premium sales and for text adoption procedures, write to Customer
Service Manager, Abbeville Press, 137 Varick Street, New York, NY 10013 or call
1-800-Artbook.

Library of Congress Cataloging-in-Publication Data

Delmas, François-Xavier.
  [Guide de dégustation de l'amateur de thé. English]
  The tea drinker's handbook / François-Xavier Delmas, Mathias Minet, Christine
Barbaste.
      p. cm.
  Includes bibliographical references and index.
  ISBN 978-0-7892-0988-7 (hardcover : alk. paper) 1. Tea—Guidebooks. 2. Tea—
History. 3. Tea tasting. I. Minet, Mathias.
II. Barbaste, Christine. III. Title.

  TX817.T3D513 2008
  641.8'77—dc22

                                          2008014288

Visit Abbeville Press online at www.abbeville.com